Mystics and Zen Masters

Books by Thomas Merton

The Ascent to Truth
The Behavior of Titans
Bread in the Wilderness
Conjectures of a Guilty Bystander
Disputed Questions
The Hidden Ground of Love
Life and Holiness
The Living Bread
Love and Living
Mystics and Zen Masters
The New Man
No Man Is an Island
The Nonviolent Alternative
Seasons of Celebration
The Secular Journal of Thomas Merton
Seeds of Contemplation
Seeds of Destruction
The Seven Storey Mountain
The Sign of Jonas
The Silent Life
Thoughts in Solitude
The Waters of Siloe

POETRY

Emblems of a Season of Fury
A Man in the Divided Sea
The Strange Islands
Selected Poems
The Tears of the Blind Lions
The Tower of Babel
Figures for an Apocalypse
Thirty Poems

TRANSLATIONS

Clement of Alexandria
The Wisdom of the Desert

Thomas Merton

MYSTICS AND ZEN MASTERS

THE NOONDAY PRESS • NEW YORK
A division of Farrar, Straus and Giroux
New York

Acknowledgment is made to the editors of *Jubilee, The Critic, Cross Currents, Continuum, Cithara, Sponsa Regis, Season,* and *The Lugano Review,* in whose pages some of these articles first appeared in somewhat different form.
First edition, 1967
Thirteenth printing, 1997

Ex parte ordinis

Nihil obstat	Fr. M. Benjamin Clark, o.c.s.o.
	Fr. M. Shane Regan, o.c.s.o.
Imprimi potest	Fr. M. Ignace Gillet, o.c.s.o.
	Abbot General
	Rome September 9, 1965
Nihil obstat	Edward J. Montano, s.t.d.
Imprimatur	Terence J. Cooke, d.d.
	Vicar General
	Archdiocese of New York
	January 24, 1967

The nihil obstat and imprimatur are official declarations that a book or pamphlet is free of doctrinal or moral error. No implication is contained therein that those who have granted the nihil obstat and imprimatur agree with the contents, opinions or statements expressed.

CONTENTS

PREFACE

There was a time, and not far distant, when the writings even of Christian mystics were regarded with a certain trepidation in Catholic contemplative monasteries. And it is true that the mystics are not for everyone. It is also true that the vogue for certain forms of Oriental mysticism is not necessarily a sign of greater spiritual maturity in the West. But it certainly seems that if anyone should be open to these Oriental traditions and interested in them, it should be the contemplative monks of the Western monastic orders. Though there are many important differences between the various traditions, they do have very much in common, including a few basic assumptions which set the monk or the Zen man apart from people dedicated to lives that are, shall we say, aggressively noncontemplative.

What are some of these assumptions? They are usually caricatured as a grossly pessimistic rejection of the material world, as an aspiration to escape in a spiritual realm of angels and pure essences or as annihilation in a negative void. In reality, when we examine them more closely, the great contemplative traditions of East and West, while differing sometimes quite radically in their formulation of their aims and in their understanding of their methods, agree in thinking that by spiritual disciplines a man can radically change his life and attain to a deeper meaning, a more perfect integration, a more complete fulfillment, a more total liberty of spirit than are possible in the routines of a purely active existence centered on money-making. That there is more to human life than just "getting somewhere" in war, politics, business—or "the Church." They all agree that the highest ambition lies beyond ambition, in the renunciation of that "self" which seeks its own aggrandizement in one way or another. And they agree that a certain "purification" of the will and intelligence can open man's spirit to a higher and more illuminated understanding of the meaning and purpose of life, or indeed of the very nature of Being itself.

Far from being suspicious of the Oriental mystical traditions, Catholic contemplatives since the Second Vatican Council should be in a position to appreciate the wealth of experience that has accumulated in those traditions. Research like that of R. C. Zaehner, to mention only one of the most recent scholars, now enables us to evaluate these other traditions more correctly. Books like Dom Aelred Graham's *Zen Catholicism* have shown that Zen has something to say not only to the curious scholar, the poet, or the aesthete, but to the ordinary Christian who takes his Christianity seriously. Jesuits in Japan have made retreats in Zen monasteries and one of them has written a *History of Zen* which will be discussed here in some detail. Another has recently written a theological study of the *Cloud of Unknowing* (a fourteenth-century mystical tract) compared with Zen. In other words, Catholics are now asking themselves, in the words of the Council, how other mystical traditions strive to penetrate "that ultimate mystery which engulfs our being, and whence we take our rise, and whither our journey leads us" (*Declara-*

tion on Non-Christian Religions, n. 1). In doing so, they are guided by the Council's reminder that "the Catholic Church rejects nothing which is true and holy in these religions. She looks with sincere respect upon those ways of conduct and of life, those rules and teachings which, though differing in many particulars from what she holds and sets forth, nevertheless often reflect a ray of that Truth which enlightens all men" (id. 2). Not only must the Catholic scholar respect these other traditions and honestly evaluate the good contained in them, but the Council adds that he must "acknowledge, preserve and promote the spiritual and moral goods found among these men as well as the values in their society and culture" (ibid.).

It is in this spirit that the present essays dealing with Oriental religion have been written. The author has attempted not merely to look at these other traditions coldly and objectively from the outside, but, in some measure at least, to try to share in the values and the experience which they embody. In other words, he is not content to write about them without making them, as far as possible, "his own." Obviously, no one can expect to be completely successful in such an endeavor; still less can a Westerner confidently assume, on the basis of his own studies, that he has "understood" Zen. It takes more than study to penetrate Zen. If I dare to publish here several essays on Zen, it is only because I have been assured by experts in Zen (including the late Dr. Suzuki) that this would not be a sheer waste of time.

In writing of Zen, needless to say, it is Zen I am trying to explain, not Catholic dogma. Zen is not theology, and it makes no claim to deal with theological truth in any form whatever. Nor is it an abstract metaphysic. It is, so to speak, a concrete and lived ontology which explains itself not in theoretical propositions but in acts emerging out of a certain quality of consciousness and of awareness. Only by these acts and by this quality of consciousness can Zen be judged. The paradoxes and seemingly absurd propositions it makes have no point except in relation to an awareness that is unspoken and unspeakable.

This is a free-wheeling and wide-ranging book which is more than ecumenical. Strictly speaking, "ecumenism" concerns itself only with the "household of the faith"; that is to say, with various Christian Churches. But there is a wider "oikoumene," the household and the spiritual family of man seeking the meaning of his life and its ultimate purpose. The horizons of this book extend beyond the established forms of Christianity. However, aspects of the Christian tradition itself are not neglected. The Patristic Age, early monasticism, the English mystics, seventeenth-century mystics, Russian Orthodox spirituality, the Shakers, Protestant monastic communities are treated here, sometimes in detail, sometimes in passing. All these studies are united by one central concern: to understand various ways in which men of different traditions have conceived the meaning and method of the "way" which leads to the highest levels of religious or of metaphysical awareness. The aim of these studies is practical rather than speculative. The intuitions and conclusions formulated here may, it is hoped, be of some use to those who are personally interested in that "way" and that awareness.

Abbey of Gethsemani
Advent, 1966

Mystics and Zen Masters

MYSTICS AND ZEN MASTERS

A rather unexpected point of departure for a discussion of Zen, and its relevance in the crises of modern society, is furnished by a recent book[1] by Professor R. C. Zaehner. *Matter and Spirit,* as his work is called, is a lively defense of Teilhardian evolutionism. Its explicit aim is to "see the religious situation today through Teilhard de Chardin's eyes." Therefore, of course, it goes back to the beginning of conscious life; and this, for Zaehner and Chardin, was man's "fall." From this beginning it traces the growth of consciousness and spirituality through the ages of religious individualism up to the point of crisis where we stand today—on the threshold of a "new era," which will be one of "convergence" or the "noösphere."

The "dying civilization" in which "individualism was dominant" is now at an end. Its spiritual death throes are expressed in the despairing pessimism of the existentialists. But their hopelessness is not something Professor Zaehner takes seriously. It is little more than an expression of our economic and social chaos. It is a confession of incapacity to face the future, and a masochistic collapse into defeat and self-pity in the present. Note that no distinction is made between the various kinds of existentialism. Not all are negative!

Marxism, on the other hand, says Zaehner, has dared to face the future and (as he argues with the help of some interesting and little-known quotations from Marx and Engels) it has already created a mystique of the "convergence of spirit and matter." This gives Marxism right of citizenship in that new world which is to come and to which individualism, existentialism, and "passive forms of mysticism" cannot gain admittance.

But Marxism itself has, as Zaehner observes, fatal weaknesses. Its ideal of ultimate solidarity of a "sum total of human minds working together in space and time and converging in an infinite mind" (Engels) cannot be realized, because Communism has no personal "center" on which to converge. The mystique of "convergence" demands a human and indeed a divine cornerstone on which to build the structure of (redeemed) Man. Zaehner is not unwilling to give a polite nod in Stalin's direction, admitting that Stalin did his best to be the kind of god-man on which everything could be built. ("Old Stalin was no fool when he established himself alone as such a center," p. 195.) But, in fact, Communism has no human and personal center. It is looking for one, and though the Soviets have not yet woken up to the fact, the center that Marxism is looking for is the one true cornerstone, Christ.

> This is what the Church, for all its palpable defects and frequent stupidities, stands for and offers: the ultimate solidarity of each in all—the ideal of Marx which the Marxists themselves can never achieve—an organism of persons in all their variety united around the Person who is the center of circumference of them all, Christ. (p. 205)

It is not my intention to discuss Teilhard de Chardin, or Marx, or even to take up what might be considered controversial points in this interesting book of Zaehner's. The book itself is characteristic of avant-garde Catholic thought in the era of the Second Vatican Council: it abounds in the awareness that man and the Church are passing into a new era, a brave new world where one must face the risks and challenges of technological society, and seize this decisive opportunity to attain the adulthood of man and of Christianity. This implies, according to the Teilhardian view, a recognition that Christianity itself is the fruit of evolution and that the world has from the beginning, knowingly or not, been converging upon the Lord of History as upon its "personal center" of fulfillment and meaning. Hence we are on "the watershed between a dying civilization based on individualism, once arrogant, now abject, and a collective civilization yet to be formed in which 'the free development of each will be the condition for the free development of all.' " We are thus in "the passage from an epoch of individual despairs to one of shared hope in an ever richer material and spiritual life."

The quotation about the "free development of each" as a "condition for the free development of all" comes from the *Communist Manifesto*. And we note that the Christian is now no longer assuming that the condition for a richer spiritual life is rejection of material abundance. We approach the time of "shared hope in an ever richer *material and* spiritual life."

As I say, I have not quoted these passages in order to quarrel with them, or in order to agree with them either. What is important is that they represent the new attitude today toward "spirituality" and "mysticism." In his other books, Zaehner has made an important contribution to the history of Christian and non-Christian mysticism.[2] He sees an evolution in mysticism from the contemplation that seeks to discover and rest in the spiritual essence of the individual nature, to a higher personalist mysticism which transcends nature and the individual self in God together with other men in the Mystical Christ. In its highest form, then, this convergence of all with all in the personal center which is Christ demands *a dying to the individual essence.* The personalist mystique is in fact basically existentialist, because centered not in a static apprehension of essence but in the leap beyond essence into freedom and act "in the Spirit" together with all whom freedom and love made one in Christ.

Now Zaehner admits that in the Oriental religions there have been various foreshadowings of this development which is becoming clear in Christianity. He has specialized in Zoroaster, who has had sight of the promised land. So too has Mahayana Buddhism. Yet all these "ancient cosmic religions" have evidently had their day, according to this line of thought, since they are "steeped in a pessimistic and passive mysticism" and can hardly adjust themselves "to the precise immensities nor to the constructive requirements of space-time" (p. 184). Little is said of Zen in particular. It is mentioned only in passing. For instance, Zaehner says that Zen and Neo-Vedanta "may satisfy some individuals for a short time [but] they plainly cannot be integrated into modern society" (p. 185).

My purpose in thus preparing my question has been to show that I intend to answer the question in quite other terms. While I can easily see, with Zaehner, that the pragmatic importance of Zen Buddhism at the present time is probably minimal, I still intend to consider it as something that might have a certain depth and intelligibility of its own which are not invalidated by the passage of time or even by the transition into a new age. But I would also like to examine whether Zen is by its very nature committed to a search for "rest in the inmost essence" of one's individual self. Is Zen meditation aimed at a purification of the self by rejection of the material world and of external concerns in order to seek fulfillment in pure interiority? Does it exalt "that inmost essence which original sin could not slay and which so often claims identity with God—FOR IN THIS ESSENCE REST IS 'SUFFICIENT AND GREAT' (ZOROASTER) AND NO NEED OR DESIRE FOR ANYTHING OR ANYONE IS ANYMORE FELT . . . Comfortably ensconced outside space and time, he no longer cares how the world is pushing forward to a common destiny in which all mankind is being knit together in an ever increasing coherence around its common center: Christ" (p. 198). Is this Zen? Is Zen incompatible with Christianity?

It is certainly true that for Zen there is absolutely no evidence of a personal center of convergence in the New Testament sense. (Though the concept of the Buddha-nature as central to all being might be considered in some way analogous to this. Yet I think the analogy would remain hemmed in by serious ambiguities.) What I intend to question is simply the idea that Zen meditation is simply a rest in individual "essence" which abolishes all need for and interest in external and historical reality, or the destiny of man.

I I

One of the most thorough recent attempts to explain Zen by tracing its history is the work of a Jesuit scholar who has spent years in Japan. This book is very clear, full of new material. It is probably the best and most comprehensive history of Zen that has yet appeared in any Western language.[3]

Father Heinrich Dumoulin is no novice in the study of Zen Buddhism. For over twenty-five years he has been publishing articles in learned Oriental journals on this subject, and in 1953 an English translation of a preliminary study, of which the present book is a full development, was published by the First Zen Institute of America.[4] Hence it is clear that we are dealing with a widely recognized Western authority on Zen, and one who, besides having a profound insight into Japanese religion and culture, is a Christian scholar and theologian. This book makes it possible for the average Christian student to advance, with a certain amount of security and confidence, into a very mysterious realm.

Some fifteen years ago I had occasion to speak with a European member of a contemplative order who was on his way back from China (where his life was endangered by the advance of the Communist armies). I asked him, in passing, if he knew anything about Buddhist contemplatives and contemplation. He shrugged, made a gesture in the air, and said: "Dreams! Dreams!" This is not an unusual response. It is a cliché generated by familiarity with apologetic texts, in which Buddhism is dismissed with two tags: "pantheism" and "nirvana." Nirvana is generally interpreted to mean something like a state of catatonic trance—a total withdrawal from reality.

Buddhism is generally described in the West as "selfish," even though the professed aim of the discipline from the very start is to attack and overcome that attachment to individual self-affirmation and survival which is the source of every woe. The truth is that the deep paradoxes and ambiguities of Buddhism have led most Westerners to treat it as a mixture of incomprehensible myths, superstitions, and self-hypnotic rites, all of it without serious importance.

The first Jesuits in Japan made no such mistakes. They had a very healthy respect and curiosity for the thought and spirituality of "the bonzes." St. Francis Xavier wrote:

> I have spoken with several learned bonzes, especially with one who is held in high esteem here by everyone, as much for his knowledge, conduct and dignity as for his great age of eighty years. His name is Ninshitsu, which in Japanese signifies "Heart of Truth." He is among them as a bishop, and if his name is appropriate, he is indeed a blessed man . . . It is a marvel how good a friend this man is to me.[5]

Though Japanese religion was then in a state of decline, the Jesuits quickly found that the Zen temples were still (in spite of serious abuses) the centers of a very real spiritual life. It is true that the many-sided manifestations of Buddhist life and thought were not always easy to grasp or entirely congenial to the Christians. Nor was it possible to expect men trained in scholastic theology and Aristotelian logic to take kindly to the outrageous paradoxes of Zen, which is aggressively opposed to all forms of logical analysis. A genuine dialogue between the Jesuits and the Zen masters was no simple matter, especially on the highest level, which Father Dumoulin does not hesitate to qualify as "mystical."

On the cultural level, however, the encounter was relatively easy. The Jesuits were entirely charmed with the subtlety, the refinement, the perfection of taste, and the good order that reigned even more in the Zen temples than everywhere else around them. Hence they did not hesitate to exercise their characteristic flair for adaptation and model the outward forms and ceremonies of their community life in Japan on those of the Zen monks. Indeed, it was altogether logical for them to do so, since they were not blinded by the illusion of so many others who tended to identify the accidental outward forms of Oriental culture with "pagan religion" or those of European culture with essentials of Christian piety. St. Francis Xavier, who seems to have been free from illusion in this respect, did not hesitate to say of the Japanese in general: "In their culture, their social usage, and their mores, they surpass the Spaniards so greatly that one must be ashamed to say so."

The famous Jesuit Visitator of the Oriental province, Valignano, strongly urged the missionaries to associate with the Zen monks. This meant participation in the quasi-religious "tea ceremony," in which the Jesuits not only took a keen interest, but which they practiced with a relatively consummate artistry, sharing with their Zen friends a real appreciation of its spiritual implications.

The uninitiated Western reader might imagine, at first sight, that the "tea ceremony" is a hieratic social formality, an external ritual without inner significance or life. Not if it is practiced as it should be. It is in the true sense an "art" and a spiritual discipline: a discipline of simplicity, of silence, of self-effacement, of contemplation. But it must be noted that it is all these things in a setting of communality and, one might

say, of "convergence." The tea ceremony, properly understood, is a celebration of oneness and convergence, a conquest
of multiplicity and of atomization, a liturgy that is not without certain spiritual features in common with the Eucharistic
repast, the primitive Christian agape. To begin with, all who
participate in the tea ceremony must first put off (as far as
possible) their artificial social and external *persona* and enter
in their simplicity, one might almost say "poverty," into the
oneness of the communion, where there is no longer any distinction of noble and commoner. There is, incidentally, a
kind of Franciscan simplicity in the spirit of the tea ceremony.

It is true that in speaking of the tea ceremony we are speaking of its spirit and ideal, which may not always be perfectly
realized, just as the spirit and ideal of the liturgy are not always realized in practice either. The fact remains that the tea
ceremony is a contemplative exercise (rather than a religious
rite) which does not manifest a spirit of individualism, withdrawal, and separation, but rather of communality and "convergence" at least in a primitive and schematic sense.

There are several instances of Zen masters who became
Christians in the early days of the Japanese mission, along
with some of the "tea masters," who were not always members
of the Zen sect.

One early Jesuit has left us a moving account of his impressions of the tea ceremony in a sixteenth-century Portuguese
manuscript, an excerpt of which has been published for the
first time by Father Dumoulin. We reproduce it here, for it
summarizes the ideas of Zen that the Jesuits acquired in this
first encounter. The writer's emphasis is on what appeared to
him to be a quasi-monastic simplicity and silence in the tea
ceremony, which he calls a "religion of solitude"—adding
later, "cenobitic solitude."

> [The "art of tea"] was established by the originators in order
> to promote good habits and moderation in all things among

those who dedicate themselves to it. In this way they imitate the Zen philosophers in their meditation, as do the philosophers of the other schools of Indian wisdom. Much rather they hold the things of this world in low esteem, they break away from them and deaden their passions through specific exercises and enigmatic, metaphorical devices which at the outset serve as guides. They give themselves to contemplation of natural things. Of themselves they arrive at the knowledge of the original cause in that they come to see things themselves. In the consideration of their mind they eliminate that which is evil and imperfect until they come to grasp the natural perfection and the being of the First Cause.

Therefore these philosophers customarily do not dispute or argue with others, rather allowing each person to consider things for himself, in order that he may draw understanding from the ground of his own being. For this reason they do not instruct even their own disciples. The teachers of this school are also imbued with a determined and decisive spirit without indolence or negligence, without lukewarmness or effeminacy. They decline the abundance of things for their personal use as superfluous and unnecessary. They regard sparsity and moderation in all things as the most important matter and as being beneficial to the hermit. This they combine with the greatest equanimity and tranquillity of mind and outer modesty . . . after the manner of the Stoics who thought that the consummate person neither possesses nor feels any passion.

The adherents of *cha-no-yu* claim to be followers of these solitary philosophers. Therefore all teachers of this art, even though they be unbelievers otherwise, are members of the Zen school or become such, even if their ancestors belonged to some other persuasion. Though they imitate this Zen ceremony, they observe neither superstition nor cult, nor any other special religious ritual, since they adopt none of these things from it. Rather they copy only their cenobitic solitude and separation from the activities of life in the world, as also their resolution and readiness of mind, eschewing laxity or indolence, pomp or effeminacy. Also in their contemplation of natural things, these practitioners imitate Zen, not indeed with regard to the goal of the knowledge of being and the perfection of original being, but rather only in that they see in those things the outer tangible and natural forms which move the mind and incite to solitude and tranquillity and detachment from the noise and proud stirring of the world.[6]

This is hardly a Teilhardian attitude, but the language is that of a sixteenth-century European Jesuit. Hence its Western and "individualist" emphasis.

III

What, exactly, is Zen?

If we read the laconic and sometimes rather violent stories of the Zen masters, we find that this is a dangerously loaded question: dangerous above all because the Zen tradition absolutely refuses to tolerate any abstract or theoretical answer to it. In fact, it must be said at the outset that philosophically or dogmatically speaking, the question probably has no satisfactory answer. Zen simply does not lend itself to logical analysis. The word "Zen" comes from the Chinese *Ch'an*, which designates a certain type of meditation, yet Zen is not a "method of meditation" or a kind of spirituality. It is a "way" and an "experience," a "life," but the way is paradoxically "not a way." Zen is therefore not a religion, not a philosophy, not a system of thought, not a doctrine, not an ascesis. In calling it a kind of "natural mysticism," Father Dumoulin is bravely submitting to the demands of Western thought, which is avid, at any price, for essences. But I think he would not find too many Eastern minds who would fully agree with him on this point, even though he is, in fact, giving Zen the highest praise he feels a Christian theologian can accord it. The truth is, Zen does not even lay claim to be "mystical," and the most widely read authority on the subject, Daisetz Suzuki, has expended no little effort in trying to deny the fact that Zen is "mysticism." This, however, is perhaps more a matter of semantics than anything else.

The Zen insight cannot be communicated in any kind of

doctrinal formula or even *in any precise phenomenological description*. This is probably what Suzuki means when he says it is "not mystical": that it does not present clear and definitely recognizable characteristics capable of being set down in words. True, the genuineness of the Zen illumination is certainly recognizable, but only by one who has attained the insight himself. And here of course we run into the first of the abominable pitfalls that meet anyone who tries to write of Zen. For to suggest that it is "an experience" which a "subject" is capable of "having" is to use terms that contradict all the implications of Zen.

Hence it is quite false to imagine that Zen is a sort of individualistic, subjective purity in which the monk seeks to rest and find spiritual refreshment by the discovery and enjoyment of his own interiority. It is not a subtle form of spiritual self-gratification, a repose in the depths of one's own inner silence. Nor is it by any means a simple withdrawal from the outer world of matter to an inner world of spirit. The first and most elementary fact about Zen is its abhorrence of this dualistic division between matter and spirit. Any criticism of Zen that presupposes such a division is, therefore, bound to go astray.

Like all forms of Buddhism, Zen seeks an "enlightenment" which results from the resolution of all subject-object relationships and oppositions in a pure void. But to call this void a mere negation is to reestablish the oppositions which are resolved in it. This explains the peculiar insistence of the Zen masters on "neither affirming nor denying." Hence it is impossible to attain *satori* (enlightenment) merely by quietistic inaction or the suppression of thought. Yet at the same time "enlightenment" is not an experience or activity of a thinking and self-conscious subject. Still less is it a vision of Buddha, or an experience of an "I-Thou" relationship with a Supreme Being considered as object of knowledge and perception. However, Zen does not *deny* the existence of a Supreme Being either. It neither affirms nor denies, it simply *is*. One might say that Zen is the ontological *awareness of pure being beyond subject and object,* an immediate grasp of being in its "suchness" and "thusness."

But the peculiarity of this awareness is that it is not reflexive, not self-conscious, not philosophical, not theological. It is in some sense entirely beyond the scope of psychological observation and metaphysical reflection. For want of a better term, we may call it "purely spiritual."

In order to preserve this purely spiritual quality, the Zen masters staunchly refuse to rationalize or verbalize the Zen experience. They relentlessly destroy all figments of the mind or imagination that pretend to convey its meaning. They even go so far as to say: "If you meet the Buddha, kill him!" They refuse to answer speculative or metaphysical questions except with words which are utterly trivial and which are designed to dismiss the question itself as irrelevant.

When asked, "If all phenomena return to the One, where does the One return to?" the Zen master Joshu simply said: "When I lived in Seiju, I made a robe out of hemp and it weighed ten pounds."

This is a useful and salutary *mondo* (saying) for the Western reader to remember. It will guard him against the almost irresistible temptation to think of Zen in Neo-Platonic terms. Zen is *not* a system of pantheistic monism. It is not a system of any kind. It refuses to make any statements at all about the metaphysical structure of being and existence. Rather it points directly to being itself, without indulging in speculation.

Father Dumoulin does not attempt to explain Zen or analyze it. He treats it with a respectful and historic objectivity. He tells us where it came from, how it developed, and what the various schools were. Though Suzuki and the other writers on Zen are generally careful to identify the Zen masters whom they quote, and to try to situate them in their context, a simple yet complete historical outline has long been badly needed. Father Dumoulin gives us the whole picture. After some early chapters on Indian Buddhism, with necessary information on the Mahayana sutras (without which Zen is not fully understandable), he speaks of the introduction of Zen to China by the semilegendary Bodhidharma, a contemporary of St. Benedict in the West (sixth century A.D.).

In point of fact, Zen was not suddenly "introduced" to China by any one man. It is a product of the combination of Mahayana Buddhism with Chinese Taoism which was later transported to Japan and further refined there. Though Bodhidharma is regarded as the first in a line of Zen patriarchs who have "directly transmitted" the enlightenment experience of the Buddha without written media or verbal formulas, the way for Zen was certainly prepared before him. The four-line verse (*gatha*) attributed to Bodhidharma, and purporting to contain a summary of his "doctrine," was actually composed later, during the T'ang Dynasty, when Zen reached its highest perfection in China. The verse reads:

A special tradition outside the scriptures (i.e., sutras),
No dependence upon words and letters,
Direct pointing at the soul of man,
Seeing into one's own nature and the attainment of buddhahood.

It is clear from this that Zen insists on concrete practice rather than on study or intellectual meditation, as a way of attaining enlightenment. The key phrase of this verse is: "Direct pointing at the soul of man," and this is practically repeated in the synonymous phrase that follows: "Seeing into one's own nature." The commonly accepted translation "seeing into the soul of man" is, however, rather unfortunate. It suggests an opposition between body-soul, spirit and matter, which is not to be found in Zen, or at least not in the way that such terms might suggest to us. This, in fact, rather disconcerted St. Francis Xavier when he conversed with his friend the Zen master Ninshitsu. The good old man did not seem to know whether or not he had "a soul." In fact, to him the concept that "a soul" was a sort of object that "one" could be considered as "having" and even "saving" was completely unfamiliar. He sought salvation, indeed, but this search could only be expressed in utterly different terms.

In other texts of Bodhidharma's verse, the word here given as soul is "mind" (*h'sin*). But "mind" (*h'sin*) is more than a psychological concept. Nor is it equivalent to the scholastic idea of the soul as "form of the body." Yet it is certainly considered a principle of *being*. Can we consider it a spiritual essence? I think not.

Suzuki says that "mind" in this sense is "an ultimate reality which is aware of itself and is not the seat of our empirical consciousness." [7] This "mind" for the Zen masters is not the intellectual faculty as such but rather what the Rhenish mystics called the "ground" of our soul or of our being, a "ground" which is not only entitative but enlightened and aware, because it is in immediate contact with God. In the Zen context, "mind" has a kind of ontological value which brings it close to the parallel term "nature" in the next line. But its connotations are existentialist, dynamic, and concrete. The New Testament term that might possibly correspond to it, though of course with many differences, is St. Paul's "spirit" or "pneuma."

It must be admitted that a great deal of study remains to be done to clarify the basic concepts of Buddhism, which have usually been translated by Western terms that have quite different implications. We have habitually taken Western metaphysical concepts as equivalent to Buddhist terms, which are not metaphysical but religious or spiritual, that is to say, expressions not of abstract speculation but of concrete spiritual experience.

As a result, we have read our abstract Western divisions into an Oriental experience that has nothing whatever to do with them, and we have also presumed that Oriental contemplation corresponded in every way with Western philosophical modes of contemplation and spirituality. Hence the mystifying use of terms like "individualism," "subjectivism," "pantheism," etc., one on top of the other, in our discussion of something like Zen. Actually these terms are worse than useless in this case. They serve only to make Zen utterly inaccessible.

The Zen insight, as Bodhidharma indicates, consists in a direct grasp of "mind" or one's "original face." And this direct grasp implies rejection of all conceptual media or methods, so that one arrives at mind by "having no mind" (*wu h'sin*): in fact, by "being" mind instead of "having" it. Zen enlightenment is an insight into being in all its existential reality and actualization. It is a fully alert and superconscious *act* of being which transcends time and space. Such is the attainment of the "Buddha mind," or "Buddhahood." (Compare the Christian expressions "having the mind of Christ" [1 Cor. 2:16], being "of one Spirit with Christ," "He who is united to the Lord is one spirit" [1 Cor. 6:17], though the Buddhist idea takes no account of any "supernatural order" in the Thomist sense.) The Zen insight is the awareness of full spiritual reality, and therefore the realization of the emptiness of all limited or particularized realities. Hence it is not accurate to say that the Zen insight is a realization of our own individual spiritual nature, or (as Zaehner would say) of our "pre-biological unity."

One might ask if our habitual failure to distinguish between "empirical ego" and the "person" has not led us to oversimplify and falsify our whole interpretation of Buddhism. There are in Zen certain suggestions of a higher and more spiritual personalism than one might at first sight expect. Zen insight is at once a liberation from the limitations of the individual ego, and a discovery of one's "original nature" and "true face" in "mind" which is no longer restricted to the empirical self but is in all and above all. Zen insight is not *our* awareness, but Being's awareness of itself in us. This is not a pantheistic submersion or a loss of self in "nature" or "the One." It is not a withdrawal into one's spiritual essence and a denial of matter and of the world. On the contrary, it is a recognition that the whole world is aware of itself in me, and that "I" am no longer my individual and limited self, still less a disembodied soul, but that my "identity" is to be sought not in that *separation* from all that is, but in oneness (indeed, "convergence"?) with all that is. This identity is not the denial of my own personal reality but its highest affirmation. It is a discovery of *genuine identity* in and with the One, and this is expressed in the paradox of Zen, from which the explicit concept of person in the highest sense is unfortunately absent, since here too the person tends to be equated with the individual.

IV

The most critical moment in the history of Chinese Zen is evidently the split between the northern and southern schools (seventh century). This extremely complex affair nevertheless has one feature which is important for the real understanding of Zen: the events which led to the choosing of the "Sixth Patriarch," Hui Neng.

When the time came for Hung Jen, the fifth patriarch, to transmit his role and dignity to a successor, he asked each of his monks to compose a verse which would testify to the candidate's Zen insight. Presumably the one whose verse was most adequate would be worthy to succeed him as patriarch, because he would be the one whose Zen enlightenment was most authentic.

Foremost among the disciples of the old man was Shen Hsiu. He was a senior in the community, outstanding for his experience, and his succession was taken as a foregone conclusion. He composed a verse which ran as follows:

The body is the Bodhi-tree (under which Buddha was enlightened),

The mind is like a clear mirror standing.
Take care to wipe it all the time,
Allow no grain of dust to cling to it.

Anyone familiar with routine descriptions of the contemplative experience, East or West, will recognize this approach. It is, as a matter of fact, very close to Neo-Platonism. It suggests (probably more in the translation than in the original) the familiar Greek division between mind and matter, and it situates enlightenment in a state of immaterial purity in essential repose, and in the absence of concepts. It indicates a program of purification and recollection, a "liberation" of the soul from the terrestrial and temporal condition imposed on it by the body and the five senses, so that it rests in our ideal essence or nature.

As a matter of fact, this is the kind of thing that the Western reader would be perfectly ready to accept as Zen. But it is rejected with impassioned scorn by the Zen masters. Another member of Hung Jen's monastic community, who was not even a monk but an illiterate oblate working in the kitchen, reacted against the inadequacy of the verse, and posted another verse of his own, which he (and later generations of Zen masters) felt to be more satisfactory. In fact, this untrained peasant, Hui Neng, was preferred to Shen Hsiu and succeeded Hung Jen as the sixth patriarch. Here is the verse:

The Bodhi is not like a tree,
The clear mirror is nowhere standing.[8]
Fundamentally not one thing exists:
Where then is a grain of dust to cling?

Here the Western reader is likely to be both disconcerted and misled. He will seize upon the phrase "not one thing exists," in order to account for his anxieties: but if he thinks this is a statement of fundamental principle, a declaration of pantheism, he is wrong. As Suzuki says, "When the Sutras declare all things to be empty, unborn and beyond causation, the declaration is not the result of metaphysical reasoning; it is a most penetrating Buddhist experience." [9] As usual, Suzuki avoids the use of the word "mystical," but statements about the "nothingness" of beings and of "oneness" in Buddhism are to be interpreted just like the figurative terms of Western mystics describing their experience of God: the language is *not metaphysical* but poetic and phenomenological. The Zen insight is a direct grasp of being in itself, but not an intuition of the nature of being. Nor can the Zen insight be described in psychological terms, and to think of it as a subjective experience "attainable" by some kind of process of mental purification is to doom oneself to error and absurdity. This error came to be described as "mirror-wiping Zen," since it imagines that the mind is like a mirror which "one" (who?) has to keep clean. To illustrate this, here is another well-known Zen story:

A Master saw a disciple who was very zealous in meditation.
The Master said: "Virtuous one, what is your aim in practicing *Zazen* (meditation)?"
The disciple said: "My aim is to become a Buddha."

Then the Master picked up a tile and began to polish it on a stone in front of the hermitage.

The disciple said: "What is the Master doing?"
The Master said: "I am polishing this tile to make it a mirror."

The disciple said: "How can you make a mirror by polishing a tile?"
The Master replied: "How can you make a Buddha by practicing *Zazen*?" [10]

The capital importance of this story is that it shows, once for all, what the Zen of Hui Neng is not. It is not a technique of introversion by which one seeks to exclude matter and the external world, to eliminate distracting thoughts, to sit in silence emptying the mind of images, and to concentrate on the purity of one's own spiritual essence, whether or not this essence be regarded as a mirror of the divinity. Zen is not a mysticism of introversion and withdrawal. It is neither quietism nor Hesychasm. It is not "acquired contemplation."

On the other hand, I believe one must not interpret stories like this to mean that the school of Hui Neng attached no importance whatever to meditation, or thought that no preliminary discipline was required: enlightenment would come suddenly all by itself. Dumoulin himself seems to have interpreted Hui Neng's doctrine of "sudden enlightenment" in this way, for he says: "The elimination of all preliminary stages and the renunciation of all preparatory exercises is the typical Chinese element in the Zen of Hui Neng" (p. 96).

It is true that Hui Neng did revolutionize Buddhist spirituality by discounting the practice of formal and prolonged meditation, referred to as *zazen* ("sitting in meditation"). He placed no confidence in self-emptying introversion. Yet it would be misleading to think that the "renunciation of preparatory exercises" means "no preparation" or the rejection of formal *zazen* means "no meditation." This way of interpreting Hui Neng accounts for the common opinion of Westerners that his spirituality, and that of Zen in general, is "quietistic." Hui Neng was no quietist. On the contrary, he was reacting *against* a quietistic type of spirituality. But his reaction was not activistic either. Yet we can say it was dynamic. It was a breakthrough into something quite original and new. He refused to separate meditation as a means (*dhyana*) from *enlightenment as an end* (*prajna*). For him, the two were really inseparable, and the Zen discipline consisted in seeking to realize this wholeness and unity of *prajna* and *dhyana* in all one's acts, however external, however commonplace, however trivial. For Hui Neng, *all life was Zen.* Zen could not be found merely by turning away from active life to become absorbed in meditation. Zen is the very awareness of the dynamism of life living itself in us—and aware of itself, in us, as being the one life that lives in all.

When, in his verse about the "mirror," Hui Neng rejected the "mirror wiping" concept of meditation, he was therefore not rejecting meditation itself, but what he believed to be a totally wrong attitude to meditation. We may sum up the "wrong" attitude in the following terms.

1. This wrong attitude assumes and gives primacy to a central ego-consciousness, an awareness of an empirical self, an "I" which, with all the good intentions in the world, sets out to "achieve liberation" or "enlightenment." This is the familiar empirical ego which is aware of itself, observes itself, remembers itself, and seeks ways to preserve and perpetuate its self-awareness. This "I" seeks to affirm itself not only in its actions, and its thoughts, but also in contemplation. In stripping off the exterior and sensible trappings of superficial experience, the ego seeks to realize its own spiritual nature more perfectly. This implies a rejection of one's sensible and active self in order to attain to an inner "silent" self, which is still, however, our "ego."

2. The empirical and self-conscious self then views its own thought as a kind of object or possession, and in so doing accounts for this thought by situating it in a separate, isolated "part of itself," a mind, which it compares to a "mirror." This is also considered a "possession." "I *have* a mind." Thus the mind is regarded not as something I am, but something I *own*. It then becomes necessary for me to sit quietly and calmly, recollecting my faculties and reaching down to experience my "mind."

3. The empirical self then resolves to purify the mirror of the mind by removing thoughts from it. When the mirror of the mind is clear of all thought (so it imagines), the ego will be "liberated." It will affirm itself freely without thoughts. Why does it aim at this bizarre attainment? Because it has read in the sutras that enlightenment is a state of "emptiness," and "suchness." It is an awareness of an inner and tran-

scendental mind. Presumably if all thoughts of material and contingent things are kept out of the mirror, then the mirror will be filled with the pure spiritual light of the Buddha mind, which is a kind of "emptiness."

At best, this contemplation is an ascent from the external and empirical consciousness to a higher and more general consciousness of one's spiritual nature. The lower self is then dissolved in the consciousness of a universal ideal *nature* which transcends the external concrete self.

What has happened is that this clinging and possessive ego-consciousness, seeking to affirm itself in "liberation," craftily tries to outwit reality by rejecting the thoughts it "possesses" and emptying the mirror of the mind, which it also "possesses." Thus, "the mind" will be in "emptiness" and "poverty." But in reality, *"emptiness" itself is regarded as a possession, and an "attainment."* So the ego-consciousness is able, it believes, to eat its cake and have it. It renounces its empirical autonomy in order to sink into its spiritual, pre-biological nature. But since this nature is regarded as one's possession, the "spiritualized" ego thus is able to affirm itself all the more perfectly, and to enjoy its own narcissism under the guise of "emptiness" and "contemplation."

Now as Hui Neng points out, I think quite rightly from any point of view, this elaborate mental fabrication is a naïve and pointless artifice. Indeed, it is not only useless but deceitful and pernicious, since it induces an illusion that the empirical ego has transcended the conditions of matter and of egotistical selfhood by "using" and "managing" separate entities such as the will, the intellect, and so on. Admittedly, these faculties are all quite real, and we must certainly have some way of talking about them and dealing with them when it is necessary to do so. But since in deeper spiritual experience they do not function according to the imagery which is adequate for ordinary, everyday life, it becomes necessary to discard that imagery and to speak in other terms.

It is quite true to say that the "sun rises" and the "sun sets" according to our empirical, everyday experience. But such terminology is no longer adequate for the professional concerns of a space man. So too, the Zen masters realized that to speak of the mind as a mirror which is "owned" by the ego and which must be kept pure by the exclusion of all thoughts was, from the point of view of Zen understanding, sheer nonsense. Such language does not come anywhere near giving a proper notion of what true insight is. Hui Neng therefore described it in other terms, in which, of course, he had been anticipated by many centuries in the Mahayana sutras, particularly the *Diamond Sutra.*

For Hui Neng the central reality in meditation, or indeed in life itself, is not the empirical ego but that ultimate reality which is at once pure being and pure awareness which we referred to above as "mind" (*h'sin*). Because he contrasts it with the "conscious" empirical self, Hui Neng calls this "ultimate mind" the "Unconscious" (*wu nien*). (This is equivalent to the Sanskrit *prajna,* or wisdom.)

It must be said here that the "Unconscious" of Hui Neng is totally different from the unconscious as it is conceived by modern psychoanalysis. To confuse these two ideas would be a fatal error. As Bodidharma said, the "Unconscious" (*prajna*) is a principle of being and light secretly at work in our conscious mind making it aware of transcendent reality. But this true awareness is not a matter of the empirical ego standing back and "having ideas," "possessing knowledge," or even "attaining to insight" (*satori*). That might be all right in the Cartesian realm of scientific abstraction. But here we are dealing with the vastly different realm of *prajna*-wisdom. Hence, what matters now is for the conscious to realize itself as identified with and illuminated by the Unconscious, in such a way that there is no longer any division or separation between the two. It is not that the empirical mind is "absorbed in" *prajna,* but simply that *prajna is,* and nothing else has any relevance except as its manifestation.

Indeed, it is not the empirical self which "possesses" *prajna*-

wisdom, or owns "an unconscious" as one might have a cellar in one's house. In reality, the conscious belongs to the transcendental unconscious, is possessed by it, and carries out its work, or it should do so. Its destiny is to manifest in itself the light of that Being by which it subsists, as a Christian philosopher might say. It becomes one, as we would say, with God's own light, and St. John's expression, the "light which enlightens every man coming into this world" (John 1:9), seems to correspond pretty closely to the idea of *prajna* and of Hui Neng's "Unconscious."

This then is what Hui Neng means when he says "mirror wiping" is useless. There is no mirror to be wiped. What we call "our" mind is only a flickering and transient manifestation of *prajna*—the formless and limitless light. We cannot be enlightened by cutting the manifestation off from the original light and giving it an autonomous existence which it cannot possibly have. Another Zen master said, characteristically, that there is no enlightenment to be attained and no subject to attain it. "No one has ever attained it in the past or will ever attain it in the future, for it is beyond attainability. Thus there is nothing to be thought of except the Unconscious itself. This is called true thought." [11] Therefore Bodidharma said, "All the attainments of the Buddhas are really non-attainments." [12]

As long as the empirical ego stands back and imagines itself to be illuminated by any light whatever, whether its own or beyond itself, and strives to see things in its "own mind" as in a mirror, it simply affirms itself as distinct from a source outside itself to which it must attain, because it is "separate" and distant. But in actual fact, Hui Neng says, there is no attainment, and therefore to busy oneself about seeking a "way" to attainment is pure self-deception. Zen is not "attained" by mirror-wiping meditation, but by self-forgetfulness in the existential *present* of life here and now.

This reminds us of St. John of the Cross and his teaching that the "Spiritual Way" is falsely conceived if it is thought to be a denial of flesh, sense, and vision in order to arrive at higher spiritual experience. On the contrary, the "dark night of sense" which sets the house of flesh at rest is at best a serious beginning. The true dark night is that of the spirit, where the "subject" of all higher forms of vision and intelligence is itself darkened and left in emptiness: not as a mirror, pure of all impressions, but as a void without knowledge and without any natural capacity to know the supernatural. It is an error to think that St. John of the Cross teaches denial of the body and the senses as a way to reach a higher and more secret mystical knowledge. On the contrary, he teaches that the light of God shines in all emptiness where there is no natural subject to receive it. To this emptiness there is in reality no definite way. "To enter upon the way is to leave the way," for the way itself is emptiness.

We are plagued today with the heritage of that Cartesian self-awareness, which assumed that the empirical ego is the starting point of an infallible intellectual progress to truth and spirit, more and more refined, abstract, and immaterial.

Now this state of affairs can never be remedied by the empirical ego's merely going through gestures of purification and concentration, suppressing thought, creating a void in itself, sinking into its own essential purity, and so on. This is only another way of affirming itself as an independent, autonomous possessor now of thought, now of no-thought; now of science, now of contemplation; now of ideas, now of emptiness. The "emptiness" which the empirical ego strives to produce in itself by "wiping the mirror" clean of all thoughts is then nothing but a trick. At best it is bogus mysticism; and at worst, schizophrenia. In any case, it is pure illusion, and it makes true enlightenment impossible. This is precisely what Zaehner stigmatizes as "individualism" and "passive mysticism" in its most refined and dangerous sense.

V

As Hui Neng saw, it really makes no difference whatever if external objects are present in the "mirror" of consciousness. There is no need to exclude or suppress them. Enlightenment does not consist in being without them. True emptiness in the realization of the underlying *prajna*-wisdom of the Unconscious is attained when the light of *prajna* (the Greek Fathers would say of the "Logos"; Zaehner would say "spirit" or "pneuma") breaks through our empirical consciousness and floods with its intelligibility not only our whole being but all the things that we see and know around us. We are thus transformed in the *prajna* light, we "become" that light, which in fact we "are." We see the light in everything. In such a situation, the presence of external objects and concepts in our mind is irrelevant, for our knowledge of them is no longer obtained by thinking about them as objects. We know them in a vastly different way, as we now know ourselves not in ourselves, not in our own mind, but in *prajna,* or, as a Christian would say, in God.

This state of "enlightenment" then has nothing to do with the exclusion of external or material reality, and when it denies the "existence" of the empirical self and of external objects, this denial is not the denial of their *reality* (which is neither affirmed nor denied) but of their relevance insofar as they are isolated in their own forms. They have become irrelevant because the subject-object relationship that existed when the empirical self regarded them and cherished its thoughts about them has now been abolished in the "void." But this void is by no means a mere negation. It would be more helpful for Western minds to call it a *pure affirmation* of the fullness of positive being, though Buddhists would prefer to stick to their principle, neither affirming nor negating.

The void (or the Unconscious) may be said to have two aspects. First, it simply is what it is. Second, it is realized, it is aware of itself, and to speak improperly, this awareness (*prajna*) is "in us," or, better, we are "in it." Here of course the mirror of "mind" is not *our mind* but the *void itself,* the Unconscious as manifest and conscious in us. Hui Neng describes it in the following terms:

> When the light of Prajna penetrates the ground nature of consciousness [In this translation, Suzuki is obviously thinking of Eckhart] it illuminates inside and outside; everything grows transparent and one recognizes one's inmost mind. To recognize the inmost mind is emancipation . . . this means the realization of the Unconscious (*wu nien*). What is the Unconscious? It is to see things as they are and not to become attached to anything. . . . To be unconscious means to be innocent of the working of a relative (empirical) mind. . . . When there is no abiding of thought anywhere on anything—this is being unbound. This not abiding anywhere is the root of our life.[13]

Prajna, therefore, is not attained when one reaches a deeper interior center in one's self (Suzuki's translation, "one's inmost mind," might be misleading here). It does not consist in "abiding" in a secret mystical point in one's own being, but in *abiding nowhere in particular,* neither in self nor out of self. It does not consist in self-realization as an affirmation of one's own limited being, or as fruition of one's inner spiritual essence, but on the contrary it is liberated from any need of self-affirmation and self-realization whatever. In a word, *prajna* is not *self*-realization, but realization pure and simple, beyond subject and object. In such realization, evidently "emptiness" is no longer opposed to "fullness," but emptiness and fullness are One. Zero equals infinity.[14]

> Another Zen Master was asked how this enlightenment could be attained.
> He answered: "Only by seeing into nothingness."
>
> Disciple: "Nothingness: but is this not something to see?" (I.e., does it not become an object—the empty mirror, unstained by "thought"?)

Master: "Though there is the act of seeing, the object is not to be designated as *something*."

Disciple: "If this is not to be designated as 'something' [object], what is the seeing?"
Master: *"To see where there is no something* [object], *this is true seeing, this is eternal seeing."* [15]

Where there is a "something," a limited or defined object, there is less than Act, therefore not "fullness." Once again, "emptiness" of all limited forms is the fullness of the One: but the One must never be regarded as an isolated form. To avoid this temptation, the Zen masters speak always of emptiness.

V I

It is impossible to get a real grasp of Zen if one does not understand the distinction between the two concepts of "mind" propounded by the Southern School of Hui Neng and the Northern School of Shen Hsiu. This resolves itself into a real grasp of the difference between the two verses ascribed (at least by posterity) to the two contestants for the title of Sixth Patriarch.

It is possible to misunderstand the true import of Hui Neng if one is unduly anxious to bring Zen a little closer to conventional Western ideas of contemplation, so that the Zen experience can be more clearly demonstrated to be something akin to supernatural mysticism, that is to say, to an "I-Thou" experience of God. To reconcile Zen with this type of union with God is a very difficult task, because it seems to involve one, again, in the subject-object relationship which is discarded by the Zen experience of void. But is it after all necessary to cling to this one viewpoint? Is Martin Buber's formula absolutely the only one that validly describes this ultimate spiritual experience? Is a personal encounter with a personal God limited to an experience of God as "object" of knowledge and love on the part of a clearly defined, individual, and empirical subject? Or does not the empirical self vanish in the highest forms of Christian mysticism? It is my opinion that even the contemplation of the void as described by Hui Neng has definite affinities with well-known records of Christian mystic experience, but space does not permit us to quote texts here.

In any event, here is how Father Dumoulin describes the "void" and "unconsciousness" of Hui Neng:

> The resolving of all opposites in the Void is the basic metaphysical doctrine of the Diamond Sutra on which Hui Neng founds his teachings. The *absence of thoughts which is achieved in the practice of contemplation by the suppression of all concepts* is regarded as the primal state of mind whose mirror light clings to no concept . . . The absence of all concepts indicates that the mind adheres to no object *but rather engages in pure mirror activity.* This absolute knowing *constitutes the unlimited activity of inexhaustible motion in the motionlessness of the mind . . . All objects are cleared away by contemplation of the void, and personal consciousness is overcome.*[16]

It is true that Hui Neng, following the *Diamond Sutra,* aims at "resolving all opposites in the void," and if by "personal consciousness" we mean the self-awareness of the empirical ego, then it is true that this is "overcome" in the Zen of the Southern School. Yet it seems to me that the language in which Father Dumoulin describes the Zen of Hui Neng does not clearly distinguish it from the "mirror wiping" of Shen Hsiu. The reason is that he speaks, in the passages which I have italicized, of *dhyana* (Zen, meditation) as a means for attaining a certain definite state of mind, a "purity" which underlies one's ordinary thought and which is recovered, uncovered, or what you will, by "the suppression of all concepts." This would be nothing more or less than "wiping the mirror" of primal consciousness clean of conceptual thought, thus revealing the presence of an inner purity, regarded as a distinct and more fundamental reality than the "everyday mind." Thus, according to this view, there would be three realities to consider: the primal mirror activity of *prajna* (enlightenment, contemplation, wisdom), the obscured and erroneous everyday mind in which the mirror is defiled with concepts, and the *dhyana* or means by which one passes from the second to the first, by emptying the "mirror" of concepts. According to this view, which seems to me to be that of Shen Hsiu, there is a definite objective, a specific state of mind "to be attained": a state of mirrorlike purity which is enlightenment. It is the object of striving and self-purification. The individual monk sets himself this aim, this object, this definitely limited state of consciousness, "pure mirror activity," and when he succeeds in attaining it, he is conscious of the fact that he is no longer in that other state, the "everyday mind," but is now in a higher and more perfect state, that of absolute purity.

As against this, Hui Neng affirmed that "from the first, not a thing is"; that is to say, the attaining is a non-attaining, because the "purity" of *sunyata* is not purity and void considered as an object of contemplation, but a non-seeing, a non-contemplation, in which precisely it is realized that the "mirror" or the original mind (of *prajna* and emptiness) is actually a non-mirror, and "no-mind." This apophatic statement is therefore much more forceful and absolute than the cataphatic positive statement of Shen Hsiu which makes it seem that in the beginning there is a primal mirror consciousness as a specific object to be brought back to awareness by the suppression of thought.

In a word, for Shen Hsiu, the enlightenment and "seeing" of Zen consists in an awareness of primal mirrorlike purity, and the "mirror light" of the mind is the basis, or "stand," upon which contemplation solidly rests. This "stand" is a "purity" existing as something entirely apart from and "beyond" the confusion and darkness of the "everyday mind." It is a primordial reality to be sought as an objective basis for contemplation. For Hui Neng there is no primal "object" on which to stand, there is no stand, the "seeing" of Zen is a non-seeing, and as Suzuki says, describing Hui Neng's teaching, "The seeing is the result of having nothing to stand on." [17] Hence, illumination is not a matter of "seeing purity" or "emptiness" as an object which one contemplates or in which one becomes immersed. It is simply "pure seeing," beyond subject and object, and therefore "no-seeing." Suzuki also admits that Hui Neng does at times use terms that suggest the other type of Zen, but there are nevertheless texts which formally exclude the "mirror wiping" of Shen Hsiu. For example:

> There are some people with the confused notion that the greatest achievement is to sit quietly with an emptied mind, where not a thought is allowed to be conceived. . . .

> When you cherish the notion of purity and cling to it, you turn purity into falsehood . . . . Purity has neither form nor shape, and when you claim an achievement by establishing a form to be known as purity, you obstruct your own self nature and are purity bound.[18]

"Purity" or "nirvana" or "illumination" is regarded as an objective form by those who make it the object of "attainment" in meditation, but "when outwardly a man is attracted to form, his inward mind is disturbed," even if this "form" is of the highest and most spiritual nature. On the other hand, true *dhyana* for Hui Neng consists in living in the midst of "form" and "beings" without being obsessed by or attached to any of them. What is *dhyana* then? It is not to be obstructed in all things . . . it is not to get attached to "purity." And "those who recognize an objective world and find their mind undisturbed are in true *dhyana*." It is the exact opposite of Shen Hsiu, for whom peace and illumination consisted in preferring inner purity to external objects. Hui Neng entirely transcends the apparent opposition, and his "illumination" is the sure and unshakable experience that this opposition is illusory.

A disciple of Hui Neng, arguing with a representative of the Northern School on this point of meditation as an essential means to recover an "inner illumination" which purifies the mind and makes one see into one's "self-nature" (one's original nature, or the "Buddha nature," *prajna*), replied:

> If you speak of an illumination taking place inside and outside, this is seeing into the mind of error. . . . This exercising in meditation owes its function ultimately to an erroneous way of viewing the truth . . .[19]

In a word, to view the secret inner purity of the mirror light as a separate entity which can be objectively "sought" and "attained" by meditation is to imagine *something that is not there*. "From the first, not a thing is." There is "nothing there" and this "nothing" that is there is *"sunyata*, emptiness, no-mind, the non-objective presence of no-seeing," and it seems much more like the *todo y nada* of St. John of the Cross than the illuminated inner self of the Neo-Platonists.

That is why the Zen masters of Hui Neng's school were so insistent on the fact that "Zen is your everyday mind." If you cannot find the emptiness of *prajna* in the very middle of concepts and contradictions, you cannot find it anywhere at all, because in fact it is nowhere in the first place. For that reason it is foolish to assert that "it is not in everyday things but in primal mirror activity." Since it is nowhere, we do not need to leave the point where we are and seek it somewhere else, but to forget all points as equally irrelevant because to seek the unlimited in a definite place is to limit it and hence not to find it.

This I think is the chief originality of Southern Chinese Zen, and it must be clearly brought out to distinguish it from the other forms of contemplation, both Asian and Western. The great merit of Hui Neng's Zen is that it liberates the mind from servitude to imagined spiritual states as "objects" which too easily become hypostatized and turn into idols that obsess and delude the seeker. In this, the Zen of Hui Neng comes rather close to the Gospels and St. Paul, though on an ontological rather than on a specifically religious level.

VII

Though Father Dumoulin is not sympathetic toward Hui Neng, he gives us a warmly appreciative picture of the Japanese Zen master Dogen (thirteenth century), whose enlightenment took place in an austere and severely disciplined Chinese Zen monastery where meditation was practiced "literally all day and night." [20] Hence, Dogen's Zen will be substantially the same as Shen Hsiu's. As described by Father Dumoulin, the enlightenment of Dogen resembles the deliverance from passion with which we are so familiar in Western mysticism (the *apatheia* of the Evagrian school), and it is represented as volitional rather than intellectual. In point of fact, Dogen was enlightened when the master rebuked one of the monks who had fallen asleep in his meditation, exclaiming: "In Zen, body and mind are cast off, why do you sleep?" [21] Here we have expressions to which Christian ascetic tradition has accustomed us. This view resembles the *bios angelikos* of Greek monasticism, the angelic life "out of the body" and even "above the soul" in a certain sense.

While Hui Neng resisted the trend that set meditation up in its own right as the ascetic means par excellence to attain illumination, Dogen not only gave himself with total generosity to *zazen* (sitting in meditation) and taught his disciples the best method, but "he saw in *zazen* the realization and fulfillment of the whole law of the Buddha." Among Buddhists, his approach is called the religion of "*zazen* only" and is regarded as "the return to the pure tradition of Buddha and the patriarchs." [22]

Interesting pages in Father Dumoulin's history treat of Dogen's teaching on meditation, on the proper way to sit, to breathe, etc. Together with the bodily discipline of "sitting," there is also a necessary interior discipline of detachment, of passionlessness, and of inner peace. Curiously enough, on one point Dogen seems to rejoin Hui Neng, or to come close to a similar result, when he teaches the Zen monk *not to desire any special experience* of enlightenment. And here, Father Dumoulin is quite sympathetic to Dogen's admonition: "Do not think about how to become a Buddha." He comments: "The purposelessness upon which Dogen insists above all is not difficult to comprehend *if one grasps that enlightenment is already present in zazen itself.*" [23]

Now this is and is not like Hui Neng. It is like Hui Neng in that it warns the monk not to look for enlightenment as a special psychological state. But it is completely unlike Hui Neng when it states that *zazen* contains in itself the substances and reality of enlightenment, so that the mere fact of persevering in meditation is, in practice, to "be enlightened." In Father Dumoulin's words: "Why should one harbor desires and dream about the future when in every instant of the sitting exercise one already possesses everything?" and "Every moment of *zazen* exists in the realm of the Buddha and is infinite." [24]

Perhaps the reason why the contemplation of Dogen appeals more immediately to the Western mind is that this description implies the action of a certain kind of religious faith, a surrender and an abandonment which Father Dumoulin obviously associates with Western models. One detects a hint of Caussade, for instance, in these words: "Dogen censures the disciples who, devoid of understanding, await a great experience and thereby neglect the present moment." [25] In addition, Father Dumoulin praises the Zen of Dogen because it is "endowed with high ethical spirit" and is never without a stern and joyous asceticism, based on "a sense of the transiency of earthly things."

Thus we have Dogen teaching both that sitting and meditation are the whole of Buddhism, and that, in Father Dumoulin's words, "nothing is more harmful than the conscious purpose of seeking Buddhahood by means of meditation." [26] Has he combined Shen Hsiu and Hui Neng? In practice, such a combination would not be possible except in terms of pure verbalism, and there remains a vast difference between Dogen and Hui Neng. Dogen and the so-called Soto school of Zen in Japan follow the lines laid down by Shen Hsiu: emphasis on meditation, asceticism, and method. The Rinzai school, which follows Hui Neng's teaching, while not abandoning meditation, takes a totally different view of it, and instead of emptying the mind of concepts by "quiet sitting," it seeks to plunge the Zen disciple into *satori*, or a metaphysical intuition of being by non-seeing and emptiness, through struggle with the *koan*.

Hence we reach a further paradox in Hui Neng. With him, non-seeing and no-mind are not renunciations but fulfillments. The seeing that is without subject or object is "pure seeing." The mind that is emptiness, void, and *sunyata* is the *prajna* mind, the metaphysical ground of being. So in reality, where Hui Neng prescribes a detachment from meditation and from inner psychological states, in order to favor this ontological intuition of the ground of being, Dogen follows a way of quiet and tranquil meditation which renounces seeing and intuition in order to dwell in an affective silence of the passions. Why does Hui Neng protest against this kind of meditation so vehemently? Because, as far as he is concerned, it is not only not illumination but it effectively prevents the real (ontological) intuition of *Chen-hsing* (seeing into the ground of being), *sunyata* (emptiness), and *prajna* (wisdom-contemplation), by turning *dhyana* (meditation) into an obstacle instead of a means. According to his view, if one merely rests in the tranquil silence of meditation, meditation becomes "an artificial construction which obstructs the way to emancipation." And if, in addition, one asserts that this tranquil resting is the same as enlightenment, because enlightenment is hidden and implicit within it, then the error is a hundred times worse.

Note that in the context of Christian meditation, based on theological faith, and not entirely dependent on the purity of ontological insight, the quiet meditation of Dogen could in fact turn into supernatural contemplation. Faith would be enough to effect the transition because it would provide not merely a psychological assurance that one had gained possession of his object, but, as St. John of the Cross teaches, since "faith is the proximate means of union with God" as He is in Himself, in His invisibility and seeming "emptiness" (as regards our own intellect, to which He is "pure darkness" and "night"),[27] if one's meditation is a resting in faith, then it does in fact attain to the infinite source of all supernatural light. The approach which seeks to find in Zen a form of spirituality akin to Christian mysticism might then argue that the devotedness and ethical purity of those who meditate according to Dogen's way seem to indicate that, without knowing it, they have stumbled upon a hidden and primitive form of theological faith. Though he does not assert this clearly, I believe that Father Dumoulin is at least inclined to take this line of thought in maintaining the possibility of true mysticism among the Zen masters. This leads him to take a special interest in the Dogen school, which is less paradoxical and more ascetic than the Rinzai sect and gives evidence of profound piety. This amounts, in the end, to judging their "mysticism" not on its intellectual illumination but on evidence of its sincerity and good will.

The Rinzai school, with its meditation on the enigmatic and sometimes frankly absurd *koan* riddles, with its resort to violent and unpredictable responses on the part of the master, with its deliberate impieties (one Zen master actually burned a wooden statue of Buddha in order to keep himself warm on a cold winter night), is hardly calculated to inspire confidence in the Christian who is looking for the kind of pious behavior that is traditionally expected in the modern novice or the budding contemplative in a Christian religious order. The least that can be said about some of the Zen masters of the Hui Neng and Rinzai tradition is that they would hardly meet the norms set up for the canonization of saints by the Church of Rome. This would seem to be enough to disqualify them for all time from any plausible claim to be mystics. And indeed they themselves are the loudest in renouncing any such claim.

But if we take another look, and if we remember some of the stories told of the Christian saints and mystics (the Desert Fathers and the first Franciscans, for example), we will have to admit that they show a spirit of freedom and abandon which is to us less disconcerting only because we have heard the stories so often and they fit into a familiar context. But rather than speculate on the stories that are told about these people, be they Christian mystics or Chinese Zen masters, it is more profitable to examine the texts bearing on the ultimate "illumination," and here again we return to Hui Neng and his tradition, as representing the purest and most original exemplars of the Zen spirit.

Here once again we must be quite clear that when Hui Neng speaks of "non-seeing" and "no-mind" he is, first of all, not describing a psychological state but a metaphysical intuition of the ground of being. And second, we must remember that his "non-seeing" is in fact "seeing." Thus, what we have is a breakthrough in which subjective and psychological consciousness is transcended and there is an awareness which does not look at being (or the void) as an object but enters into the self-awareness of the being-void which is the *prajna mind.* Here again, a Western writer about Zen and Yoga who is usually very alert gives a somewhat misleading description. In an otherwise excellent article on no-mind in the *Zen Dictionary,* Ernest Wood has this: "So Hui Neng demanded *sunyata* [emptiness], the avoidance of all qualities, as prerequisite to true seeing." This supposes that for Hui Neng emptiness was a psychological term designating a psychological state of emptiness, whereas he really means it to be a metaphysical term designating the void of pure being. Once again, the illumination of the Hui Neng school is a breakthrough which does not simply produce an enlightened state of consciousness or superconsciousness in the experience of the individual—which for Buddhism would be a fundamental error and evidence of "ignorance" (*avidya*)—but which allows being itself to reveal its light, which is no-light and void.

The Zen intuition of Hui Neng is then an intuition of the metaphysical ground of all being and knowledge as void. This void itself is infinite. Suzuki loves to repeat the formula that for Zen "zero equals infinity," and in this he is close to the *todo y nada* of St. John of the Cross. The infinite emptiness is then infinite totality and fullness. The ground of this void is *sunyata*, but the pure void is also pure light, because it is void of all (limited) mind: and the light of the pure void manifests itself in act. But since this can be translated into positive terms, pure void is pure Being. And pure Being is by that very fact pure illumination. And the illumination springs from pure Being in perfect Actuality. This is only an intellectual intuition, but one which penetrates far more deeply than mere metaphysical speculation. This is the light of an experience of the ground of being, the light therefore of pure ontological contemplation. But to a Christian perhaps the most extraordinary thing about it is that it sees the primal ontological constitution of being or void in a Trinitarian relationship.

Suzuki brings this out in speaking of a descendant of Hui Neng, namely Ma Tzu, who started out with a "mirror-wiping Zen" and left it to take up the Zen of the Southern School. In fact, it was Ma Tzu who was sitting in meditation (*zazen*) when his master took up the tile and polished it, teaching him that just as one could not make a tile into a mirror by polishing it, so one could not become a Buddha by sitting in meditation. Suzuki comments that at this time Ma

Tzu "had no idea of the self-seeing [*prajna-dhyana*, Hui Neng school] type [of Zen], no conception that self-nature which is self-being was self-seeing, that there was no Being besides Seeing which is Acting, that these three terms, Being, Seeing, and Acting, were synonymous and interchangeable." [28] This quite remarkable passage, which as far as I know has not been commented on or developed, suggests not a *doctrine* of a Trinitarian structure of being, but an *experience* of the ground of being as pure void which is light and act because it is fullness and totality.

Thus, there is in the "void" of Hui Neng a surprising Trinitarian structure that reminds us of all that is most characteristic of the highest forms of Christian contemplation, whether in the Cappadocian school, the Augustinians and Franciscans, Ruysbroeck and the Rhenish mystics, or St. John of the Cross and the Carmelites. Needless to say, this intuition is not theological and not even explicitly or manifestly religious, but the least that can be said about it by a Christian is that it certainly gives us food for thought. And this "Trinitarian structure" is this: the ground of all Being is pure Void (*sunyata*-emptiness), which is *prajna*, light illuminating everything in a pure Act of being-void without any limitation. The ground-Being is not distinct from itself as Light and as Act. And to this basic constitution of being there corresponds the threefold disposition of the mind in illumination. First, the ground which is Void; second, the emptiness and nowhereness of no-mind which is *dhyana* (right meditation) and illumination; and third, the act of realization, or *prajna*, in which the void and light are so to speak let loose in pure freedom and power to give and spend in action this self which is no-self, this void which is the inexhaustible source of all light and act, and which has broken through into our own life, bursting its limitations and uniting us to itself so that we are lost in the boundless freedom and energy of *prajna*-wisdom.

This means inevitably a fulfillment in love, which is what

one seemingly least expects in Hui Neng, but it is an ineluc-
table consequence of the Trinitarian structure of being which
his Zen perceives and reveals. And in point of fact I can say
that for Daisetz Suzuki, who is certainly the most authoritative and accomplished interpreter of the Rinzai tradition, the
"most important thing of all is love." This he himself told me
in a personal conversation in which I feel that he intended, by
this remark, to sum up all that he had ever written, experienced, or said.[29]

It remains now to conclude this brief essay by returning to
Professor Zaehner's reservations about Zen. Is Zen then to be
classed without further qualification among a whole collection of spiritualities of inwardness, withdrawal, inner purity,
and quiet contemplation which simply take a man out of the
world and make him indifferent to all forms of worldly life
and action? Does it offer him nothing but the injunction to
reject all forms of ordinary and human experience as trivial,
gross, worldly, and profane? Certainly, if Zen is to consist in
simply sitting quietly away from everything and "guarding
the mind" to keep it spotlessly clean of all concepts, then it is
surely open to this criticism. But if the Zen of Hui Neng is
what we have tried to show it to be, then it is anything but a
mystique of passivity and of withdrawal. It is not a resting in
one's own interiority but a complete release from bondage to
the limited and subjective self.

It is evident that when we understand the true originality
of Hui Neng we see that his Zen is not a "liberation" from
matter in order to "bind" us to interior purity, *dhyana*, illumination, and so on. It is a liberation from all forms of bondage to techniques, to exercises, to systems of thought and of
spirituality, to specific forms of individual spiritual achievement, to limited and dogmatic social programs. Hui Neng's
aim was the direct awareness in which is formed the "truth
that makes us free"—not the truth as an object of knowledge
only, but the truth lived and experienced in concrete and existential awareness. For this reason it is axiomatic in the Zen

of Hui Neng that works and external concern should in no way be regarded as obstacles to Zen; on the contrary, Zen is manifested in them as well as anywhere else, including eating, sleeping, or the humblest material functions. If the Zen of Hui Neng is properly understood, we see that it is in fact a necessary condition for the "convergence" which Zaehner looks for. But it is not by itself a sufficient condition. We must also look to the transcendent and personal center upon which this love, liberated by illumination and freedom, can converge. That center is the Risen and Deathless Christ in Whom all are fulfilled in One.

VIII

We now have a complete version in English of Hui Neng's *Platform Scripture,* with facing Chinese text. The work has been done with great care by Professor Wing-Tsit Chan of Dartmouth and is supplemented by a long and detailed introduction. It is published in a series issued by the Asian Institute of St. John's University, New York, under the general editorship of Dr. Paul K. T. Sih.

Hui Neng, the sixth Zen patriarch, was probably not himself the author of the *Platform Scripture,* which is, however, the official manifesto of his "Southern School," the most successful as well as the most characteristically Chinese school of Zen Buddhism. All authorities seem to agree that Hui Neng's Zen is "pure Zen," and that the later masters can be judged according to their closeness to the *Platform Scripture.* In point of fact, this is the only Chinese Buddhist text that attained the status of a scripture in the sense of a sutra. That is to say, it is the only Chinese Zen text that has found its way into what we might call, for want of a better analogy, the "Mahayana canon." At the same time, while recognizing the authenticity of the *Platform Scripture,* Zen masters in the past have also showed themselves quite reluctant to let their disci-

ples rest on it as on an authoritative book, since in the transmission of the Zen tradition one of the essential characters is
that the Zen experience must be communicated *"without the
sutras."*

The cardinal importance of the *Platform Scripture* is that
it claims to give the most exact description of what Hui Neng
meant by Zen enlightenment, with his characteristic insistence that it was to be attained suddenly, and not as the result
of quietistic meditation or any other previous discipline. Hui
Neng is completely non-doctrinal, concrete, and, one might
say, existential in his view of Zen as a unity that cannot be
divided into stages or degrees such as "meditation" and "contemplation" (or *prajna*-wisdom).

In order then to fully appreciate the importance of this
text, one must be aware of the statements it makes on these
characteristic points. Here is where, without being able in the
least to judge the relative merits of different translations, we
must note that it would be highly desirable if the key terms in
Zen were somehow standardized in English so that they might
be identified from one translation to the next. It is unfortunate that Professor Wing-Tsit Chan and other authorities,
such as Dr. Suzuki, who is followed by a host of articulate
disciples, do not use the same terminology at all. Thus, the
reader who is unprepared for this will tend to pass over the
most important parts of the sutra without realizing what he
is reading. Doubtless, if Professor Wing-Tsit Chan is determined to use "calmness" instead of "meditation," he has a
good reason for doing so. It is that Hui Neng tends to down-
grade the importance of meditation as a distinct and formal
exercise. Nevertheless, the word "calmness" is not of a nature
to suggest the crucial point raised by Hui Neng, a point
which is at the heart of Chinese Zen.

If a non-expert might be permitted a suggestion, it would
be this: that whenever these important terms are used, irre-
spective of how they might be translated, some indication

should be given of their importance. One way to do this would be to furnish, in brackets, the Chinese or Sanskrit equivalents, or both, as these have gradually become rather familiar to students of Zen who are nevertheless not Orientalists.

CLASSIC CHINESE THOUGHT

We of the West still hold instinctively to the prejudice that our world and our civilization are the "whole world" and that we have a mission to lead all others to the particular cultural goals we have set for ourselves. But the world is bigger than we have imagined, and its new directions are not always those that we ourselves have envisaged. The destiny of the whole human family has, it is true, been practically in our hands for four hundred years. But times are changing. Asia and Africa are beginning to claim their active share, for better or for worse, in directing the course of civilization and the fortunes of mankind. At such a time it is vitally necessary for the West to understand the traditional thought of the great Asian cultures: China, India, and Japan. This is necessary not only for specialists, but for every educated person in the West.

The cultural heritage of Asia has as much right to be studied in our colleges as the cultural heritage of Greece and Rome. Asian cultural traditions have, like our own ancient cultures, been profoundly spiritual. It was perhaps with good

reason that the Chinese and Japanese regarded the first European traders as "barbarians from the West" and sought to
protect their people against a baleful influence by excluding
them. Rare indeed were the Europeans who, like the first Jesuits in China, were able to evaluate correctly the profound
Catholicity of Confucian philosophy. If the West continues to
underestimate and to neglect the spiritual heritage of the
East, it may hasten the tragedy that threatens man and his
civilizations. If the West can recognize that contact with Eastern thought can renew our appreciation for our own cultural
heritage, a product of the fusion of the Judeo-Christian religion with Greco-Roman culture, then it will be easier to defend that heritage, not only in Asia but in the West as well.

The great traditions of China[1]

One of our most facile generalizations about Chinese thought
is that there are "three traditions" corresponding with the
"three religions of China": Confucianism, Taoism, and Buddhism. This cliché is all the more tempting to an American
because it reminds him of a familiar classification at home:
Catholicism, Protestantism, and Judaism in America. Actually, there is not the faintest resemblance between the ancient
religious situation in China and the present one in America.
Oriental religions, while they may differ in philosophy and
belief, have a way of interpenetrating quite freely with one
another. Chinese Buddhism is in fact an amalgam of Taoism
and the "Great Vehicle" (Mahayana Buddhism) of India.
The Taoism that still goes by that name is in fact much further from the original Taoism of Lao Tzu than Zen Buddhism, which preserves intact the living thought of the *Tao
Te Ching,* while popular Taoism is a hodgepodge of quasi-
magical rites, folklore, and superstition. As for Confucianism,
it is certainly not a religion in the same sense as Christianity.
Confucianism is less a "faith" than a sacred philosophy, a way

of life based on archaic religious wisdom, and capable of coexistence with some other faith in religious revelation. As the first Jesuits in China believed, it should not be impossible to remain essentially a Confucian and yet to become a Christian, since Confucianism is nothing more or less than natural ethics in a very refined and traditional form: the natural law expressed in a sacred culture. This thesis was of course violently disputed by those Catholics who did not understand the real nature of Confucianism and who were misled into believing that Confucian rites were by their nature idolatrous. This was certainly never true of pure and authentic Confucianism.

Buddhism has been the most important popular religion in China, for it brought to the masses a definite message of salvation: but it has not influenced Chinese thought as much as primitive Taoism or, especially, Confucianism. As Buddhism is a relatively late arrival, we shall not be concerned with it in this essay. It does not belong to the classic creative period of Chinese philosophy.

The greatest, most universal, most "catholic" and most influential school of Chinese thought is the *Ju* school, founded by Kung Tzu, or "Master Kung," whose name was latinized by early missionaries as Confucius. We shall call him Kung Tzu, and if we have occasion to refer to his greatest disciple, known to the West as Mencius, we shall call him by his Chinese name: Meng Tzu. Since Lao Tzu, the mystic, and father of Taoism, evidently did not interest the early Jesuits, he never became "Laotius." Nevertheless, his fascinating work, the *Tao Te Ching* (The Way and Its Power), has perhaps been more often translated than any other Chinese classic.

The sources of classic thought

Kung Tzu and Lao Tzu lived in the sixth century B.C. (though in the case of Lao Tzu no date and no biographical fact can ever be taken as certain). This made them contemporaries with Gautama Buddha in India, Pythagoras in Greece, and in Israel the prophets of the exile, such as Jeremiah, Ezechiel, and Deutero-Isaiah. The "classic period" of early Chinese thought extended down through the so-called "period of the warring states" until the third century and the establishment of a unified China. This unification of China was to a great extent the work of the "Legalists," who brought the most vital and productive age of Chinese thought to a close and perhaps did more than anyone else to create a society that would guarantee the formalization and even the ossification of classic thought for centuries to come. At any rate, by the third century the really great development of Chinese philosophy ceased, and what followed was little more than scholastic elaboration or sporadic mystical revolt.

Kung Tzu wrote nothing himself, and did not consider himself an originator but rather a formulator and a defender of the unwritten traditions of the archaic past. Indeed, when we look at prehistoric China through the eyes of Kung Tzu, and consider the book of primitive odes collected by him, we are astonished at the depth and sophistication of the culture that he sought to preserve in its highest and most perfect form through ages which, he thought, would probably be ages of decadence.

Lao Tzu evidently shared Kung's reverence for the past, but he went back even further into the archaic world and was suspicious of any systematization or social order as "artificial." In his mind, government, politics, and even ethical systems, no matter how good they might be in themselves, were a perversion of man's natural simplicity. They made man competitive, self-centered, aggressive, and ultimately they led him into obsession with delusive ideas about himself. From these delusions came hatreds, schisms, factions, wars, and the destruction of society. Lao Tzu's ideal of society was the small primitive community consisting of nothing more than a few villages inhabited by simple, self-forgetful men in complete harmony with the hidden, ineffable *Tao*.

It was when the Great Tao declined
That there appeared humanity and righteousness.
It was when knowledge and intelligence arose
That there appeared much hypocrisy.
It was when the six relations lost their harmony
That there was talk of filial piety and paternal affection.
It was when the country fell into chaos and confusion
That there was talk of loyalty and trustworthiness.[2]

Those who cannot cope with the paradoxical simplicity of this archaic and mystical view of the world imagine that Lao Tzu is scorning the virtues of humanity and righteousness (the foundation stones of the Confucian ethic). On the contrary, he is trying to preach a doctrine which to Westerners seems oversubtle: that the *reality* of humanity and righteousness is right there in front of your nose if only you will practice them without self-conscious reflection, or self-congratulation, and without trying to explain and justify your acts by ethical theory. In other words, reflection and self-consciousness are what begin the *vitiation* of true moral activity, according to Lao Tzu. As soon as man becomes aware of doing good and avoiding evil, he is no longer perfectly good. Ethical rationalization makes possible that schizoid division between words and acts, between thoughts and deeds, which (as Hamlet well knew) finally reduces honest activity to complete helplessness, or else lays the way open for political or religious crooks to do all the evil they like in the name of "righteousness."

For Lao Tzu, the worst way of creating a wise and just society was to set men apart and prepare them, school them, to be wise men, rulers, "superior men" (which of course was just what Kung Tzu wanted to do). For Lao Tzu, if one were to be righteous he should first of all fly all thought of righteousness, and put out of his mind any ideal image of himself as a "righteous man."

He who knows glory but keeps to disgrace
Becomes the valley of the world.

Being the valley of the world
He finds contentment in constant virtue,
He returns to the uncarved block.

The cutting up of the uncarved block results in vessels,
Which in the hands of the sage become officers,
Truly, "a great cutter does not cut . . ."

This kind of thought is definitely left of center. And there is no denying it sounds dangerous. It seems to be a revolt against reason and order. The only one who can safely follow Lao Tzu is the man who is already on the way to being a saint and a sage. Indeed, that is the implicit assumption made by Taoism: it is a philosophy that would have worked very well in the Garden of Eden, and if Adam and Eve had stuck to the *Tao,* there would have been little difficulty for the rest of us in doing so. But from the moment a man is immersed in confusion and carried away by the passions and eccentricities of a bewildered and not always upright society, he has little hope of finding himself merely by shutting his eyes and following the *Tao.* The *Tao* may be within him, but he is completely out of touch with it, just as he is out of touch with his own inmost self. Recovery of the *Tao* is impossible without a complete transformation, a change of heart, which Christianity would call *metanoia.* Zen of course envisaged this problem, and studied how to arrive at *satori,* or the explosive rediscovery of the hidden and lost reality within us.

The result of the practical anarchism which is implicit in Taoist doctrine was that Taoism had really little to offer a man who wanted to struggle—as most men must—with the problems of life in society. All it could offer was a kind of evasion from society. Those who really understood it could make this evasion *upward* into the transcendent, but the majority, less capable of wisdom, made the evasion downward into the Freudian id, an all too obvious consummation. Consequently, the anarchist tendencies of Taoism played straight into the hands of the extreme right wing of Chinese thought—the Legalists, who were to build a totalitarian China and deliver it over into the polite Confucian hands of the Son of Heaven.

Confucian humanism

Before we consider the Legalists, let us take a look at the *Ju* (Confucian) school in the center. When Lao Tzu disparaged "humanity" or "human-heartedness" (*Jen*), he was talking about the very essence of *Ju*. The foundation of Confucian system is first of all the *human person* and then his relations with other persons in society. This of course sounds quite modern—because one of our illusions about ourselves is that we have finally discovered "personality" and "personalism" in the twentieth century. Such are the advantages of not having had a classical education, which would do us the disservice of reminding us that personalism was very much alive in the sixth century B.C., and that, in fact, it existed then in a much more authentic form than it does among us with our "personality tests" and "personality problems" (the ultimate carving of the Taoist uncarved block!).

Ju is therefore a humanist and personalist doctrine, and this humanism is religious and sacred, as we shall later see. The development of *Ju* was intellectual and ethical, objective, social, and one might even say democratic. The greatest thing about it is its universality. Even modern Chinese Communists sometimes appeal to Kung Tzu and his basic doctrines on the formation of the person and his place in society. However, the Communists would do better to claim as their ancestors the totalitarian Legalists, who unified China by pretty much the tactics now being used by Mao Tse-tung.

The basic wisdom of Kung Tzu lies not so much in his knowledge of human nature as in his faith in man. This he shares with Meng Tzu, his disciple, who gave his belief an immortal expression in the "Ox Mountain parable." The Ox

Mountain, once thickly wooded, was near a center of population out of which men came with axes and cut down the trees. When the trees began to grow again, they set their flocks to graze on the mountainside, and the flocks ate up the green shoots. No one would believe the mountain had once been wooded. So too with man: he is naturally inclined to virtue, but his actions, in a greedy and grasping society, so completely destroy all evidence of his innate goodness that he appears to be naturally evil. (See the last section of this chapter.)

The Confucians believed that a society governed by a just and "human-hearted" prince would once again bring out the concealed goodness in the subjects. Men would once again be themselves, and would gradually recover the ability to act virtuously, kindly, and mercifully. But this was no matter of sentimental good will and paternalist gestures of kindness. The society in which such results were to be obtained must be very seriously and firmly held together by a social order that draws its strength not from the authority of law but from the deep and sacred significance of liturgical rites, *Li*. These rites, which bring earth into harmony with heaven, are not merely the cult of heaven itself but also the expression of those affective relationships which, in their varying degrees, bind men to one another.

Confucianism is not just a collection of formalistic devotions which have been so loosely dismissed by us as "ancestor worship." The Confucian system of rites was meant to give full expression to that natural and humane love which is the only genuine guarantee of peace and unity in society, and which produces that unity not by imposing it from without but by *bringing it out from within men themselves*. Kung Tzu believed, then, that men *could* be good, but that for them to actualize these potentialities they had to live in a society that fully respected their hidden goodness, respected them as persons, with sacred and God-given rights, and educated them in the same respect by a wholly sacred cultural organism that embraced every aspect of their lives. This is the true meaning of Confucianism, and we must not interpret *Ju* merely as a kind of sentimental humanitarianism that breathes abstract "good will" to all men while emptying their pockets.

If Kung Tzu was practical, it was not with a facile, utilitarian pragmatism but with a sacred sense of the "will of heaven" inscribed in the very nature of man. Kung therefore respected the *Tao,* but unlike the Taoists he did not concentrate on the *Tao* alone. He set his gaze clearly on man, and he saw that if the will of heaven was to have any meaning on earth, it would have to be in some way reflected in man's society. He could not afford to be an anarchist. He persisted in trying to educate the good prince and the wise ministers who would bring about his desired ends. He never had any immediate success in practical politics, but he did succeed in founding a system of education which, for all its eventual limitations, was able to survive, and to form generations of scholars who were to be the glory of their nation and a singular credit to the human race.

However, the picture is not all as bright as this might suggest. If one had to be a sage to live up to the doctrine of Lao Tzu, one also had to be a man of profound humility, insight, and patience to be fully loyal to the principles of *Ju.* All China, at least all the ruling class of China, was supposed in theory to be educated on Confucian lines: but many, and not the least successful of Chinese statesmen, were men who, with an outward façade of *Ju,* were inwardly either pedants or rigid and heartless conformists or unprincipled crooks.

To situate the Legalists correctly, let us review the three tendencies in Chinese tradition. In the center, we have the Confucian line, which believes in the goodness of human nature and seeks to educate it, bring it to light, patiently and humanely by a sacred culture that expresses love and educates men in love, *Jen.* The *Ju* school does not seek to interfere with human nature, but definitely tries to help it.

The Taoists tended to be less concerned with man than

with *Tao*. They were suspicious of everything that savored of education and "help." They thought man would do a lot better if fewer people tried to monkey with his nature and "help" him to be wise and just. They felt that the hidden *Tao* would be perfectly able to manifest itself and work out its hidden and inscrutable meaning in man if man would only let himself and his nature alone. The mystics then preached a way that is not a way, a "returning to the root," a deep respect for reality in its primitive and inscrutable state as an "uncarved block." Theirs was a way of "non-action," which is falsely interpreted as pure quietism when in reality it is a policy of non-interference and an abstention from useless and artificial action. Taoism is not complete non-action but rather non-activism. It appears to be antinomian, but this apparent antinomianism (inherited by Zen) must be carefully and properly understood. Those who fool with it do so at their own risk, and court ruin.

Legalism

The right-wing Legalists are just the opposite. Not only do they interfere with the course of nature, but they interfere with it as thoroughly and completely as they possibly can. In every conceivable way they bring man under the rule of organization and of law. In every possible sphere, subjective spontaneity is replaced by objective decrees and sanctions, rewards and punishments. The Legalists not only refuse to respect the "uncarved block" of life and nature, but they take it upon themselves to carve it as thoroughly as possible, even if that means carving it right out of existence.

In general, the Legalists took a pessimistic view of man: his nature could not be left to itself because it was evil, and hence it had to be whipped into good action, against its own spontaneous instincts, by absolute authoritarianism. This ineradicable selfishness of human nature could not be corrected, and to try to correct it, or bring it back to a supposed primitive order and rightness, as did Meng Tzu, was a delusion. No, the Legalist would simply accept the inevitable and *make use of* man's depravity, his greed, his fears, his lusts, his self-interest, in order to bring about certain political ends. These ends can best be summed up in the one word: *power (shih)*.

Chinese Legalism goes back to a Confucian root, in the scholar Hsun Tzu (third century B.C.), who was loyal to the *Ju* school while being completely agnostic and skeptical. So much so that it can be said of him that "the Chinese people lost their faith in Hsun Tzu's time and have not yet found it." [3] Liu Wu-Chi adds what may perhaps be a really gross exaggeration: "From now on religion had to go underground, so to speak, and never again would it become the chief concern of Chinese intellectuals except for a few erratic souls." [4]

Two students of Hsun, Han Fei Tzu and Li Szu (one of whom eventually killed the other), became the founders of Legalism.

Pure Legalism discards all concern for moral and supernatural sanctions. The rites, the wisdom, the "human-heartedness" of *Ju* are of no use to it. Law replaces everything else, including morality, religion, and conscience: for law in this tradition does not appeal to the sanction of conscience. It relies, much more effectively from their pragmatic point of view, on punishment—and on extremely severe punishment. Objective standards of right and wrong are thrown out of court. The only standard is the arbitrary will of the ruler. And in order to make sure that everyone conforms to the will of the ruler, the whole of society must become a network of espionage in which groups and individuals are mutually responsible for each other and are obliged to inform on each other regularly and in detail. Even language, especially the language of law, means nothing except what the ruler means it to mean. And presumably the ruler can change his mind whenever he likes, since he is responsible neither to heaven nor to *Tao*. Perhaps, indeed, his change of mind is dictated by heaven or by *Tao*, who knows? He alone is the judge of that. But if his decisions do not work . . .

The goal of Legalism is to make the state so powerful that all its enemies are wiped out. Then there will be peace. This doctrine is not confined to Asia or to the third century B.C.

A few lines from Arthur Waley will fill in some details of this somber picture:

> What prevents the people spontaneously falling in with the ruler's plans is that he takes a long view, whereas they take a short one. He knows that by sacrificing every other activity to food production and preparation for war a state can become so strong that at every battle it will overthrow an enemy's army . . .
>
> The ruler's subjects, on the other hand, are incapable of taking long views. What they hate is toil and danger, what they want is immediate ease and peace, and they are too stupid to see that ultimate safety can only be secured by immediate discomfort and danger . . . [If the ruler keeps them in order with severe laws] no greater service to the people could be imagined; but there are some so stupid as not to realize this and to insist upon regarding the ruler's measures as tyranny. These stupid critics want order to exist in the state but are opposed to every measure that is calculated to produce order . . . Severe laws and heavy punishments are what the people hate; but they are the only means by which order can prevail. Compassion and sympathy on the part of the ruler towards his subjects are what the people approve of; but it is through these that a country falls into danger . . . "It is a misfortune for a prosperous country not to be at war; for in peace time it will breed the six maggots, to wit Rites and Music, the Songs (Odes) and the Book (of History), the cultivation of goodness, filial piety and respect for elders, sincerity and truth, purity and integrity, kindness and morality, detraction of warfare and shame at taking part in it. In a country that has these twelve things, the ruler will not promote agriculture and warfare, with the result that he will become impoverished . . ." [5]

The last part of this passage is quoted directly from Han Fei Tzu, and we have no difficulty in seeing that the Legalist psychology and methods are in fact very close to the methods of totalism, whether Communist or Fascist.

The four Confucian classics

It must not be imagined that the Legalists were friendly to *Ju* doctrine, though they owed something to it. On the contrary, soon after they had in effect seized power by putting the first emperor on the throne and abolishing feudalism, they set about abolishing Confucianism as well. And they nearly succeeded. Li Szu proposed the extermination of scholars as parasites. All the libraries were to be burned; especially all works of poetry, philosophy, and history were to be destroyed. Only certain chosen records, in the care of Legalist scholars, were to be preserved, along with works on divination, medicine, and agriculture. The study of law would be pursued under close surveillance. The edict was put into effect and carried out with such thoroughness that some of the ancient books were irreparably lost. Fortunately, copies of most of them were hidden and eventually recovered, at least in part. A year later, no fewer than four hundred and six *Ju* scholars were executed.

Fortunately, the Confucian school revived under the Han Dynasty (second century B.C.) and worked itself into an official position which it never lost until the twentieth century. It founded great universities, controlled the education of scholars by its system of examinations on the Confucian classics, and finally, in the tenth century A.D., caused the most important works of the school to be reproduced by block printing: the first edition of its kind in history.

Legalism may have been the actual political philosophy of many rulers of China, but it never deeply or directly affected the thinking of the people at large or even of the scholars. It may indirectly have contributed to an atmosphere of pragmatism and even of cynicism in regard to public affairs. It may have driven whole generations of Chinese, by way of reaction, to seek a brighter and more supernatural hope in the protection of the merciful Amida, whose way was the way of love and who would deliver them from the sufferings of this world and admit them to his paradise.

But the philosophy of Kung and Meng Tzu, renewed and reshaped by various scholastic revivals, continued to be the most vital and effective spiritual force in China. For centuries, the education of the Chinese scholar class was based, legally and officially, upon the study of the four Confucian classics. As soon as the Chinese boy learned to read, he began to memorize and to study the *Analects*, the *Great Learning*, and the *Doctrine of the Mean* (all three ascribed to Kung Tzu), together with the *Book of Meng Tzu*, containing the sayings ascribed to Meng. Anyone who wants to understand anything about China should read and meditate on these four books. This teaching continues to exercise a vital influence in China today. What is its peculiar strength?

In answering this question we shall try to arrive at some estimate of the *Confucian spirit*. This may not be quite as easy as it appears.

The basis of Kung's philosophy, which is essentially practical, is what is known in the West by the rather vague term of "natural law." But this must not be taken to mean a law abstracted or deduced from our nature. It is the *Tao* itself, but the ethical *Tao*, the way of man, rather than the metaphysical *Tao* or the inscrutable way of God. The main difference between the *Ju* school and the Taoists is that the latter are concerned with the metaphysical, the former with the ethical *Tao*. Needless to say, this comparison itself is not always clear, except in the *Doctrine of the Mean*, or *Chung Yung*, which is one of the four Confucian classics, and which was a kind of Confucian reply to Taoism. Actually, to call the *Chung Yung* the *Doctrine of the Mean* is very inadequate. Ezra Pound's rendering, the "Unwobbling Pivot," is perhaps closer to the author's intention. Other suggestions by various translators include the "Working Center" and the "Functioning Mean" or the "Mean in Action." The point of the book is that at the very center of man's being is an intimate, dynamic principle of reality. It is not merely a static concept or essence, but a "nature" constantly seeking to express its reality in right action. In this way, the hidden reality of heaven communicates itself to the man who is in harmony with it by his actions. *Reality* is the goal, and reality in act is the "axis" or "pivot" of man's being. The "superior man" is one who finds this axis in himself and lives always centered upon it. Other men do not find the center, the axis, and spend their lives aimlessly carried this way and that by winds of fortune and of passion. Their center is not in themselves but somewhere outside them, and their lives are consequently a turmoil of frustration, self-seeking, and confusion.

The starting point of Kung's teaching is that there is a transcendent and objective reality (the metaphysical nature of which is never discussed) called "heaven." And there are other realities, the changing, contingent realities of earth and of man, which can be in order or in disorder. They are in order when they are in accord, or in "harmony," with "heaven"—with the ultimately real. They are in disorder when they are out of harmony with the highest principles, with the will of heaven. One might compare this to the doctrine of the sapiential books of the Bible, as well as with the Gospels.

The whole philosophy of Kung is much more than a philosophy: it is a *wisdom,* that is to say, it is not a doctrine, but a *way of life* impregnated with truth. One only comes to know the doctrine by living the truth which it contains, and that truth is not a partial truth but the whole meaning of existence, both for the person and for the society to which he belongs.

One can only fully live the Confucian doctrine by living in

a religious society governed by a sacred ritual, which is a practical "acting out" of the wisdom immanent in nature.

One might almost say that for Kung "rites" or *Li* were the visible expression of the hidden reality of the universe: the manifestation of heaven, or, we would say, of divine wisdom, in human affairs and in the social order. It is not enough for the divine order to be present metaphysically: or enough for man to bring it into his own life or the life of society by moral conduct. The will of heaven is something that has to be *celebrated* in earthly society, and celebrated with beauty and solemnity. Without this element of splendor and harmony, wisdom is not complete, it can never be mature, it can never be completely beautiful. One might say that it is the splendor of *Li* (in all its sobriety and truth) which gives a dynamic and productive quality to wisdom. For when man participates in *Li* by faithfully performing the rites which are called for by his given situation and by his relationships to others, he thereby is awakened, grows, and is transformed. At the same time his society (whether the family, the city, or the state) grows and is transformed with him.

The Great Learning

The so-called *Great Learning* (*Ta Hsio*) attributed to Kung Tzu is a brief but rich treatise which is so concrete and condensed that we can easily miss its point. When translated into a Western language derived from Latin or Greek, any Chinese text tends to lose most of the concreteness and solidity of its meaning. We are apt to skip through the *Great Learning* catching at words like "good government," "self-knowledge," "discipline" as we go by. And we put it aside. Another treatise on self-cultivation for the sake of social service!

But that is not the *Great Learning*.

The whole meaning of the *Great Learning* is that right action depends on the awareness of the person acting. Awareness of what? Of himself, of his own responsibility, of his abstract ethical ideal to which he tries to conform, of the desires that he seeks to satisfy? None of these things. It means awareness of the personal root and the inner truth which is the center and source of all well-ordered action. However, this personal root is not mere subjective sincerity, since it is conditioned by appreciation of the objective nature of things. It is not mere rationalization, it is embodied in action itself. The order of society depends on awareness, right action, and self-discipline in all its members from the ruler to the least of common men. The peace and order of the community depend on the discipline of awareness by which each member recognizes what is to be done by him, or what properly accords with his identity and function in the community.

The *Great Learning* is by no means a matter of introspective self-awareness, still less of hypersubjective self-consciousness. It is objective, concrete, and dynamic. It is a way of enlightenment, of clarification by *intelligent action*. It is a way of acting that clarifies reality by being itself clear, direct, definite, and true, and thus bringing the agent into harmony with the objectively real, not in a metaphysical sense so much as in a practical, social, and religious sense. And this contact with the real, the ethical *Tao*, is celebrated, solemnized, and clarified by rites. Thus, moral action is at the same time contemplative and liturgical. Symbolic ceremony gives morality a character of deeper realization. The Confucian ethic is not only not automatic, not the product of inert routine. It is more than merely spontaneous. It is the *fruit of spiritual awareness*.

This concept of awareness is often translated as "sincerity." Ezra Pound sees it as a matter of meaning, of clarity and precise signification, which he describes as "the sun's lance coming to rest on the precise spot verbally." It is a matter of semantic focus, as well as a sapiential clarification of what was hitherto unknown and inarticulate, the bringing forth of the unconscious and the obscure into the focus of clarity by

meaningful action at the right moment, with the right purpose, in the right manner, with the proper splendor of rite,
that is to say, with sacred and aesthetic awareness and with the
correct definition of what was to be done.

This, to my mind, is a splendid and civilized concept of
ethical action. It is magnificently human, contemplative,
noble, and productive. When one grasps this Confucian outlook on life and on human activity, one realizes in a flash its
implications for the meaning of Christian conduct—a meaning which has been to such a great extent emptied of religious
content and emasculated by abstractness in our cerebral
Western culture. It is quite clear, though, that this archaic
Chinese concept accords with the unspoken presuppositions
of a thought like that of St. Thomas Aquinas, who, though he
uses the technical language of Greek philosophy, is nevertheless fully concrete in this sapiential sense because he is a contemplative: not a Platonic contemplative in love with incorporeal essences, but a Christian contemplative who sees the
divine light in every being. For everything exists "insofar as it
is known by God." [6]

If we miss this note of sacred awareness at the heart of
Kung's doctrine, we miss the point of the whole doctrine and
open the way to its secularization. And this is perhaps what
too often happened, in the scholastic revivals of *Ju* philosophy, in which its technical aspects were more and more emphasized at the expense of the living reality.

The *Great Learning* remains the key to classic Chinese
thought.

Conclusions

The starting point of Confucian education is then the cultivation of the person. When a man is wise, that is to say, when
he enters freely into the clarity of meaningful action and is
nourished and developed by the splendor and significance

with which "heaven" invests even the most ordinary and simple actions of human (social) existence, he is able to bring his wisdom to act in harmony with the wise acts of those around him. But this is at the antipodes of Legalism. The Legalist is by definition not wise in this sense at all. He simply conforms to the ruler's will in order to advance himself by serving the ruler's policy, which is always a policy of power and self-assertion. Here we come closer to certain modern and pragmatic misconceptions concerning the development of the person: that is, the development of aggressiveness, of astuteness, of attractiveness, of diplomatic skills; in a word, the ability to *succeed*. "Personality" in this sense is the power to impose yourself and your wishes on others. For Kung Tzu, wisdom by no means consists in imposing your will or your "personality" on somebody else, and making him serve your own ends by domination or by flattery. It is not that this is "wrong" according to some abstract standard, but before all else it is unhealthy because it is unreal. A man who acts like this is untrue to himself and at the same moment, by the same token, untrue to heaven, whose will is embedded deep in his very heart. He can only act so because he has failed to get to the root of good action. He does not really know himself.

The purpose of Kung's teaching, and this is why it became the foundation stone of official Chinese education, was to form a governing class of humane and enlightened scholars. We have indicated above that this intellectual elite sometimes participated more fully in the government and sometimes were pushed out of the way almost completely by Legalists. In practice, they always had to compete with the crafty, uneducated opportunists who were the court eunuchs. But in spite of the corruption, the iniquity, and the perversion of human nature that were able to flourish in this climate of official cynicism, the *Ju* scholars as a whole remained untouched by what was around them and the Confucian tradition remained pure. Otherwise it could not have borne the fruits that we know. Christopher Dawson has said:

The result [of Confucianism] has been that in China alone among the advanced civilizations of the world, the law of nature had not been a philosophical abstraction but a living force which has had a religious appeal to the heart and conscience of the people . . . In this way Chinese civilization seems to have solved certain fundamental problems of the social and moral order more successfully than any other known culture.[7]

So much for the past of Confucianism. What about the future? Since the fall of the Manchus and the end of the empire, there have been movements of strong reaction against *Ju* philosophy, and Chinese thinkers have demanded that it be thrown out altogether as a retrograde force that makes all vital contemporary thought impossible. At the same time, others have sought to perpetuate *Ju* in the form of an official national "religion," which, as we have seen, is also incongruous and absurd. With the coming of Chinese Communism, we might expect that the days of *Ju* are numbered. But is this exact?

Certainly Red China, in its efforts to create a new thought along with a new society, has reacted emphatically against all the traditional social elements of Confucianism that are associated with the old China: especially its ritual and sacred tradition, and above all its emphasis on basic relationships and on the family. Mao Tse-tung is on record as detesting Confucius. There can be no doubt that the traditional *Ju* philosophy and culture, in the rigidly fixed form which it finally acquired after centuries of application and interpretation, is now a thing of the past. China will never return to the days of mandarins and the official examinations in scholastic Confucianism, complete with the "eight-legged essay." Yet, though Communism is generally critical of and unfriendly to the tradition of Kung Tzu, some Communist writers are not afraid to appeal to the *Great Learning* and doubtless to other Confucian classics as sources for a living Chinese thought. It is possible that *Ju*, much pruned and "adapted," may still have an influence in modern China, though we may remark in passing that Communist China would do better to point to Legalism as the Chinese fountainhead of its "tradition."

The future of Confucianism lies perhaps outside China itself, in its future impact in the West. We hopefully look forward not to an age of eclecticism and syncretism, certainly, but to an age of understanding and adaptation that will be able to synthesize and make use of all that is good and noble in all the traditions of the past. If the world is to survive and if civilization is to endure or rather perhaps weather its present crisis and recover its dimension of "wisdom," we must hope for a new world culture that takes account of all civilized philosophies.

The Christian scholar is obligated by his sacred vocation to understand and even preserve the heritage of all the great traditions insofar as they contain truths that cannot be neglected and that offer precious insights into Christianity itself. As the monks of the Middle Ages and the scholastics of the thirteenth century preserved the cultural traditions of Greece and Rome and adapted what they found in Arabic philosophy and science, so we too have a far greater task before us. It is time that we begin to consider something of our responsibility. Jesuit scholars have already pointed the way by contributing to the numerous excellent translations of Oriental texts. Benedictines can hardly find it difficult to understand and to admire the tradition of Kung Tzu, which has in it so many elements in common with the tradition and spirit of St. Benedict.

The Ox Mountain Parable of Meng Tzu

In the fourth and third centuries B.C., in an age (like ours) of war and chaos, Meng Tzu (Mencius) built on the philosophical and spiritual foundations which had been laid by Confucius. One of his central intuitions was that human nature was basically good, but that this basic goodness was destroyed by evil acts, and had to be restored by right education, education in "humaneness." The great man, said Meng Tzu, is the man "who has not lost the heart of a child." This statement was not meant to be sentimental. It implied the serious duty to preserve the spontaneous and deep natural instinct to love, that instinct which is safeguarded by the mysterious action of life itself and of providence, but which is destroyed by the willfulness, the passionate arbitrariness of man's greed. In contrast to Meng Tzu were Mo Tzu and the Legalist school, which wanted man to be forced into the path of an abstract universal love by the force of the law (Mo Tzu), or else made to obey arbitrary power by the threat of punishment (the Legalists). Since, according to them, man was basically evil, his evil tendencies had to be harnessed and exploited by the power of the ruler.

But Meng Tzu believed that man was good, and that the function of a wise and merciful ruler was to bring out the goodness in his subjects by education. The Ox Mountain story is a parable of mercy. Note especially the emphasis of Meng Tzu on the "night wind," which is here rendered "night spirit," the merciful, secret, and mysterious influence of unconscious nature which, according to him, as long as it is not tampered with, heals and revives man's good tendencies, his "right mind." Our text is based on a literal translation from the Chinese, found in an appendix to I. A. Richards' *Mencius on the Mind.*

THE OX MOUNTAIN PARABLE

i

Master Meng said: There was once a fine forest on the Ox Mountain,
Near the capital of a populous country.
The men came out with axes and cut down the trees. Was it still a fine forest?

Yet, resting in the alternation of days and nights, moistened
    by dew,
The stumps sprouted, the trees began to grow again.
Then out came goats and cattle to browse on the young shoots,
The Ox Mountain was stripped utterly bare.
And the people, seeing it stripped utterly bare,
Think the Ox Mountain never had any woods on it at all.

ii

Our mind too, stripped bare, like the mountain,
Still cannot be without some basic tendency to love.
But just as men with axes, cutting down the trees every
    morning,
Destroy the beauty of the forest,
So we, by our daily actions, destroy our right mind.

Day follows night, giving rest to the murdered forest,
The moisture of the dawn spirit
Awakens in us the right loves, the right aversions.

With the actions of one morning we cut down this love,
And destroy it again. At last the night spirit
Is no longer able to revive our right mind.

Where, then, do our likes and dislikes differ from those of
    animals?
In nothing much.
Men see us, and say we never had in us anything but evil.
Is this man's nature?

iii

Whatever is cultivated rightly, will surely grow.
Whatever is not cultivated rightly must surely perish.
Master Kung (Confucius) said:

Grasp it firmly and you will keep it.
Grasp it loosely, and it will vanish out of your hand.
Its comings and goings have no fixed times:
No one knows its country!

Of man's right mind, of this only does he speak!

LOVE AND TAO

A hundred years ago America began to discover the Orient and its philosophical tradition. The discovery was valid, it reached toward the inner truth of Oriental thought. The intuitions of Emerson and Thoreau were rich in promises that were not afterward fulfilled by successors. America did not have the patience to continue what was so happily begun. The door that had opened for an instant, closed again for a century. Now that the door seems to be opening again (and sometimes one wonders if it is the door of the same house), we have another chance. It is imperative for us to find out what is inside this fabulous edifice. From where we stand, we can descry the residents dressed in our kind of clothing and engaged in our kind of frantic gesturing. They are tearing the place apart and rebuilding it in the likeness of our own utilitarian dwellings, department stores, and factories. Not that there is anything wrong with industrial production, with its higher standard of living. Yet we know, or should know, by this time, that our material riches unfortunately imply a spiritual, cultural, and moral poverty that are perhaps far greater than we see.

In this quandary we cannot help regarding an effort such as that of the Institute of Asian Studies, at St. John's University, as a real, though seemingly modest, benefaction. Here, in contrast to some other institutions where zeal and organized efficiency go together with a lack of spiritual perspective, we find rather an emphasis on the primary and the sapiential. Under the direction of Dr. Paul K. T. Sih, a well-known Chinese Catholic scholar, two of the most fundamental and traditional Chinese philosophical texts have been handsomely published in excellent translations, with facing Chinese versions. No better choice of a translator could have been made for the *Tao Te Ching* than Dr. John C. H. Wu, whose rendering is superb. More than this, Dr. Wu is able not only to translate Lao Tzu's words but also to interpret his life. He is remarkable as a Catholic who has brought over into his fervent life of Christian faith all the humility, the sense of dependence on the unseen, and the sapiential awareness of the hidden patterns of life which, in Taoism, foreshadowed their fulfillment in the Gospel of Christ. The translator of the *Hsiao Ching* is a Maryknoll missionary sister with a profound knowledge and love of Chinese classical thought. She has done her task superlatively well.

Both these works are of such fundamental importance that a mere review calling attention, in stereotyped images, to their various qualities, would hardly be adequate.

Everyone knows in a vague way that the *Tao Te Ching* is poetic, and indeed that it is great poetry. Most people know that it usually impresses Westerners as more than a little quietistic. Hence they treat it with condescension as a quaint impractical document of an ancient day when no one bothered much about progress. Perhaps they do not realize that some of the wisdom of the *Tao Te Ching*, which so often reminds one of the Sermon on the Mount, is absolutely necessary for us not only to progress but even to survive.

As for the *Hsiao Ching*: this is less well known in the West than the *Tao* classic. But it is no less characteristic of China. Here in this "Classic of Filial Love" we find not so much a Confucianism that is arbitrarily opposed to Taoism, as what I would venture to call a *Confucian kind of Taoism*. We must not imagine that the classic Confucianism of the third century B.C. was something purely formalistic and external, without respect for the interior, the hidden mystery in which all life has its invisible roots. On the contrary, we shall see that filial love was, for these Confucians, the taproot which was sunk most deeply in the mystery of the ethical *Tao* and which, unless it was cut by selfishness, kept both the individual and society in living contact with the mysterious will of heaven.

Classics and masters

The word "Ching" which is found in the titles of these and other celebrated Chinese texts, is roughly translated as "classic." It means something more than just "book" and yet it does not have the connotations that "classic" has come to have for us. In the West, a classical work is one of the "highest class" because it embodies the peculiar literary and stylistic excellence we find in the great writers of Greece and Rome. The classical writers of Greece and Rome are those whose style is most pure and admirable. But a "Ching" is not a classic in this sense. It might be more helpful to consider the word "Ching" as corresponding to "Bible." Remember that our word "Bible" comes from the Greek *ta biblia*, or "the books." And not simply "the books," but precisely the books as contrasted with some other vehicle of tradition; that is to say, with the oral tradition. Words like "Ching" and "Bible" then, far from referring to what we would now call "Great Books" as distinct from books of a lesser literary value, mean simply the ancient traditions as contained in books rather than as orally transmitted. Such books then are not so much the ornaments and jewels of a culture as its mind and its memory, though that is not accurate if we remember that oral transmission of wisdom is more important than transmission in writing.

Hence a "Ching" is an *authoritative* book. Not that it has been written by an authoritative man (a "classical scholar" or even a "philosopher"), but that it goes back to an authority higher than man. One hesitates to use the word supernatural in connection with Chinese thought, yet the fact that the *Tao Te Ching* distinguishes a *Tao* that can be known and spoken of from the *Tao* which is unknown and unable to be named authorizes us to find here something that corresponds with our notion of God above and beyond the cosmos. After all, did not Dr. Wu, when he translated the Gospel of St. John into Chinese thirty years ago, start out with the words: "In the beginning was Tao, and Tao was with God, and Tao was God"?

If we want to understand the position of writers like these ancient Chinese philosophers, we must compare them not only with Plato or Parmenides but also with the Hebrew scribes, the transmitters of the wisdom tradition in the so-called sapiential books of the Old Testament. The ideogram which represents Tzu, in Lao Tzu (Master Lao), means both "master" and "child." Indeed, we find this ideogram combined with another in the word *hsiao*, meaning filial love. There the "son" is seen bearing the "father" on his shoulders. A master is therefore a child of the ancient Fathers, who bears their tradition with him and transmits it to future generations. Or rather, to be much more accurate, a master is a child who, like Lao Tzu, knows how to draw secret nourishment in silence from his "mother" the Tao.

Hence, we see that a master is not merely one who learns and repeats authoritative forms of words passed on from the time of the ancients; he is one who has been born to his wisdom by the mysterious all-embracing and merciful love which is the mother of all being. He is one who knows the unknown not by intellectual penetration, or by a science that wrests for itself the secrets of heaven, but by the wisdom of "littleness" and silence which knows how to receive in secret a word that cannot be uttered except in an enigma. This enigma is not a verbal riddle but the existential mystery of life itself. The wisdom of the *Tao Te Ching* leads therefore to Zen, which is at least ideally a transmission without any "Ching," passed on unaccountably from master to disciple not by means of written words but by seemingly absurd *koans,* accompanied, on occasion, by kicks and clouts on the head.

The classic of Tao

The literal translation of the title *Tao Te Ching* is the "Book of the Way and Its (Hidden) Power." If there is a correct answer to the question: "What is the *Tao?"* it is: "I don't know."

> Tao *can be talked about but not the eternal* Tao,
> *Names can be named, but not the Eternal Name.*
> *As the origin of heaven and earth it is nameless:*
> *As "the Mother" of all things it is namable.*

It is like an "empty bowl that can never be filled." It is like the hole in the center of the hub of a wheel, upon which all the spokes converge.

> *We make doors and windows for a room;*
> *But it is these empty spaces that make the room livable. . . .*

> *Look at it, but you cannot see it!*
> *Its name is* Formless.

> *Listen to it, but you cannot hear it!*
> *Its name is* Soundless.

Grasp at it, but you cannot get it!
Its name is Incorporeal.

It is the formless form, the imageless image. It is a "fountain spirit" of inexhaustible life and yet never draws attention to itself. It does its work without remark and without recognition. It is utterly elusive: if you think you have seen it, what you have seen is not the *Tao*. Yet it is the source of all, and all things return to it "as to their home."

The whole secret of life lies in the discovery of this *Tao* which can never be discovered. This does not involve an intellectual quest, but rather a spiritual change of one's whole being. One "reaches" the *Tao* by "becoming like" the *Tao*, by acting, in some sense, according to the "way" (*Tao*). For the *Tao* is at once perfect activity and perfect rest. It is supreme act, *actus purissimus*. Hence human activity, even virtuous activity, is not enough to bring one into line with the *Tao*. Virtuous activity tends to be busy and showy, and even with the best intentions in the world it cannot avoid sounding the trumpet before itself in the market place.

He who cultivates the Tao *is one with the* Tao;
He who practices Virtue is one with Virtue;
And he who courts after Loss is one with Loss.

The way of loss is the way of whirlwind activity, of rash endeavor, of ambition, the accumulation of "extraneous growths." It is the way of aggression, of success. The way of virtue is the Confucian way of self-conscious and professional goodness, which is, in fact, a less pure form of virtue. St. Thomas would say it works *humano modo* rather than with the divine and mysterious spontaneity of the gifts of the Holy Ghost. But the way of *Tao* is just that: the way of supreme spontaneity, which is virtuous in a transcendent sense because it "does not strive."

High virtue is non-virtuous;
Therefore it has virtue.
Low virtue never frees itself from virtuousness,
Therefore, it has no virtue.

The "sage," or the man who has discovered the secret of the *Tao,* has not acquired any special esoteric knowledge that sets him apart from others and makes him smarter than they are. On the contrary, he is from a certain point of view more stupid and exteriorly less remarkable. He is "dim and ob-scure." While everyone else exults over success as over a sacri-ficial ox, he alone is silent, "like a babe who has not yet smiled." Though he has in fact "returned to the root," the *Tao,* he appears to be the "only one who has no home to re-turn to." He is very much like the One who has nowhere to lay His head, even though the foxes may have holes and the birds of the air their nests. He who has found the *Tao* has no local habitation and no name on the earth. He is "bland like the ocean, aimless as the wafting gale." Again we remember the Gospels: "The wind blows where it pleases . . . even so is every man who is born of the Spirit" (John 3:8).

The way of the sage is the way of not-attacking, not charg-ing at his objective, not busying himself too intently about his goals. The Chinese ideogram for this is, unfortunately, hardly able to be translated. The "active" symbol in it looks like a charging horse. *Wu wei* is a Taoist and Zen technical expres-sion, and perhaps it is better left as it stands. Dr. Wu coins an English expression for it: "non-ado," and one can see what is at the back of his mind. It recalls the Shakespeare title *Much Ado About Nothing.*

The Japanese Zen artist and poet Sengai has left us two Japanese characters, *Bu Ji,* which are a work of art in them-selves and eloquent of the spirit of *Tao. Bu Ji* means "noth-ing doing." I can say that there is more energy, more creativ-ity, more productiveness in these two powerful signs created by Sengai than in all the skyscrapers of New York, and yet he dashed them onto paper with four strokes of his brush.

Hence *wu wei* is far from being inactive. It is supreme activity, because it acts at rest, acts without effort. Its effortlessness is not a matter of inertia, but of harmony with the hidden power that drives the planets and the cosmos.

The sage, then, accomplishes very much indeed because it is the *Tao* that acts in him and through him. He does not act of and by himself, still less for himself alone. His action is not a violent manipulation of exterior reality, an "attack" on the outside world, bending it to his conquering will: on the contrary, he respects external reality by yielding to it, and his yielding is at once an act of worship, a recognition of sacredness, and a perfect accomplishment of what is demanded by the precise situation.

The world is a sacred vessel which must not be tampered with or grabbed after.

To tamper with it is to spoil it, and to grasp it is to lose it.

The power of the sage is then the very power which has been revealed in the Gospels as Pure Love. *Deus caritas est* is the full manifestation of the truth hidden in the nameless *Tao,* and yet it still leaves *Tao* nameless. For love is not a name, any more than *Tao* is. One must go beyond the word and enter into communion with the reality before he can know anything about it: and then, more likely than not, he will know "in the cloud of unknowing."

The sixty-seventh chapter of the *Tao Te Ching* is one of the most profound and the most akin to Christianity. In the *Tao,* "which is queer like nothing on earth," are found three treasures: mercy, frugality, and not wanting to be first in the world. And the extraordinarily profound statement is made

Because I am merciful, therefore I can be brave . . .
For heaven will come to the rescue of the merciful and protect
    him with its mercy.

Again one hears echoes of the Gospel: "Blessed are the merciful . . ." "Perfect love casteth out fear." Comparing Dr. Wu's translation with that of Lin Yutang in the Modern Library edition of Lao Tzu (another extremely interesting translation, with parallel passages from the poet and sage Chuang Tzu), we find new perspectives. (It is often necessary to read a translated Chinese text in two or more versions.)

> *If one forsakes love and fearlessness,*
> *   forsakes restraint and reserve power,*
> *   forsakes following behind and rushes in front,*
> *He is doomed!*
>
> *For love is victorious in attack*
> *   And invulnerable in defense,*
> Heaven arms with love
> Those it would not see destroyed.

The word which Lin Yutang translates as "love" and Dr. Wu as "mercy" is in fact the compassionate love of the mother for the child. Once again, the sage and the wise ruler are men who do not rush forward to aggrandize themselves, but cherish, with loving concern, the "sacred" reality of persons and things which have been entrusted to them by the *Tao*.

It must be remembered that the *Tao Te Ching* is basically not a manual for hermits but a treatise on government, and much is said there on war and peace. It is a manual that our leaders might be expected to read, and doubtless some of them might do so with profit. One of its most astute sayings is that in a war the winner is likely to be the side that enters the war with the most sorrow.

> *To rejoice over a victory is to rejoice over the slaughter of men!*
> *Hence a man who rejoices over the slaughter of men cannot*
> *   expect to thrive in the world of men.*
> *. . . Every victory is a funeral.*

The classic of filial love

The paradoxical brilliance of the *Tao* classic contrasts with the simplicity of the *Hsiao Ching,* a primer of Chinese Confucian ethics and one of the first texts formerly studied by Chinese schoolboys. But this makes it even more interesting, in some respects, than the better known *Tao Te Ching.* Many who would be secretly irritated by the apparent subtlety of the *Tao* classic might prefer to meditate on the "Classic of Filial Love." It is a revelation of the deepest natural wisdom, and its intuitions are surprisingly "modern." In fact, we are here on the same ground as Freud, and substantially the same conclusions that were reached by Freud more than twenty centuries later are here exposed in all simplicity and without benefit of the Oedipus complex.

One might be tempted to imagine that this treatise is designed merely to keep sons in subjection to their parents and hence to exalt parental authority for its own sake. It is doubtless true that the rigid formalism of Confucian ethics became, after two thousand years, a somewhat suffocating system. But, in its original purity, the Confucian ideal is basically *personalistic.* The fundamental justification for filial piety is that our person is received as a gift from our parents and is to be fully developed out of gratitude toward them. Hence, the astounding fact that this filial piety is not simply a cult of the parent as such, but a development of one's own gifts in honor of the parents who gave them to us. Then, when we reach manhood and our parents are old, we make a fitting return to them by loving support. This basic attitude is said to be "the foundation of virtue and the root of civilization."

If a child can enter fruitfully and lovingly into the five basic relationships, he will certainly develop into a good citizen and a worthy leader, supposing that to be his vocation. The five basic relationships are those of father to son, marked by *justice;* mother to son, marked by *compassion,* or merciful love; the son to his parents, marked by *filial love;* the elder brother to his younger brother, marked by *friendship;* and the younger to the elder, marked by *respect* for his senior.

Thus, we see a wonderful organic complex of strength from the father, warmth from the mother, gratitude from the son, and wholesome respectful friendship between brothers. "He who really loves his parents will not be proud in high station; he will not be insubordinate in an inferior position; among his equals he will not be contentious. To be proud in high station is to be ruined; to be insubordinate in an inferior position is to incur punishment; to be contentious among one's equals leads to physical violence. As long as these three evils are not uprooted, a son cannot be called filial even though he feast his parents daily on three kinds of choice meat." On such a ground grows up a love that reaches out through society and makes it the earthly image of the invisible order of heaven.

The *Hsiao Ching* then shows how this love has various ways of coming to fruitful development in all the levels of society, from the Son of Heaven down through the princes and scholars to the peasants. "From the Son of Heaven to the commoners, if filial piety is not pursued from beginning to end, disasters are sure to follow." The society of love (compare the works of Pseudo-Dionysius) is hierarchical. The lower depend on the higher in this exercise of love. The emperor is at the summit. All depends on him, and he should ideally be capable of the widest and most all-embracing love. For he must love all his subjects and care for their needs. In so doing, he embodies the "heavenly principle" on earth and imitates heaven, who loves all alike. He also has a duty to share with his subjects this knowledge of heavenly love, and this he does by means of *ritual and music.* In other words, the nation which lives by love grows in love by liturgical celebration of the mystery of love: such are the Christian terms in which we might expand this primitive intuition.

It is important to notice that in all this there is no such

thing as blind subservience to age and to authority. On the contrary, one of the basic duties of filial love is to correct the father when he is wrong, and one of the basic duties of the minister is to correct his prince when he errs. This, of course, was the ideal. The pungent humor of Chuang Tzu shows us many occasions when in practice this kind of "filial love" was not appreciated.

Conclusions

Christopher Dawson has remarked on the "religious vacuum" in our education. It is absolutely essential to introduce into our study of the humanities a dimension of *wisdom* oriented to contemplation as well as to wise action. For this, it is no longer sufficient merely to go back over the Christian and European cultural traditions. The horizons of the world are no longer confined to Europe and America. We have to gain new perspectives, and on this our spiritual and even our physical survival may depend.

THE JESUITS IN CHINA

The sixteenth-century Jesuit missionaries in China and Paraguay have become legendary for the inspired and farsighted originality of their apostolate. Yet the legend has not always been well understood, nor has the full reality been made public. Only in recent years have we begun to appreciate the significance of Matthew Ricci entering Peking with his map of the world, his clock, his telescope, and his hydraulic machines. These were more than ingenious toys with which to beguile his way into the forbidden city. (Contrary to legend, Ricci was *not* called into the emperor's presence to wind up the clock when it first ran down.)

When Ricci dressed as a Confucian scholar, this was not a Jesuitical disguise. The Jesuits wore the traditional robes of the Chinese scholar because they earned the right to do so just as seriously as any other Chinese scholar. They won themselves a place among the mandarins by their knowledge of science and philosophy. When Father Aleni commented on Confucius, in perfect literary Chinese, before the Academy of

Foochow, he was not putting on a show: he really had something to say. He knew what he was doing. His discourse was appreciated on its own merits, not as a tour de force. But when the rumor of such strange missionary procedures filtered out of China, distorted, expanded, and confused, they caused scandal in the West. They disturbed other Christians who had no knowledge of the situation and who had no way of distinguishing between Confucianism and idolatry.

It was almost impossible to get into China in the first place. St. Francis Xavier had, of course, failed. Michele Ruggieri, and then Ricci, had made their way into the Celestial Kingdom. A handful of Jesuits followed them. The missionaries were never to be more than a handful in the Ming Dynasty. For various good reasons, the Jesuits had the China mission all to themselves for over half a century. Perhaps this air of exclusive proprietorship and of esoteric mystery tantalized the other missionaries, who were stamping with impatience in the Philippines, trying to find out what was going on in China and looking for a way in.

It must be said that those who waited outside, who heard the mysterious reports that came from inside China, and who were horrified by what they heard, had quite a different kind of apostolate in mind. Indeed, some of them frankly wanted to repeat in China the exploits of Mexico and of Peru, where the cross had followed the cannon and now reigned in undisputed sovereignty over the converted empires of the Incas and the Aztecs. Why not do the same in China? Were not the Chinese pagans, idolaters, whose idolatry violated the natural law? Was not war a just means of rectifying this harmful disorder and opening the way for the preachers of the cross? Not all went this far. But many felt, and declared, that the Jesuit emphasis on mathematics, on astronomy, on scholarly discussion, on philosophical dialogue, hardly merited the name of an "apostolate." Were not these "purely natural means"? Was not the supernatural message of Christianity being falsified, if not totally obscured? Were not the Jesuits, furthermore, failing to promulgate the laws of the Church regarding fasts and holy days of obligation? Worst of all, were not the Jesuits themselves turning into Confucians? Were they not scandalously permitting idolatrous worship of Confucius and of the spirits of ancestors? All these misunderstandings grew from the fact that neither Confucian ethics nor the Chinese civilization could be properly evaluated without long study and careful adaptation.

The Jesuit China mission was far more than a "new approach" to a new and difficult mission field. The legend of the subtle Jesuit diplomatist who always has an ace up his sleeve has obscured the true meaning and profound importance of Ricci's "originality." He not only made an intelligent diagnosis of a totally unfamiliar condition, but he also, by implication, diagnosed *his own* condition and that of Western Christian civilization as a whole. In confronting the culture, the philosophy, and the religion of China, he immediately took stock of Catholicism as he had known it in Italy, and in the light granted him by the Holy Spirit he distinguished what was essentially Christian and truly Catholic—that is, universal—from cultural and accidental accretions proper to a certain time and place. Guided by the Holy Spirit, he was able to sacrifice all that was secondary and accidental. Like a true missionary, he divested himself of all that belonged to his own country and his own race and adopted all the good customs and attitudes of the land to which he had been sent. Far from being a shrewd "natural" tactic, this was a supernatural and Christian sacrifice, a stripping of himself in imitation of Christ, who "emptied Himself, taking the form of a servant," and of St. Paul becoming "all things to all men."

Indeed, the question that is summed up in the expression "the Chinese Rites Controversy" is basically a question of the real meaning of *natural* and *supernatural*. In the seventeenth century it was perhaps not difficult for Europeans to assume, without further investigation, that all non-Christian philosophies were "pagan" and indeed somehow diabolical. Was there any need of serious distinctions between the animism of the African jungles and the ethics of the Chinese mandarin? Did it not all eventually come to the same thing?

If that was the case, conciliation, adaptation, "dialogue," and indeed any attempt to sift out the good from the bad in Chinese thought and culture, could be made to appear a compromise that betrayed the Gospel and the cross of Christ. What was the use of half measures? Why this Jesuit diplomacy, this dressing in Chinese costume, this cult of Chinese ceremony and politeness? This was nothing but the "prudence of the world." And what good did it do? This dangerous policy was grieving the Holy Spirit, it was blocking grace, it was emptying the Gospel of meaning.

Was this the "truly supernatural" solution? On the surface it might appear to be so. But then this would imply perhaps an oversimplified and naïve and ultimately false idea of the supernatural: that in order to be "supernatural" it is sufficient to *contradict* "the natural." In this particular case, the supernatural approach would then be purely and simply to flout, denounce, and challenge all that the Chinese were used to, all that they loved, all that they revered. The "supernatural" thing was to demand, in the most aggressive and uncompromising terms, the total sacrifice of all their culture, all their traditional ideas and attitudes.

But does God demand this of men? Did He demand it of our own forefathers in the West? The early Church certainly condemned the idolatry and vices of pagan Rome: but she also adopted all that was good in Greek and Roman philosophical thought, and modeled her law, her liturgy, her daily life on classical patterns. In demanding that China sacrifice her own cultural patterns, were not these other missionaries imposing, instead, the patterns and attitudes of an alien Western culture which the Chinese could not possibly understand? Under the pretext of being "supernatural," were they not perhaps unconsciously following habitual and familiar natural patterns of their own, convinced that these patterns were supernatural simply because they were theirs?

Today, though it is by no means certain that we are much wiser than our fathers, we have at least come to the point where we can recognize that perhaps the distinction between nature and grace has sometimes been sadly confused by prejudice and ignorant generalizations.

Indeed, it is by no means certain that all prudence is natural prudence and that imprudence is the indisputable mark of grace. True, the work of God is never effectively undertaken without daring, without risk. One must risk everything, even one's very life. And the grace of the Holy Spirit leads men to make this kind of wager. If we look at Ricci, we will see that, in fact, his was the greater daring, the bolder risk. There is such a thing as the gift of counsel, which may well dictate solutions that are at first sight surprising because they go far beyond the ordinary limits and perspectives of practical conduct. Surely Matthew Ricci was guided by this spirit.

In a word, the apostolate of Ricci and the Jesuits was not necessarily "naturalism" at all. On the contrary, the Holy Spirit asks the Christian apostle to respect and preserve all that is good in the culture and philosophy of newly converted peoples. As Pope Pius XII said: "The Catholic Church is not one with western culture; she never identifies herself with any one culture, and she is ready to make a covenant with every culture. She readily recognizes in every culture what is not contrary to the work of the Creator" (letter of June 27, 1955, to the Bishop of Augsburg).

It might also be remarked that in the early Church a distinction was made between *kerygma* and *apologia* or *didascalia*. The kerygmatic apostolate was proper to the Judeo-Christian milieu. There, where for centuries the prophets had foretold the coming of the Messiah, it was necessary to announce His coming in bold and triumphant tones, summoning all to repent and follow Him. But speaking to the

Greeks in the Areopagus (Acts 17: 12–34), St. Paul took a different approach. Starting from pagan religions and philosophical thought, he proceeded to show that Christ was the fulfillment of legitimate natural aspirations of the human heart. Certainly the cross and resurrection were to be preached to the gentiles, but not until a certain preparatory teaching on the philosophical level had opened the way for this revealed message.

The desire for a vernacular liturgy is not entirely new. We know, of course, that where the Roman liturgy took shape, the laity knew and spoke Greek and Latin. Originally, all liturgies were celebrated in "the vernacular." However, it must be remembered that the "vernacular" is not purely and simply the language used in ordinary conversation. The language of the liturgy must have a *sacred* character. The vernacular, used in the liturgy, must then be a *literary* language with a certain elevation and nobility of tone. The Mass is not to be celebrated in slang.

The Jesuits in China confronted the fact that Latin presented great difficulty to the Chinese. The missionaries were concerned especially with the formation of Chinese priests, but this concern had remarkably interesting implications for the faithful. It is a mark of the deep human understanding and thorough Catholicity of the Jesuit mission in China.

In January, 1615, the Holy Office granted to the Chinese Jesuits three remarkable permissions, which were solemnly promulgated in a brief of June 27 by Pope Paul V.

First of all, they were permitted to celebrate Mass with their heads covered, since in China the uncovered head was a sign of disrespect.

Then they were allowed to translate the Scriptures into literary Chinese.

Finally, it was permitted for Chinese priests of the Society *to offer Mass and recite the breviary in literary Chinese*. No distinctions were made as to the different parts of the Mass or office; all could be said in Chinese. This permission, further-more, has never been revoked. Unfortunately, it has never been used.

The permission was granted only for Chinese priests of the Society of Jesus. Of course, there were as yet no liturgical books in Chinese, and in any case the first Chinese priest of the Society was ordained only in 1664, almost forty years after the permission was granted. For that reason the Jesuit fathers in China deemed it prudent to refer the matter to Rome once again, before taking advantage of the indult. By this time a new Congregation, the *Propaganda,* had come into existence, and China being a mission country, the matter was referred to it. Furthermore, the Jesuits had now been under heavy fire for several years, constantly delated to Rome for their "unorthodox" and "novel" methods. The atmosphere was charged with tensions and animosities. Hence the *Propaganda* did not act. In spite of the support of Popes Alexander VII and Innocent XI, attempts to get the permission confirmed failed in 1678, 1686, 1698, and 1726. The permission, therefore, though never revoked, could never be used.

Another and far more momentous question was that of the famous "Chinese Rites." The Jesuits had been extremely liberal in making concessions to the Chinese Christian converts, permitting them to observe traditional family rites and customs by which respect was shown to the memory of ancestors. Since the whole fabric of Chinese society rested on the classical relationships and the "filial piety" (*hsiao*) which expressed them, and since the careful study of Confucianism had shown the Jesuits that these rites were not in any sense idolatrous or superstitious, these customs were integrated into the Christian life without too much difficulty. This involved no compromise, once the true nature of the rites was understood.

The Jesuits also permitted Confucian scholars converted to the faith (and the finest of the early Chinese converts belonged to this class) to participate in customary acts of respect for the memory of Confucius. These "rites" again were, when properly understood, no more idolatrous than the respect we in America pay to the national flag.

The most momentous consequence of the ban of the "Chinese Rites" was that a Confucian scholar could not become a Christian without abandoning his office and position in society, and a Christian could not, as Ricci and his followers had done, become a member of the intellectual elite.

The controversy over the Chinese rites reflected first of all the scandal and the profound shock which was felt by non-Jesuit missionaries who had a less clear idea of the true nature of Chinese customs. But it soon involved much more than this. National and international political issues became connected with the debate. The accommodations made by the fathers of the Society were first forbidden, in 1645. Then they were permitted, after satisfactory explanations, in 1656. But when the issue became too heated and the confusion too great, the Holy See finally took the safer and more conservative course in order to limit the spread of the controversy. The Chinese rites were solemnly banned in 1704 and again in 1715 and 1742. Only after the passage of two centuries did Pope Pius XII finally reverse the decision, and permit the wise adaptations that had been requested by the Jesuit fathers in the seventeenth century. On December 8, 1939, almost at the beginning of his pontificate, Pius XII raised the ban. But by that time China was filled with pragmatism and materialism, and the structure of the newly formed republican state was being undermined by Communism.

The story of the Jesuit missionaries in China easily lends itself to romantic treatment. Indeed, the wonderful adventures of Ricci in Peking have sometimes been related with more zest than accuracy. But now we have a clear, well-documented, and thoroughly trustworthy history of the Jesuit Chinese missions in the Ming Dynasty. Father George H. Dunne, S.J., himself a former missionary in China, has set himself the task of getting the story straight, disposing of legends, and restoring a proper perspective on the "Chinese Rites" question. His book[1] draws heavily on the Jesuit archives in Rome, and on others, and though he is impatient of all melodrama, this is an exciting story to read. In fact, it is all the more exciting because it is not fanciful but, as far as we can judge, historically true.

The truth of the Jesuit mission in China cannot help but inspire us. Here were men who, three hundred years ahead of their time, were profoundly concerned with issues which we now see to be so important that the whole history of the Church and of Western civilization seems to be implicated in their solution. We admire first of all the brilliance, the courage, and the fidelity of these scholar-missionaries. Some of them were saints; some were great scientists; all of them were true Christians and religious, and in their human limitations they displayed an honesty and a compunction which are all the more moving to us since they show us something we can imitate.

Father Adam Schall, who stands out as one of the most engaging and unforgettable of characters, certainly did many things with which we might be inclined to disagree. He was placed at the head of the bureau of Chinese calendar reform (for which he deserves nothing but praise). He turned his hand to the production of cannons to defend Peking against the Manchus, a decision for which he has been understandably criticized. He adopted a Chinese orphan as his grandson, which he later admitted was an imprudence, though it is one for which we cannot help loving him.

In the end, when he fell from the highest pinnacle of imperial favor and was condemned to be dismembered alive, he did not lose his courage or his fabulous irony. He escaped execution, and later avowed all the errors of his religious and missionary life (not including the cannons) with an exemplary compunction.

But the history of the Jesuit missions in China is not simply the history of heroic men and their acts of wisdom or of daring. It is the story of Christ in China: a kind of brief epiphany of the Son of Man as a Chinese scholar. All too brief, alas. But the old tradition of the wise men from the East has always obscurely called for this epiphany. Why was it never fully realized? There are no simple answers to this question. One of the chief merits of Father Dunne's book is that the delicate problem of the Chinese rites controversy is treated with exceptional tact. The contesting policies of various religious orders were of course a factor in the dispute. But Father Dunne makes quite clear that this was not the real explanation for the animosity with which the struggle was carried on. Certainly the Jesuits and the Mendicants favored different approaches to the Asian apostolate. But we must not oversimplify. A Dominican, Father de Azevedo, was discussing Oriental philosophy with the scholars of Cambodia when the Jesuits were doing the same in China. Unfortunately, de Azevedo did not get much encouragement for his efforts. He was excommunicated. (The Jesuits in Japan helped him to get back on his feet after this tragic rebuff.)

Father Dunne's book has the merit of making clear the fact that national and imperialist rivalries had a much more decisive influence in the controversy than emulation between missionary orders.

FROM PILGRIMAGE TO CRUSADE

The "sacred journey" has origins in prehistoric religious cultures and myths. Man instinctively regards himself as a wanderer and wayfarer, and it is second nature for him to go on pilgrimage in search of a privileged and holy place, a center and source of indefectible life. This hope is built into his psychology, and whether he acts it out or simply dreams it, his heart seeks to return to a mythical source, a place of "origin," the "home" where the ancestors came from, the mountain where the ancient fathers were in direct communication with heaven, the place of the creation of the world, paradise itself, with its sacred tree of life.[1]

In the traditions of all the great religions, pilgrimage takes the faithful back to the source and center of the religion itself, the place of theophany, of cleansing, renewal, and salvation. For the Christian there is, of course, Jerusalem, the Holy Sepulchre, where the definitive victory of life over death, good over evil, was won. And there is Rome, the center of the Catholic Church, the See of Peter, the place of indulgence and forgiveness. There are also grottoes and springs blessed by visitations of the merciful Mother, sites of repentance and of healing. There are countless tombs of saints, places of hierophany and of joy.

Christian pilgrimages to Jerusalem, which simply followed the example and pattern of much older Jewish pilgrimages, began in the fourth century A.D. St. Helena's pilgrimage and the finding of the True Cross took place in 326. Less than ten years later, the splendid Basilica of the Holy Sepulchre was dedicated. It would attract thousands of pilgrims from the West. Already, in 333, a pilgrim from Bordeaux, in France, was writing about his visit to the Holy Places. One of the liveliest and most interesting of all written pilgrimages is that of the nun Aetheria,[2] who probably came from Spain and visited not only the Holy Places in Jerusalem but the monks of the Egyptian desert and of Palestine, even going through the Arabian desert to Mount Sinai, where there was as yet no monastery, but where there were colonies of hermits living in huts and caves. Large numbers of these anchorites escorted her enthusiastically to the summit of the mountain, where appropriate texts from the Bible were read, Mass was sung, *eulogiae* or spiritual gifts (consisting of fruits from the monks' orchard) were passed around, and the joys of the Christian life were generally celebrated in the very place where God had given the Law to Moses. Note that at this same time St. Gregory of Nyssa was writing his life of Moses,[3] which is in fact a description of the mystical itinerary and ascent of the monk to God in "dark contemplation." The geographical pilgrimage is the symbolic acting out of an inner journey. The inner journey is the interpolation of the meanings and signs of the outer pilgrimage. One can have one without the other. It is best to have both. History would show the fatality and doom that would attend on the external pilgrimage with no interior spiritual integration, a divisive and disintegrated wandering, without understanding and without the fulfillment of any humble inner quest. In such pilgrimage no blessing is found within, and so the outward journey is cursed with alienation. Historically, we find a progressive "interiorization" of the pilgrimage theme, until in monastic literature the "peregrinatio" of the monk is entirely spiritual and is in fact synonymous with monastic stability.[4]

Aetheria's account of her pilgrimage tells us much about the liturgy of fourth-century Jerusalem, where the Holy Sepulchre was regarded as the normal station for daily celebration of the Eucharist, and where the True Cross was set up under the roof of the same basilica, on what remained of the rock of Calvary (Aetheria calls it simply the *martyrium*—the place of martyrdom or of witness). Note that even though Calvary was there, the Eucharist was celebrated specifically at the Holy Sepulchre, not on Calvary. The sacred events of the New Testament were reenacted liturgically at the place where they actually happened. The liturgy of other places in the Christian world was simply intended to reproduce and remind the pilgrim of what he could see in its perfection at Jerusalem. Jerusalem was in every sense the "center of the world," not only in terms of ancient geography, but in the more important and sacred sense. It was the center par excellence of *Truth*, the place of the *True* Cross, of which all other crosses would be mementos and representations; the place of the true Holy Sepulchre, which would be recalled by the sepulchres of the martyrs in each altar of sacrifice: the place where the Saviour had truly walked, spoken, preached, healed, suffered, risen, ascended. The places themselves in their reality bore witness to that truth: but they were, far more than that, sacraments of truth and of a special life-giving presence.[5] If Jerusalem was the place of the *anastasis,* the resurrection, the regions around it were filled with the *martyria,* where the apostles and saints had borne witness to the power of the resurrection. Finally, there were the monks in all the deserts of Syria, Palestine, Arabia, and Egypt who were living witnesses of the resurrection. The pilgrimage of Aetheria was, then, a sacred journey to the center from which the whole Christian world was charged with the true presence of the resurrection and glory of the Saviour.

II

The fall of Rome to the Barbarians in the beginning of the sixth century and the invasions that poured down over the East as well as over Western Europe temporarily cut off the Holy Land from the West. Though Jerusalem was then practically inaccessible to most European Christians, pilgrimages continued unabated elsewhere. But now they received a new character, imprinted upon them by the Celtic monks of Ireland.

Peregrinatio, or "going forth into strange countries," was a characteristically Irish form of asceticism. The Irish *peregrinus,* or pilgrim, set out on his journey, not in order to visit a sacred shrine, but in search of solitude and exile. His pilgrimage was an exercise in ascetic homelessness and wandering.[6] He entrusted himself to Providence, setting out with no definite aim, abandoning himself to the Lord of the universe. Since Ireland is an island, this meant entrusting oneself to the hazards of sea travel, and there are records of Irish *peregrini* who simply floated off aimlessly into the sea, abandoning themselves to wind and current, in the hope of being led to the place of solitude which God Himself would pick for them. In this way, some came to Wales or Cornwall or to the isles of western Scotland. Others, doubtless the majority, made use of their considerable skill in navigation and followed indications that had perhaps come to them down years of seafaring tradition. Such were St. Columba, founder of the great monastic center at Iona,[7] and St. Brendan, whose legendary voyages[8] are thought, by some, to have brought him even to America. This has still to be convincingly proved. But there is historical evidence that Irish monks were in Iceland[9] before the coming of the Danes in the eighth century, and they had also visited the Faroe Islands, as well as the Shetlands and the

Orkneys, not to mention Brittany, which was entirely popu-
lated by Welsh and Irish colonists, mostly monks, in the sixth
century.

It is true, of course, that many of these pilgrimages brought
Irish monks into inhabited places where the natives were willing and ready to receive the Christian message. The monks
then became missionaries. The main reason for their journeys
was not the missionary apostolate but the desire of voluntary
exile.[10]

An *Old Irish Life of St. Columba* (a panegyric, not to be
confused with the essentially historical life by Adomnan) describes the pilgrim spirit as belonging to the very essence of
Christianity:

> God counselled Abraham to leave his own country and go in
> pilgrimage into the land which God had shown him, to wit the
> "Land of Promise." . . . Now the good counsel which God en-
> joined here on the father of the faithful is incumbent on all the
> faithful; that is to leave their country and their land, their
> wealth and their worldly delight for the sake of the Lord of
> the Elements, and go in perfect pilgrimage in imitation of
> him.[11]

The example of Abraham inspired many other Irish pilgrims, including Saint Cadroe, and his companions, who went
forth to seek the land which the Lord "would show them." [12]

It was, of course, the vision of the "Land Promised to the
Saints" that inspired the fabulous voyage of Brendan and his
monks. In Celtic pilgrimages there is a reawakening of the
archaic mythical theme of the "return to paradise" [13] under
the guidance of God or of His angels. But this is something
more than "mere myth." The mystic spirituality of the Celtic
monks is built on a charism of pilgrimage and navigation.

The objective of the monk's pilgrimage on earth may be
imaginatively described as the quest of the "promised land"
and "paradise," but more theologically this goal was described as the "place of resurrection" [14]—the place divinely

appointed, in which the monk is to settle down, spend the rest of his days in solitude, doing penance, praying, waiting for the day of his death. To leave Ireland in search of this privileged place was to "go on pilgrimage for the love of God" (*peregrinari pro Dei amore*) or "in the name of God." If the pilgrimage were a "navigation," then the monk was seeking for a "desert in the sea." [15] The Irish had a predilection for lonely islands.[16] In the voyage of St. Brendan, one of the Faroe Islands covered with wild sea birds becomes transformed into a monastic and liturgical paradise, the place par excellence for the celebration of the Easter mystery.[17] The Holy Sepulchre has been replaced by the Desert Island. In any event, the object of pilgrimage is to take the monk to his peculiar and appointed place on the face of the earth, a place not determined by nature, race, and society, but by the free choice of God. Here he was to live, praise God, and finally die. His body would then be buried in this spot, and would there await the resurrection. The pilgrimage of the Celtic monk was not then just endless and aimless wandering for its own sake. It was a journey to a mysterious, unknown, but divinely appointed place, which was to be the place of the monk's ultimate meeting with God.

In the eighth and ninth centuries, when communication with the East was once again open, Irish monks went on pilgrimages to Egypt and the Holy Land, and in many cases their desire was either to settle at a Holy Place and die there, or else to find "the place of their resurrection" on the way back, and remain there, often as recluses, or solitaries living in completely enclosed cells built against the wall of a Church.[18] Thus, the ninth and tenth centuries record the presence of scores of Irish monks living in cities of Germany, Burgundy, Lorraine, etc., either as scholars teaching in schools or as recluses.[19]

Soon there were many secondary aims in the pilgrimage. Monks went to spend a time in *peregrinatio* with other monks and in monastic centers where they could find instruction and example. Or else they went to obtain liturgical and other books,[20] which they copied in their own monasteries. The five pilgrimages of St. Benedict Biscop to Rome are famous examples of this. Others went to Rome to obtain relics needed in the dedication of monastic churches or altars.[21] Some even went on pilgrimages in the hope of martyrdom;[22] others to escape death at the hands of invading Vikings.

Whatever one may think about some of the special forms taken by the Celtic *peregrinatio*, the records, historical as well as literary, bear witness to a profound spiritual integration in the culture from which this practice emerged. The external and geographic pilgrimage was evidently, in most cases, something more than the acting out of psychic obsessions and instabilities. It was in profound relationship with an inner experience of *continuity* between the natural and the supernatural, between the sacred and the profane, between this world and the next: a continuity both in time and in space.[23] For the Celt, as for archaic and primitive man, the true reality is that which is manifested obscurely and sacramentally in symbol, sacrament, and myth. The deepest and most mysterious potentialities of the physical and bodily world, potentialities essentially sacred, demanded to be worked out on a spiritual and human level.

The pilgrimage of the Irish monk was therefore not merely the restless search of an unsatisfied romantic heart. It was a profound and existential tribute to realities perceived in the very structure of the world, and of man, and of their being: a sense of ontological and spiritual dialogue between man and creation in which spiritual and bodily realities interweave and interlace themselves like manuscript illuminations in the Book of Kells. This resulted in an astounding spiritual creativity which made it impossible for the Celtic monk merely to accept his existence as something static and "given," or his monastic vocation as a juridically stabilized and sedentary existence. His vocation was to mystery and growth, to liberty and abandonment to God, in self-commitment to the apparent irrationality of the winds and the seas, in witness to the wisdom of God the Father and Lord of the elements. Better perhaps than the Greeks, some of the Celtic monks arrived at the purity of that *theoria physike* which sees God not in the essences or *logoi* of things, but in a hierophanic cosmos; hence the marvelous vernacular nature poetry of the sixth and seventh century Celtic hermits.[24]

As Dom Jean Leclercq points out,[25] pilgrimage was to remain a "form of hermit life" and a logical though exceptional, constituent of the monastic vocation.

III

In the meantime, quite a different concept of "pilgrimage" was growing up in Irish circles.

The penitential systems of Ireland and Anglo-Saxon England in the sixth to the tenth centuries completely transformed the old concept of ecclesiastical penance.[26] In primitive Christianity, the only formal penance imposed by the Church was public penance, and in the earliest times this could be performed only once. The transition to private and indefinitely repeatable penance was made under Celtic influence. One of the most important forms of penance was *peregrinatio,* pilgrimage, or exile, especially to an island, *relegatio in insulam.*[27] Instead of doing public penance in full view of the local church (for instance, by remaining outside the church in penitential garb, fasting and performing other prescribed works until reconciled), the penitent was sent off into exile, either perpetual or temporary. He might be sent to a lonely island, or simply turned out into the alien world to wander without a specified goal. The penitent just "peregrinated." Only after the eighth century is the penitent sent to a specific place, or perhaps to a distant bishop to *receive* a penance, and then when he returned to his own church, after giving proof that his penance was completed, he was absolved. We must always remember that at this time absolution was given only after the penance had been completed. After the ninth century, the goal of the penitent pilgrim was most often Rome, where he was sent to have the Pope decide his case and impose a suitable penance and send him back to his own bishop for absolution. Some penitents preferred to go direct to Rome, over the head of their own bishop, but this was reproved.[28]

It is not quite exact to regard this *peregrinatio* as a purely private and face-saving form of penance. On the contrary, it had a semi-public character[29] and was imposed for scandalous faults. The penitent pilgrim was driven forth as an outcast, dressed in rags or sackcloth, barefoot, perhaps even wearing a chain.[30] He was under strict obligation to keep moving, for he was a "wanderer" ("Let him not spend the night twice in the same place," said one of the Penitentials).[31] He was not allowed to bear arms, and was therefore sent totally defenseless among strangers who might be barbarians and pagans (for instance, the Picts in Scotland or many of the inhabitants of lands east of the Rhine). The pilgrim who was carrying out a canonical penance wore a distinctive garb and badge. The pilgrim thus became a familiar figure in the Europe of the Dark Ages, and he was easily recognizable as a sacred person. If he were a canonical penitent, he was, like Cain, one on whom the curse of God rested, one who was being punished and healed, whom *man might not touch* (Gen. 4:13–15). He was, so to speak, a holy outcast, a consecrated tramp, living under a mystery of execration and protection, overshadowed by inscrutable love, a mystery and portent to every man. It was a sacred duty to protect him, feed him, give him shelter, and show him his way. Failure to shelter and protect pilgrims was declared to be the reason for punishment by an invasion of Lombards in southern France.[32] Since one could not count even on the faithful to respect the pilgrim and penitent, these travelers were sometimes provided with official letters of identification.[33] Special hostelries for the numerous Irish and Anglo-Saxon pilgrims were provided both at the chief places of pilgrimage and on the way there, and the Anglo-Saxon hostelry in Rome was supported by taxation in England.[34] Thus the penitent pilgrim, though cast out, had a very definite and indeed privileged place in the Church.

Pilgrimage or perpetual exile was usually given as penances for the worst crimes:[35] murder, incest, sacrilegious sins of violence or lust; and if the penitent was convinced of his need for penance and forgiveness, there is no question that he would take his penance seriously. Unfortunately, when it became common to send the worst offenders on pilgrimage as penance for grave crimes, large numbers of criminals were in effect turned loose, to live an irresponsible and wandering existence in common.[36] They naturally tended to band together, and when they did, their influence on each other was perhaps not much help in carrying forward their repentance and conversion.

Alcuin complained, in a letter,[37] of the dangers that came from associating with the riffraff of the roads, the jugglers, the thieves, and the pilgrims of various shades and dispositions who were met everywhere. Even genuine pilgrims who fell in with these others tended to suffer grave damage from their contact, and St. Boniface lamented that there was hardly a city on the way from England to Rome that did not have a few fallen Anglo-Saxon women living there as whores.[38] They were among the many for whom pilgrimage, on the Continent, was hardly a spiritual success. Note that on the Continent especially, pilgrimage was imposed as penance on clerics and monks who were considered scandalous and even incorrigible, doubtless as a last resort.[39] In fact, since the monk was already living in a public state of penance, he was not able to perform the ordinary public penance according to the ancient and solemn discipline. The paradoxical result of the penitential pilgrimage in the Middle Ages was to *increase* scandal by turning loose clerics and monks of disordered life to wander in public in situations that invited them to further sins that could hardly be kept hidden.[40] There was consequently a strong reaction on the part of the eleventh-century reformers against the "gyrovagues" or wandering monks.[41]

We have seen that pilgrimages were originally intended as expiation, by a defenseless and nonviolent, wandering existence, of the worst crimes of violence. Now in the ninth and tenth centuries, even killing in war was regarded as a sin requiring expiation.[42] In the Anglo-Saxon penitential of Theodore of Canterbury, a soldier who killed a man in war was obliged to a forty-day fast even though he might have killed his enemy in the "ordinary line of duty," under obedience to his officer. Later penitentials distinguished between offensive and defensive killing. One who attacked an enemy and killed him was obliged to do penance. One who killed another in self-defense was not obliged to do penance, but was *counseled* to do so for the good of his soul. Burchard of Worms, in the eleventh century, equated killing in war with ordinary homicide and assigned seven years of penance, without distinction as to offense or defense.[43]

Pilgrimage was not usually given as a penance for killing in war. But persons who had accumulated many penances for various sins might find themselves faced with a staggering burden of penitential "tariffs" to pay off. In order not to have to fast and do penance for scores of years, they had their multiple penance commuted to a single pilgrimage, which took care of everything.

With this, the systematization of pilgrimage began, and pilgrimages were imposed by the Inquisition as afflictive punishments.[44] The Church recognized places of major pilgrimage, such as Jerusalem and Rome, Canterbury and Compostela. There were also minor places of pilgrimage such as Le Puy, St. Gilles, Rocamadour, in France.[45] Ponce de Léras, a twelfth-century brigand in the central mountains of France, abandoned his life of brigandage, made restitution, went on pilgrimage to Compostela, and returned to settle down in a Cistercian monastery he had founded.[46] This was a standard medieval pattern for a successful conversion of life. As a matter of fact, it introduces us to a new pattern, in which "wandering eremitism" is no longer favored as an ascetic ideal, and in which the *peregrinatio* of Abraham is imitated by the monk who leaves "the world" for the cloister and stability of the monastery. In the eleventh and twelfth centuries we find frequent attacks upon "false hermits" who wander about. The monk who has entered the cloister will no longer leave to wander further afield. His perfection will consist in his stability.[47] However, as Dom Leclercq points out,[48] the monk in the cloister will read the narratives of saintly pilgrims as his "adventure stories." He will also take a passionate interest in the Crusades. As a matter of fact, in the case of the Crusades, an exception will be made. Many Cistercians accompanied the Crusades as chaplains, and Cistercian foundations were made in the Near East. In any case, the same spiritual crisis which led to monastic reforms in the eleventh and twelfth centuries led at the same time to a revival of itinerant eremitism and also, above all, to the great mass-*peregrinatio* of the Crusade.[49]

IV

It is often thought that the sole or chief reason for the Crusades was the fact that Christian pilgrims suffered harassment from the Moslems who were masters of Jerusalem.[50] It is certain that the popular enthusiasm that drove thousands of knights and common soldiers to the East in 1095 was an eruption of zeal for the liberation of the Holy Sepulchre. But it must be remembered that the first idea of the Crusade, which goes back to Gregory VII in 1074, was a project for the defense of Constantinople, an essentially "ecumenical" venture, by which it was hoped that the union of Greek and Latin against the Turk would heal the schism that had begun in 1054. Actually Constantinople was a holy city and a place of pilgrimage. The First Crusade was itself an enormous pilgrimage, a holy war preached and organized by the Church, led by an armed bishop, Adhemar, ordinary of Le Puy, one of the "minor" places of pilgrimage in France. The various armies converged on Constantinople, and then went on to take Jerusalem.

Pilgrimages to Jerusalem had opened a familiar way to the armies of the Cross. In the first half of the eleventh century, Robert II, Duke of Normandy, had to make a barefoot pilgrimage to Jerusalem to expiate the murder of his brother, Duke Richard III.[51] In 1073, Count Theodore, murderer of Conrad, Archbishop of Trier, went to Jerusalem. These two examples among many[52] show that the Crusaders were not all launching out into the unknown. Noblemen who had done penance and visited the Holy Sepulchre were now also attracted by the prospect of settling in this most sacred of lands, and having castles of their own in Judea or Galilee, there to await the second coming of Christ and the resurrection.

In the mind of Pope Urban II, the Holy Crusade was to be not only a great unification of Christendom against the Turk, but a magnificent and general act of repentant faith that would culminate in the moral reform and total renewal of Christendom. The "land of promise" which the Holy Father envisioned was a general state of holiness, unity, and perfection in the whole Church, East and West, a Christendom united and renewed in peace at the Holy Sepulchre.

Since the ninth century, very serious and sustained efforts had been made to limit wars among Christians. While promulgating the Crusade, the Council of Clermont (1095) also made the "Truce of God" of general obligation. This prohibition of fighting, from Septuagesima to Trinity Sunday and from Wednesday to Monday all year, had previously been imposed by local councils. Pope Urban was seeking a paradise of peace in Christendom, united in defense of the Holy Land, which symbolized the peace promised to all men of good will. As a Catholic historian observes,[53] "he commanded Christians to make a truce to all hostility that sprang from private interests. Thus the very notion of war was altered under the influence of the Roman Pontiff." War was now to be waged only in obedience to the Church, which was intent upon restricting the use of violence to what was absolutely necessary for the defense of Christendom. In the sense that the Crusade was expected to unify Christendom and consolidate Christian power in a way that would permanently subdue Islam and hold off all future aggression from without, it was explicitly considered a "war to end wars." This eschatological hope accounted in part for the tremendous expectation and enthusiasm of the first Crusaders.[54] War against the infidel now became a sacred duty for all because it was the pledge of unity and peace within Christendom as well as of permanent peace for the Christian world. Hence, the Crusade was considered one of the greatest and most meritorious good works. There was no "Truce of God" in killing Turks, because the sooner the great work was accomplished, the better it would be for all.

But above all, in the intentions of the Popes, the Crusade remained essentially a pilgrimage, but a mass pilgrimage of all Christians united in the expectation of the imminent return of Christ. The eschatological hope was expressed in the hymns and marching songs of the Crusaders.[55] Just as pilgrimage had been the commutation of all other penances, so now the Crusade, the super-pilgrimage, amply satisfied for the sins of a whole lifetime, even a lifetime of brigandage, lechery, murder, blasphemy, impiety, anything. The Crusade became the *epitome of all penance*. In fact, there was a great deal of penitential ardor among the first Crusaders. They fasted and prayed before battles and multiplied processions and acts of devotion. They were in general dedicated to a true spirit of poverty and austerity befitting pilgrims. The proof of one's profound and sincere conversion and loyalty to Christ and His Church was one's readiness to undergo hardship and privation, and do battle against an enemy who, quite naturally, came to be regarded as the incarnation of all the forces of evil. St. Bernard emphasized that the presence of infidels at the Holy Sepulchre was an outrage and insult to the Saviour.[56]

Urban II at Clermont urged the faithful to take up arms against an "abominable . . . impure people . . . [who had] ravaged and stained the holy places." [57] He had barely uttered his call when the cry went up everywhere: *Deus vult!* "God wills it!" The same cry, "It is written!," had launched the Moslems, a people of pilgrimage, upon the holy war.

It has been noted about St. Bernard (who preached the Second Crusade) that a deep vein of Augustinian pessimism about fallen man in a world of sin colored his ideas.[58] For St. Bernard, salvation outside a monastery was, to say the least, extremely difficult and doubtful. Though he was himself not friendly to pilgrimages for monks, he felt that the Crusade offered a unique opportunity for penance and salvation for multitudes of Christians who would otherwise most certainly be damned. "I call blessed the generation that can seize an opportunity of such rich indulgence as this blessed, to be alive in this year of God's choice. The blessing is spread throughout the whole world and all the world is called to receive the badge of immortality." [59] But if this is the case, then the Crusade is a Jubilee open to everyone—not only to an elite but to all sinners. It is not merely a question of a challenge to noble knights: there is a terrible moral risk for anyone who refuses to take this unique opportunity.[60]

St. Bernard even more than Urban II believed that the Crusade was a providential opportunity for the total renewal of feudal society.

With exaltation and immense relief, the first great army of repentant sinners started for the East, assured by Pope Urban himself that if they died on the expedition they would possess eternal life without further delay. "The robbers and pirates," said Oderic Vital, "criminals of every sort, moved by grace, came forth from the abyss of their wretchedness, disavowed their crimes and forsook them, and departed for the far-off country." [61]

Thus we see that in the course of time the peaceful and defenseless pilgrimage, the humble and meek "return to the source" of all life and grace, became the organized martial expedition to liberate the land promised to Abraham and his sons. It is surely significant that in the Middle Ages this conception of the Christian life became deeply embedded in European man: the "center," the "source," the "holy place," the "promised land," the "place of resurrection" becomes something to be attained, conquered, and preserved by politics and by force of arms. The whole Christian life and all Christian virtue then takes on a certain martial and embattled character. The true life of Christian virtue now becomes a struggle to death with pagan adversaries who are wickedly standing in the way of one's divinely appointed goal and perversely preventing fulfillment of a "manifest destiny."

Meanwhile, of course, certain ambiguities appeared in this conception of the Christian life as a mystique of martial and political organization. In the Second Crusade these ambiguities made themselves decisively felt: if the Crusade is a war to annihilate the enemy, then strategy comes first and the army should besiege Aleppo. If it is primarily a pilgrimage, then the crusading pilgrims should go up to Jerusalem. Yet the king had not made a vow to conquer Aleppo, only to go to Jerusalem.[62] Thus, the concept of an essentially embattled Christian society tended to become inseparable from the Christian outlook, one might almost say the Christian faith. Christian eschatology in the West took on a very precise historical and social coloring in centuries of combat against the Turk. It was defense of Western Christendom against Eastern and pagan autocracy and power.

It would be naïve to underestimate the sincerity and the deep spiritual motivation of the Crusades, just as it would be naïve to ignore the fact that the violence, the greed, the lust, and the continued depravity of the worst elements continued unchanged. In point of fact, the Crusades had an immense effect on European and Christian society in the West. They certainly opened the way to renaissance and modern Christendom. But the paradise of spiritual benefits that had been hoped for was never attained. On the contrary, from the point of view of East-West relations in Christendom, the Crusades were a disaster. They certainly made all reunion between Rome and Constantinople unthinkable.

Above all, the Crusades introduced a note of fatal ambiguity into the concept of pilgrimage and penance. What was intended as a remedy for sins of violence, particularly murder, now became a consecration of violence. There is, of course, a distinction between war and murder, and the sacrifice entailed by warfare can certainly be regarded as "penitential." But a man prone to violence and passion, a potential or actual murderer and sadist, is not likely to make too many fine distinctions when he discovers that he can now not only kill people legitimately, but even offer his acts to God as "good works" and as "penance," provided he concentrates on infidels, regarded as the embodiment of all evil.

We know that the Crusaders did not confine their warlike activities to what was juridically "holy." The sack of Christian Constantinople and the internecine battles among the Crusaders themselves are there to prove it.

Finally, a very interesting development took place in the Crusades. The mystique of sacred love was, in the twelfth century, very close to the courtly love of the troubadours. But we find, curiously enough, that a typical troubadour, Jaufré Rudel, who took part in the Second Crusade, could sing in the same breath of the love for little Jesus in Bethlehem and of a more secular love for the "distant lady" in whose "service" the loyal knight will risk death and imprisonment. The Crusade becomes merged with the romance of courtly love. At the same time the sacred element tends to be neglected by those who, like Bertrand de Born, are engrossed in the martial glory and exploits of the knights.[63]

V

So much for the East. There remained the fabulous paradise of the West. It is curious that in the folklore tradition of Spain, the "Lost Island" of the West, identified with the Brendan legend to the point that it was given Brendan's own name, remained the paradisiacal refuge to which the kings of Spain and Portugal might flee from Moorish invasions,[64] just as in the Celtic legend the "land of promise" in the western ocean was evidently regarded as a place of refuge from the Norsemen.

Christopher Columbus was most probably aware of the Brendan legend[65] as well as of such classic medieval descriptions of the "Lost Island," or Perdita, as that of Honorius of Autun (or more exactly, William of Conches):

> There is a certain island of the Ocean called Perdita, and it excels all the lands of the earth in the beauty and fertility of all things. Found once by chance, it was later sought again and not found, whence it is called Perdita. To this isle, Brendan is said to have come.[66]

The description has all the mythical qualities of the lost paradise, and Columbus's idyllic description of his landfall on Hispaniola showed that the new land appeared to him to be in every way an earthly paradise. He did not believe he had discovered Perdita, however, and Spanish expeditions in search of the "Lost Island" continued even after the discovery of the American mainland.

Brendan's Island was marked ("tentatively") on maps as late as the eighteenth century.[67] It was even formally renounced by Portugal in the Treaty of Evora (1519), so that if it ever were found it was already assigned in advance (by the Apostolic See) to his Catholic majesty of Spain.

In one word, the Renaissance explorers, the conquistadores, the Puritans, the missionaries, the colonizers, and doubtless also the slave traders and pirates, were in their own way deeply influenced by the mythical paradisiacal aspect of the Americas. But it was a paradise into which they could not penetrate without the most profound ambiguities.

They came, in a way, as "penitents" or as men seeking renewal, deliverance from the past, the gift to begin again. But at the same time the pattern of this renewal forbade neither self-enrichment nor the free enjoyment of the opportunities which the "paradise" so generously offered (native women). And it prescribed, above all, as a sort of vestige of crusading ardor and as an earnest of absolution, an uncompromising zeal in the subjection of the infidel—and, of course, in his conversion. It was also a good thing to build churches at home with Inca gold. While St. Theresa of Avila was following her interior and mystic itinerary (not without some very energetic peregrination about Spain, founding Carmels[68]), her brother was in the Kingdom of Quito getting rich. When he returned to Spain, he financed the Carmel of Seville (where St. Theresa enjoyed the view of the river with the gallant ships of the Armada back from the Indies). And there is no reason to doubt the depth and sincerity of his inner life, troubled only by certain violent reactions, which his sister, though she had never experienced such things, did not find surprising.

There was in the Indies the lush and tempting beauty and fantastic opulence of nature. There were the true and legendary riches, from the mines of San Luis Potosí to the lake of Eldorado and the fountain of eternal youth. There were the Indians and their cities, appearing now as idyllic "noble savages" in utopian communities, now as treacherous devils indulging in infernal tricks and sunk in the worst forms of heathenism.

Thus, the European white man set foot on the shores of America with the conflicting feelings of an Adam newly restored to paradise and of a Crusader about to scale the walls of Acre.

The mentality of the pilgrim and that of the Crusader had

fused together to create a singular form of alienation: that of the Puritan "pilgrim father" and that of the conquistador. Centuries of ardent, unconscious desire for the Lost Island had established a kind of right to paradise once it was found. It never occurred to the sixteenth-century Spaniard or Englishman to doubt for a moment that the new world was entirely and rightly his. It had been promised and given to him by God. It was the end of centuries of pilgrimage. It was the long-sought land of promise and renewal, where the old deficiencies and limitations no longer existed: the land of the new beginning not only for the individual but for society itself. The land of refuge from persecution. The land of peace and plenty, where all the iniquities and oppressions of the old world were forgotten. Here peace and unity were bought at the price of Christian courage in battling with the wilderness and with the infidel. To conquer and subjugate the native population was not regarded as an unjust aggression, as usurpation or as robbery and tyranny but on the contrary as proof of one's loyalty to all the values dear to the European and Christian heart since Charlemagne.

It is true, however, that some of the missioners had a different and more mystical view of paradise. But their solution was only more logically and consistently paradisiacal; as in the primitive and religious Jesuit utopias in Paraguay, or the communities of Vasco de Quiroga in Mexico.

These were, indeed, admirable and virtuous efforts. But for the greater part, the pilgrims were rushing upon the Lost Island with a combative ferocity and a wasteful irresponsibility that have tainted the fruits of the paradise tree with bitterness ever since.

Somehow it has been forgotten that a paradise that can be conquered and acquired by force is not paradise at all.

So the story of man's pilgrimage and search has reached the end of a cycle and is starting on another: now that it is clear that there is no paradise on earth that is not defiled as well as limited, now that there are no lost islands, there is perhaps some dry existentialist paradise of clean ashes to be discovered and colonized in outer space: a "new beginning" that initiates nothing and is little more than a sign of our irreversible decision to be disgusted with the paradises and pilgrimages of earth. Disgust with paradise, but not with crusades! The new planet is apparently to be the base for a more definitive extermination of infidels, together with the mass of less agile pilgrims so occupied in keeping body and soul together that they cannot be singled out as pilgrims to a promised land.

And yet the pilgrimage must continue, because it is an inescapable part of man's structure and program. The problem is for his pilgrimage to make sense—it must represent a complete integration of his inner and outer life, of his relation to himself and to other men.

The Bible has always taken man in the concrete, never in the abstract. The world has been given by God not to a theoretical man but to the actual beings that we are. If we instinctively seek a paradisiacal and special place on earth, it is because we know in our inmost hearts that the earth was given us in order that we might find meaning, order, truth, and salvation in it. The world is not only a vale of tears. There is joy in it somewhere. Joy is to be sought, for the glory of God.

But the joy is not for mere tourists. Our pilgrimage is more than the synthetic happy-making of a vacation cruise. Our journey is from the limitations and routines of "the given"— the *Dasein* which confronts us as we are born into it without choice—to the creative freedom of that love which is personal choice and commitment. Paradise symbolizes this freedom and creativity, but in reality this must be worked out in the human and personal encounter with the stranger seen as our other self.

As long as the Inca, the Maya, the Mestizo, the Negro, the Jew, or what have you, confronts us as *Dasein*, as a lump of limited and nonnegotiable *en-soi*, he will seem to stand in the way of our fulfillment. *"L'enfer, c'est les autres,"* [69] and we will seek paradise by combating his presence, subduing him, enslaving him, eliminating him.

Our task now is to learn that if we can voyage to the ends of the earth and there find *ourselves* in the aborigine who most differs from ourselves, we will have made a fruitful pilgrimage. That is why pilgrimage is necessary, in some shape or other. Mere sitting at home and meditating on the divine presence is not enough for our time. We have to come to the end of a long journey and see that the stranger we meet there is no other than ourselves—which is the same as saying that we find Christ in him.

For if the Lord is risen, as He said, He is actually or potentially alive in every man. Our pilgrimage to the Holy Sepulchre is our pilgrimage to the stranger who is Christ our fellow-pilgrim and our brother. There is no lost island merely for the individual. We are all pieces of the paradise isle, and we can find our Brendan's island only when we all realize ourselves together as the paradise which is Christ and His Bride, God, man, and Church.

It was in this spirit that St. Francis went on pilgrimage—on his own original kind of "crusade"—to meet the Soldan: as a messenger not of violence, not of arrogant power, but of humility, simplicity, and love.[70]

And it was in this spirit that Pope John XXIII wrote *Pacem in Terris.*

VIRGINITY AND HUMANISM
IN THE WESTERN FATHERS

A scholar with a profound understanding of both antiquity and the Middle Ages has said that "every true humanism delights spontaneously in the world and in the book." [1] But if this statement is true, how can we seriously assert that there was ever any such thing as a "patristic humanism," or worse still, a "monastic humanism"?

The age of the Fathers, the age of the first monks, was, of course, an age in which "the world" was rejected with uncompromising and single-minded intensity of purpose. Also the monks were, it is often thought, hostile to study: if not to the study of Scripture, then at least to the study of the classics and the grammarians. Besides this, the term "humanism" is often associated in the popular mind with an anti-Christian humanism which summarily rejects the Church or even God, on the grounds that religious faith keeps man alienated, suppressing his deepest and most vital energies, and preventing his full human development as an individual and as a member of society. The very idea of humanism tends to acquire a flavor of impiety and irreligion.

But when we know the Fathers better, we see that a great deal depends on what one means by "the world." Certainly it has never been Christian to reject the "world" in the sense of the cosmos created by God, dwelt in by the Incarnate Word, sanctified by the presence and action of the Mystical Christ, and destined to be transformed with man in a new eschatological creation. In this sense, the Fathers took the deepest and most spontaneous delight in the world, and the early monks believed they could already see paradise again in the landscape around them, even though it might be the arid desert of Egypt. As for the "book," we know how the Fathers loved the Bible. We know too that they could not refrain from quoting the classics, even while commenting on the Bible.

The purpose of the present essay is to point out how the Latin Fathers, even though they may at times have felt a certain amount of personal conflict in their struggle to reconcile the reading of the classics with the meditation on the Word of God (and the case of Jerome's famous dream[2] is typical), were most uncompromising in their defense of basic human values. This defense is very clear and forthright in their writings to or about virgins.

Not that they always urged the "more illustrious portion of the flock of Christ"[3] to read Ovid. Far from it. Yet their concern for the education of Christian virgins, and for their full, integral formation in every aspect of a joyous and positive Christian life, reflects all that is deepest and best in the humanism of Christian antiquity. To this humanism of the Fathers we can always profitably return as to a pure source of the Christian spirit.

We must not narrow the idea of humanism to the mere study of the classics or of the liberal arts, though this study and the disciplines connected with it are certainly essential. True Christian humanism is the full flowering of the theology of the Incarnation. It is rooted in a totally new concept of man which grew out of the mystery of the union of God and man in Christ. Christian humanism is therefore much more than the humanism of the Stoa or of the Academy sprinkled with a few drops of holy water and made official by a Papal brief. It is the full realization of man's dignity and obligations as son of God, as image of God, created, regenerated, and transformed in the Word made Flesh.

In writing about the way Christian virgins should dress, St. Cyprian is not content to praise that *disciplina custos spei*, the external discipline which preserves the purity of the theological virtues within the soul.[4] Virginal purity, itself manifested by external modesty, is a spiritual light which proclaims the glory of the presence of Christ in a human temple. "Let us radiate the light of God and bear it everywhere in a pure and stainless body." [5] Therefore the question of modest dress, the use of makeup, or attendance at the public baths is more than a matter of personal decency and self-protective caution. The glory of God and of Christ is involved. The virgin is the *illustrior portio gregis*, and we must note the implications of the "light-bearing" in the adjective *illustrior*. She not only bears the lamp of virtue and almsgiving (the light of the virgin's lamp is active charity), but she is herself a lamp kindled with the light of Christ. She is a more perfect replica of that image of God which is in all the "illuminated"—the baptized. The Church, the stainless Bride of Christ, cannot but concern herself more particularly with the purity of virgins since that purity is her own glory. The purity of the virgin is closely connected with the purity of the faith itself.[6] It is the purity of truth. The virgin is what a redeemed human person really ought to be. Hence, a twofold reason why she should not use cosmetics: on the one hand, if she paints her face she transforms it into a lie, making it other than God wanted it to be. This of course is a trope even in secular satire. But the meaning here is deeper. She in a certain sense yields up the freedom of the children of God and returns to what St. Paul would call captivity under the "elements of this world" (Gal.

4:3) since she implicitly wants to be desired with an erotic love. But the realm of *eros* is also the realm of death.

The house of Hymen and of pleasure is also, unfortunately, the house of cruel pain. The wife in the ancient world was more or less the husband's property, a thing rather than a person, and she was not always treated with gentleness or consideration.[7] The virgin was by her consecration liberated by Christ from the tyranny of a pagan or half-converted husband.

Hence, the virgin had an obligation to preserve the eschatological freedom, which enabled her to manifest in the world, in a really prophetic witness, the future state of glory promised to all the baptized. "Be precisely what God your maker made you; be such as the Father's hand created you. Keep an uncorrupted face, a pure neck, a form without adulteration," says St. Cyprian,[8] and adds, above all: "Keep, O virgins, keep what you have begun to be, keep that which you will one day be. That which we will all be you have begun to be. You have already laid hold on the glory of the resurrection even in this present life."[9]

The eschatological humanism of Christian virginity as understood by St. Cyprian is therefore not the mere denial of the world, of love, and of man. It is the conquest and transformation of man and the world in the divinizing power of the resurrection. It is the victory of Christ over suffering, anguish, misery, and the whole realm of death of which sexual love is but a part.

It must not be forgotten that the Fathers also saw in virginity the return to the paradisiacal perfection of man's beginning, the recovery of the innocence, the purity, and the familiarity with God for which man was originally created. St. Ambrose says that "in the sacred virgins we see on earth that angelic life which we once lost in Paradise."[10] St. Jerome[11] adds that if married life is appropriate to man after the fall, the virginal life is characteristic of Paradise. In a word, virginity is man's "normal" state, a state of personal and spiritual freedom above the vicissitudes of terrestrial existence, which is always lived in the shadow of death and in which sex provides a means of survival, not for the person, but only for human nature. Christian virginity is therefore the highest affirmation of human values and aspirations, for it is the liberation and fulfillment of the human person in union with God in Christ.

II

Demetrias, a daughter of Roman aristocrats who had fled from the sack of Rome into North Africa and had there, to the consternation of the whole Roman world, suddenly renounced a brilliant marriage in order to consecrate her life to Christ, was praised by Jerome for her courageous assertion of *Christian liberty*.[12] In defying the possible censure of her parents (who, as a matter of fact, fully approved her resolution) and of society (which, at any rate, wondered at it), Demetrias had followed the footsteps of the virgin martyr Agnes. Jerome evokes the savage turmoil of Rome in flames, echoing with the cries of women violated by Barbarians. He recalls the obscene nuptial lampoons sung at weddings.[13] The "Fescenninan Songs" represent the victory of lust, the triumph of unregenerate nature and indeed of the Prince of this world asserting his power over all flesh. But the Christian virgin conquers the flesh and her victory is the victory of Christ. Jerome exults over the triumph of Christ in the purity of Demetrias. Again, here is the theme of divine truth shining gloriously in the liberty of the virgin who asserts her freedom against the insistence of the flesh and the tyrannical demands of social convention.

If we look closely, then, at the idea of "the world" in these patristic writings on virginity, we see that it is always the corrupt pagan society in which human love and honor tend to be debased. The virgin is one who conquers this debased and confused society precisely because she not only has the grace of Christ but unites with it supreme human qualities of soul and body. By no means will Jerome consent to the practice of certain unfortunate parents (*miseri parentes*) who, weak in Christian faith, consecrate to God only the daughters who will never be able to attract a husband.[14]

St. Ambrose, in his succinct little tract *De Institutione Virginis*[15] (On the Education of a Virgin), blends mysticism and humanism together in a manner that merits a much more detailed study than we can attempt here. The full maturity of the Christian life is attained in a virginal union with Christ which itself implies *the perfect integration of the whole human person*. Union with Christ implies His entrance into a personality which is perfectly united in all its three traditional elements of body, soul, and spirit—*corpus, anima, spiritus*.[16]

This treatise of St. Ambrose's is particularly interesting for its outspoken defense of women in general. Basing himself on the creation narrative of Genesis, and on St. Paul's doctrine of the mystery of Christ typified in the union of Adam and Eve, the mystical humanism of Ambrose declares that man without woman is physically and spiritually incomplete, and that woman is in a very deep sense the "glory" of man, his spiritual completion, his "grace," without whom he cannot fully possess or recover his true being in Christ.

Indeed, man was made of the earth, but woman was made of man as a kind of figure of that grace which Christ came to bring,[17] a figure of spiritual life and of the Church.

We are therefore far from the pessimism of Augustine. On the contrary, St. Ambrose vehemently exonerates Eve of full responsibility in the fall of man: she was deceived by a superior being, and man, deceived by her, his inferior, is therefore without excuse![18] With Eve, original sin was error: with Adam, it was sin, and Adam's fault exculpates Eve from all guilt, since he is the more responsible. Not only that, but the penalty of childbearing in suffering is for the good of Eve and it washes away, in salutary penance, the sin of Adam.[19]

We seem to be contradicting what was just said by Jerome:

that childbearing is something to be dreaded and avoided. Ambrose goes deeper: but in doing so he takes a deeply compassionate and optimistic view of woman. He defends woman against the brutal self-complacency of man, who blames her for everything and curses her as a stumbling block and temptation to him, whereas all the while it is man himself who seeks in woman that which tempts him.[20] The beauty of woman's body is a great work of God, meant to be a sign of that far greater interior beauty, the special clarity and loveliness of her spirit.[21] Indeed, St. Ambrose declares, it is quite evident that women are more generous, more virtuous, more self-sacrificing than men.[22]

Finally, in an astute observation upon Abraham's rather cowardly lie that Sarah was his sister (Genesis 20:2), Ambrose remarks that in fact Sarah was the glory of Abraham, and implies that she was far better than Abraham deserved.

This totally refreshing defense of woman gives us some indication of the depth and reality of patristic humanism. Indeed, how can there be a true "humanism" when half of the human race is ignored or excluded? Pagan humanism, the exclusive preserve of man, only exalts his complacency and justifies his selfishness with a veneer of philosophy. A humanism for men only is, as we have seen, nothing but a barbarous falsehood. The light of true humanism is kindled by the Incarnate Word.

It may be mentioned here in passing that St. Ambrose's *De Institutione Virginis* devotes many columns to the praise of Mary's virginity and to the defense of her virginal motherhood. Mary is indeed the model of all Christian virgins, as well as the crown and glory of all women. Indeed, Ambrose's glorification of women is to be understood in the light of the mystery of the virginal Mother of God.

In the life of the Christian virgin, the mystery of Mary's motherhood is reproduced spiritually and in a hidden manner. Just as Mary was the "door" by which Christ entered the world even though the door was not "opened," so too the virgin is filled with a love which is rich in material gifts, which generously gives itself everywhere in outward works of mercy, yet at the same time never yields its interior secret, which remains totally consecrated to God. The Christian virgin is, like Mary, a *porta clausa,* a "closed door" (cf. Ezechiel 46:1–2). In bodily things, she gives but does not receive human love and consolation. In spiritual things, she receives from God but does not reveal the secret communicated to her by the King. Thus, her life is integrated in a perfectly ordered love. God is loved for His own sake, and the neighbor purely and disinterestedly for the love of God.[23]

Here precisely we come to the question of the study of the word of God in the contemplative life of the Christian virgin.

There can be no question that this contemplative life has both an intellectual and a mystical aspect. The two necessarily go together. The contemplative life of the Christian virgin is centered on a deep interior meditation of the word of God, which itself leads to union with the Person of the Word. This meditation begins of course with a reading of the sacred text, which must be fully understood both in its literal and in its spiritual senses.[24] In actual fact, it is Christ Himself who opens to his virginal spouse the sense of the Scriptures in secret. It is in the word of the Scriptures that He comes secretly to her, and enters into her heart as He once entered secretly through the "closed door" of the Blessed Virgin's womb.

St. Ambrose says: "Thou are a closed door, O Virgin. Let no one open thy door once locked by the Holy One and True Who has the key of David, who opens and no one closes, who closes and no one opens: HE HAS OPENED TO THEE THE SCRIPTURES, LET NO ONE CLOSE THEM. HE HAS CLOSED THY PURITY, LET NO ONE OPEN IT." [25] A beautiful text, which shows clearly the intimate connection between virginity of body and purity of heart,[26] integrity of body and unadulterated faith, chastity in the flesh and mystical love in the spirit.

Needless to say, the spiritual understanding of the sacred text implies a certain intellectual preparation. Therefore, the

virginal life certainly requires study and education, of the
kind which we generally term "humanistic." However, the
virginal life is not merely a life of pious study. The purpose of
intellectual preparation is to open the way to receive the mystical fire like that which Elias breathed into the dead child.
The fire of mystical understanding is the guarantee of virginal purity being preserved. "Keep this fire with thee in thy
heart, it will revive thee, lest the coldness of perpetual death
steal in and take possession of thee." [27] But between the study
of the text and its mystical understanding comes a very important intermediary stage which is the chief activity of the
virgin: the rumination of the sacred text in meditation. This
is her "world," in which she lives and moves and has her
being. The Scriptures are the Paradise she has received in exchange for the society of men. "Once dead to the world I beg
thee not to touch the things of time lest thou be contaminated
by them: but at all times in psalms and hymns and spiritual
canticles withdraw thyself from the society of this world, singing to God and not to man. Do as holy Mary did, and meditate on these words in thy heart. And like a good little lamb,
ruminate in thy mouth the divine precepts." [28]

III

St. Jerome insists that his virgins and widows keep assidu-
ously to their reading. If they have embraced the life of Mary
instead of that of Martha, this means precisely that they are
intent on *doctrina* (learning)[29] rather than on labor, though
of course manual work too will always have its essential part
to play in their lives.[30] Eustochium must keep at her reading
and learn all she can: *crebrius lege, disce quamplurima.*[31]
However, the pious trope of Jerome and so many other patristic authors, including Ailred of Rievaulx,[32] about "falling
asleep on the sacred page" [33] is not exactly the most convinc-
ing witness to patristic humanism. It has a certain element of
ambiguity about it!

One might ask if the Christian virgin ought to read the Latin classics. St. Jerome anticipates this question from Eustochium and answers with an emphatic "no." She should not want to appear learned in the pagan classics, nor should she waste her time trying to write lyric poems in the ancient meters, reciting them among other learned matrons in affected tones; for "What consent can there be between Christ and Belial? What has Horace to do with the Psalter? Virgil with the Gospels? Cicero with the Apostle?" [34] And here Jerome reveals the horrible example of his own temptation and fall, the famous Ciceronian vision, in which he appears before the judgment seat of Christ, is asked what kind of a thing he claims to be, and when he replies "a Christian" he is rebuked: "Thou liest, thou art not a Christian but a Ciceronian, for where thy treasure is there thy heart is also." [35]

This, as we know, was no small crisis in Jerome's life. He had collapsed in Syria, and the monastic brethren, taking him for dead, were preparing his obsequies. The immediate cause of the collapse seems to have been the intense struggle over the classics, for he was completely unable to relinquish Cicero and Plautus even in the desert.

In his vision, having received some kind of mystical flagellation, he vowed never again to touch a pagan book.

Unfortunately, or rather perhaps fortunately, we find him a few columns later in Migne writing to Marcella on textual problems of Scripture and quoting Horace in mockery of those "two-legged asses" who, instead of agreeing with Jerome's improved translation, persist in clinging to the old familiar versions.[36]

It is well known that Jerome did not keep this "vow" never to read Cicero. But quite apart from the classics, we can see from the letters he wrote on technical Scriptural questions to his virginal correspondents that he expected them to have rather sharp intellects well prepared by thorough study to appreciate the meaning of what he was telling them.

Without going into all of Jerome's ideas about the education of virgins, let us simply examine the charming letter to
Laeta in which the old scholar of Bethlehem sketches out a
program for the training of a small child, little Paula, the
niece of Eustochium and the granddaughter of St. Paula, so
that she might grow up to be a truly "wise virgin." Here it is
a question of a very special training because the child had
been consecrated to God even before her birth. This suggests
that her parents should keep in mind the model of St. John
the Baptist. In any case, little Paula must never hear anything,
never say anything, except what pertains to the fear of God.
But let us be quite clear what this means. Not only is Paula
to be protected from vicious influences, but she is also to be
guarded against bad Latin. She must learn to speak correctly
from the very first, "lest she should learn in tender years what
must be unlearned later." [37] She must not acquire the vice of
careless diction, which might be contracted by babytalk in the
nursery. No, even in early childhood she must learn to speak
clearly and correctly. No fault of speech is to be regarded as
slight. Furthermore, she might as well begin her Greek while
she is still in early childhood.

The passage where Jerome speaks of Paula learning her letters by playing with ivory blocks with the letters carved on
them[38] needs no comment here. It is doubtless inspired by
Quintilian. Paula of course learns to speak by lisping the
"sweet psalms": *adhuc tenera lingua psalmis dulcibus im-
buatur.*[39] It is interesting to notice that Jerome anticipates
modern educational psychology when he declares that Paula
must first learn by playing and that learning must always be
pleasurable to her. It is of the greatest importance, says Jerome, to *see that she never comes to hate study.* A consecrated
virgin would, according to his way of thinking, be terribly
handicapped if in early childhood she acquired a bitter dislike of learning which she could never shake off in riper years.
Cavendum est in primis ne oderit studia, ne amaritudo

eorum praecepta in infanita ultra rudes annos transeat.[40] For this reason she should not come to associate study with punishment. She should be encouraged with rewards.

Passing over the details of Paula's spiritual formation, which is described in all the familiar and traditional language of asceticism, and recalls St. Cyprian, we come to Jerome's plan for her Scripture studies.

First of all, the child must learn not only to read Scripture daily but to give a daily account of her *lectio*.[41] Memory of course plays a very important part. She will learn parts of the Scripture by heart, not only in Latin but also in Greek.[42] At the same time she will go to church, to the "Temple of her true Father," along with her parents (never with a boy friend),[43] and there she will listen intently to the reading of the Sacred Books, realizing that it is the voice of her Spouse calling her to marriage with Him. This will help her to be deaf to the attractions of worldly music and friendships.

Her reading of Scripture is closely integrated with prayer,[44] which is to be taught by a "veteran virgin," a *virgo veterana* (a term which must not suggest a military image to our minds).

Her prayers are those of the canonical hours. She will rise in the night for "orations and psalms." She will sing hymns at daybreak (lauds). At tierce, sext, and none, she will stand in the battle line like a warrior of Christ. When the lamp is lit, she will render the evening sacrifice.[45] Prayer and Scripture study are also integrated with her manual work. She will work with her hands, spinning wool and weaving. And she will not waste her time on silks or other fine materials, but the Scripture will take the place of silks and riches in her life.[46]

Her Scripture reading will of course follow a special plan. We have already seen that in earliest childhood she learns to speak with the very words of the Psalter. Jerome returns to this in his *ratio studiorum:* "Let her first learn the Psalter, and in the Proverbs of Solomon let her be taught to live." After that, in an order which suggests Origen but which will eventually differ from him in important details, she will learn, in Ecclesiastes, "to trample down the things of this world." At the same time she will follow the examples of virtue and patience given in the Book of Job. Then she will pass on to the Gospels, "never to let them out of her hands," and she will with all the "will of her heart drink in the Acts of the Apostles and the Epistles." "When she shall have filled the storerooms of her heart with these riches, she will commit to memory the Prophets, the Heptateuch, the Book of Kings and Chronicles as well as the volumes of Esdras and Esther." [47]

We note the language of this passage. *Mandet memoriae* tells us that the terms *discat* and *cordis sui cellarium his opibus locupletare* all mean the same thing. She is to make the Sacred Books part of her very being, to treasure them in her heart and in her memory so that they fill her thoughts at all times. This was a most important aspect of the education of virgins and of monks in the early days of the Church, and remained so down until the invention of printing.

When she has learned all the rest of the Scriptures, then it will be time for her to come without danger to the Canticle of Canticles.[48]

Thus, we see that for St. Jerome the virginal life, centered on the word of God, is a harmonious and well integrated whole which culminates in the highest spiritual union, but which begins nevertheless with simple respect for spoken Latin. It is instructive to see how, for St. Jerome, there is no division, no discontinuity in this conception of the spiritual life. It begins with the fullest respect for the ordinary spoken word. It continues with the study of language, with the memorization of the inspired word of God, the constant meditation of that word, in an attitude of greater and greater interior attentiveness to the Word Himself Who speaks in the Scriptures, until at last He reveals Himself in a spiritual and personal way to His chosen one, and unites her to Himself.

IV

In résumé, we have here a perfect and integral Christian humanism. It guards against an inordinate taste for pagan poetry and myth, but it nevertheless does not really exclude anything essential to the purest tradition of Christian humanism. On the contrary, Jerome's plan of education for little Paula is simply a Christian adaptation and development of classical educational ideas as they were inherited from Cicero and Quintilian. Cassiodorus reminds us that Quintilian's idea of rhetoric could be summed up as a training "which takes a good man, expert in speech, from his earliest childhood, through a course of training in all the arts and disciplines of noble letters, as the need of the whole commonwealth calls for such a man to defend it." [49]

The Christian virgin is by no means an orator, but she is dedicated to a life of praise, in divinely inspired words which transcend human eloquence. Her praise is not the defense of civil right, but the proclamation of the freedom of the Sons of God in the Risen Christ. She nevertheless needs training in the essentials of those same "arts and disciplines of noble letters" which help her to understand and use human speech as a divinely given instrument. She will rise above the merely human use of this instrument, and carry it to a spiritual and angelic level, for her life of praise is one with the life of the angels in heaven, and is therefore a higher kind of communication.

On this highest level, it is no longer the consecrated virgin alone who speaks, praises, and sings: it is Christ Himself, her Spouse, who acts, thinks, speaks, and utters praise in her. As St. Ambrose puts it: "In all her senses and actions, Christ shines forth, Christ is her aim, Christ Himself speaks." [50]

In Laeta's family there was an old pagan grandfather, still clinging to the past, sour and bitter over the decline of the great culture of Greece and Rome, and still disdaining to submit to the new faith which all his family had now embraced.

Yet he loved little Paula, and Jerome (who may perhaps have somehow identified his own rude Ciceronian self with the surly grandfather) advises in a flash of wise spontaneity: "When [Paula] sees her grandfather, let her leap into his arms, let her cling to his neck, and whether he likes it or not, let her sing Alleluia into his ears." [51]

Surely, this is one of the most apt and perfect expressions of the true relation between the humanism of Christianity and that of the ancient classical world! In any case, it represents the final solution of Jerome's own conflict.

THE ENGLISH MYSTICS

The last few years have seen the publication of important studies on the English mystics, together with new modern versions of their writings. The present essay grew out of a review article on the more important studies printed in 1961. When the essay was submitted to *Jubilee,* where it first appeared, someone who read the manuscript remarked that he had never even known there were English mystics. It is therefore high time for all these studies and new versions to appear, and a brief introduction to the subject of English mysticism will obviously not be superfluous.

There is every reason for interest in the English mystics. They have a charm and simplicity that are unequaled by any other school. And they are also, it may be said, generally quite clear, down-to-earth, and practical, even when they are concerned with the loftiest of matters. They never seem to have thought of their life with God as something recondite or even unusual. They were simply Christians. They rejoiced to know in Christ their Creator and Redeemer. They rejoiced that in Him they had direct access to the Father of Lights.

This study, while mentioning Thomas Traherne, whose *Centuries of Meditations* also appeared in 1961, concentrates on the Roman Catholic mystics, especially those of the fourteenth century. There is no doubt that it would be important to discuss the spirituality of the seventeenth-century Anglican school, the Cambridge Platonists, the Friends, the Methodists. But the difficulties and complications of such a study make it impossible in a short essay. Suffice it to say that in William Law or Isaac Pennington one can certainly find echoes of the great fourteenth-century tradition, which was itself, as we state in the conclusion to this essay, the fruit of the English medieval monastic spirituality.

English spirituality

Cardinal Newman was too Catholic to be anything but an English Catholic. His Catholic instinct told him that universality did not demand renunciation of his English outlook and spiritual heritage. Hence, he did not follow the more romantic converts of his time. Or rather, though he was momentarily influenced by them, it was just long enough to discover with alarm that he could be untrue to himself and to his authentic sense of the English tradition. Having once wavered in the presence of the overcompensation practiced by some of his colleagues, for whom nothing was sufficiently un-English, or too aggressively Roman, he drew back in salutary fear from the abyss of exotic and baroque clichés into which he saw himself about to fall headlong. He preserved the simplicity of his English devotion, and the clarity of the English spiritual idiom.

The English mystics belong to the ancient, patristic tradition, which Newman loved and which was so thoroughly transplanted into Britain by the early monks as to become authentically part of the very essence of the English spirit. Unfortunately, at the Reformation, the mystics were forgotten by all but a few of the old English Catholics, mostly in exile. When Catholic and mystical piety returned once again to England, it was in an alien and baroque costume, so that it appeared suspicious, theatrical, and false in the English setting. Post-Reformation continental terminology, transliterated into cumbersome jargon, did not slip easily and naturally off the English tongue. Its attitudes seemed forced and artificial. But the more uncomfortable the piety of the continental Counter Reformation appeared to the new English convert, the more he thought it his duty to sacrifice his native realism and soundness of taste, submitting to what secretly appalled him: thus, "nature" bowed to the "supernatural," *ad majorem Dei gloriam*. It was the Protestants and Anglicans of the nineteenth century who rediscovered the English mystics.

But that which most genuinely glorifies God is a catholicity true enough to respect the manifold variety of races, nations, and traditions which seek their fulfillment and their *raison d'être* in Christ. Our natures do not manifest Him by being suppressed but by being transfigured by obedience to the Gospel. Just as Christ came to fulfill the Law, not to destroy it, so too He came to fulfill the authentic aspirations of the customs, traditions, and philosophies of the Greeks and "Gentiles" in general. Catholicism should then be English in England, not Italian; Chinese in China and not French; African in Africa, not Belgian. The loss of the English mystical tradition would be, in fact, irreparable. The strength, sincerity, simplicity, and naturalness of an authentic English sense would be stifled. What has perhaps happened, with the loss of the earthy and humorous naturalness of medieval English piety, has been a slow smothering of the English religious instinct, and its final reduction to a lay and despairing state of tongue-tied agnosticism.

Who were the English mystics? The custom has been to designate, by this name, the greatest and most characteristic of them, the fourteenth-century contemplatives, who first developed a mysticism that was purely in the English idiom, expressed in the rich original vernacular of their time. This pure "English school" includes four great figures above all: Richard Rolle, Walter Hilton, Julian (i.e., Juliana) of Norwich, and the author of the *Cloud of Unknowing*, whom no one has ever been able to identify. Sometimes, as in the study of the English mystics by Professor David Knowles,[1] the sixteenth-century Benedictine Dom Augustine Baker is added to this group, since he is more or less in the fourteenth-century tradition, being insular and original, a decidedly solitary and independent spirit. But one might also include some of the great medieval mystics, who, though they wrote in Latin, were distinctly English in their character: St. Ailred of Rievaulx, for instance, and Adam the Carthusian (of Witham), or the anonymous Monk Solitary of Farne.[2] A recent anthology[3] has decided to take this approach, and it contains selections from the medieval mystics only. The four great mystics of the fourteenth-century school are represented there, together with Margery Kempe, St. Ailred of Rievaulx, and St. Edmund Rich, Archbishop of Canterbury. The texts of Ailred and Edmund have never been available before in English, and are typical examples of the medieval Augustinian tradition.

Ailred of Rievaulx was a twelfth-century Cistercian abbot, friend and disciple of St. Bernard of Clairvaux, father of one of the great monastic families that peopled the valleys of Yorkshire and built the pure and severe churches whose ruins still amaze even the most hardened tourist. For Ailred, as for all his fellow Cistercians, these monasteries were "schools of charity" (*scholae caritatis*). Following the Augustinian tradition, the Cistercians taught that man was made in God's image in the sense that he was created for pure love, but he had fallen from the divine likeness by centering all his love upon himself. The monastery and monastic life were designed to reeducate and reform man's capacity to love, liberating him from fixation upon himself, teaching him to love the divine image in his fellow man, and finally leading him to love perfectly, in spirit and in truth, by returning to the source of love, God Himself. Such is the theme of Ailred's principal work, the "Mirror of Charity" (*Speculum Caritatis*).

This ascent to purity begins with ascetic labor but terminates in the repose of contemplation, the "Sabbath" of perfect love, in which God is now not only believed and known but also experienced in mystical wisdom.

But Ailred's doctrine of contemplation must be seen in the context of the cenobitic tradition. In the cloister, the monks share with one another the fruits of contemplation, not by preaching to one another, but by a spiritual friendship that bears witness to the presence of Christ in their midst. For Ailred, contemplation was shared in fraternal love, and his most original work is perhaps his dialogue *De Spirituali Amicitia* —in which the theme of Christian friendship is developed as a mystique of contemplative community life.

The best modern study of St. Ailred is unfortunately not yet available in English: it is a thesis by Father Amedée Hallier, O.C.S.O.,[4] which stresses the humanistic aspect of Ailred's thought, in its deep respect for the full integral reality of the human person, finally attained by a paradoxical stripping off of "self" and a fullness of pure love in Christ.

The mystics of the Middle Ages are not the only English contemplatives, however, and one could think of other writers that might fill out the picture. Some of them would perhaps not be as orthodox as Rolle, Hilton, and the Lady Julian: for instance, William Blake. Then there is the gentle and happy spirit of the Anglican Thomas Traherne, whose *Centuries*[5] has recently been published. He is certainly one of the most English and most paradisiacal of contemplative poets.

Hilda Vaughan, in her introduction to the *Centuries,* has rightly pointed out the close affinity of spirit between Traherne and Julian of Norwich. Both alike are enlightened by an innocence and joy that are not of this world. Both see the world with a simplicity and a wisdom given only by the Holy Spirit. This does not mean, however, that Traherne is altogether a child. He is absorbed in ontological concerns, he abounds in metaphysical conceits. He can speak in theological symbols that echo the intuitions of Julian of Norwich about the Redemption:

> You never enjoy the world aright till the sea itself floweth in your veins, till you are clothed with the heavens and crowned with the stars; and perceive yourself to be the sole heir of the whole world, and more then so, because men are in it who are every one sole heirs as well as you.[6]

He can also be more difficult, more philosophical:

> By this you may know that you are infinitely beloved: God hath made your spirit a center in eternity comprehending all, and filled all about you in an endless manner with infinite riches: which shine before you and surround you with divine and heavenly enjoyments.[7]

In either case, what is important is not a theory, not an abstract proposition, but a concrete experience, expressed now in the context of theological mystery, now in philosophical language. Yet in every case we must penetrate immediately to the central intuition, a basic Eucharistic and primitive Christian theology of praise:

> By an act of the understanding therefore be present now with all the creatures among whom you live; and hear them in their beings and operations praising God in a heavenly manner. Some of them vocally, others in their ministry, all of them naturally and continually.

And he adds a sentence that manifests the real inner spirit of the English mystics in all their love of the positive and of the concrete:

We infinitely wrong ourselves by laziness and confinement. All creatures in all nations and tongues and peoples praise God infinitely: and the more for being your sole and perfect treasures. You are never what you ought till you go out of yourself and walk among them.[8]

One of the later representatives of the tradition of the *Cloud of Unknowing* is the Capuchin Benet of Canfield, who, however, wrote mostly in Latin and French. Early translations of his *Rule of Perfection* exist, but they are not yet easily accessible. A critical edition is, we hope, soon to be published, and it will draw this little-known contemplative out of the obscurity in which he has lain hidden.

Born of Puritan gentry in Essex in 1562, William Flich went to London to read for the bar and was baptized a Catholic in 1585 by an imprisoned priest in one of the London jails. He then went to France and entered the Capuchin novitiate in 1587. There he took the name of Benet (or Benedict). Later, after a short period of imprisonment in England, he was guardian and novice master in the Capuchins, and died in 1610, regarded as a saint. Henri Brémond has a very high opinion of Benet, of whom he says: "Master of the masters themselves, of Berulle, Mme. Acarie, Marie de Beauvillier and many others, he in my opinion more than any other gave our French religious renaissance this clearly mystical character."

Benet's *Rule of Perfection* is a treatise on self-emptying by total abandonment to the will of God. Unfortunately, his treatment breaks the spiritual life up into divisions and subdivisions which bewilder more than they enlighten. He distinguishes between the *Active Life*, in which one obeys the "exterior will of God" and practices vocal prayer; the *Contemplative Life*, in which the "interior will of God" moves the contemplative from within, and prayer is totally simplified. Finally, and this is characteristic of Benet, there is the *Supereminent Life* transcending both action and contemplation in union with the "essential will of God." This is the life of the saint and the mystic, in "perfect unclothing of the Spirit." Benet's emphasis (and this is still a matter of questioning and controversy) is on the total cessation of all natural activity, and complete subjection to the divine movement "between two extremes of false rest and hurtful working," to "live constantly in the Infinite of the Divine Being and the nothingness of things."

This is of course not a pure negation. The "unclothing of the Spirit" is at the same time an illumination in "such an abundance of light that [the spirit] is clothed therewith as with a garment, transformed into it and made one with the light itself." [9]

Without further discussion of these later figures, let us concentrate our attention on the mystics of the fourteenth century and Dom Augustine Baker.

The English mystics of the fourteenth century

The fourteenth century was a period of disruption and new growth: the age of the Hundred Years' War, of the Black Death, of Joan of Arc, Langland, Dante, Occam. It was the age of Chaucer, when the spires of Norwich and Salisbury first soared into the hazy blue sky and when men first began to talk and write in the English tongue about God, love and prayer, work and war, rights and justice. In the fourteenth century, the Catholic spirit became fully, joyously, and outspokenly English. With the newfound vernacular piety, the solitary self-reliance of the hermits, the growth of independent spirit among the burghers and peasantry, there developed a kind of spontaneity and forthrightness, a courageous frankness mingled with humor which are characteristic of England. All these traits are found in the English mystics, whose humility is witty, whose ardor is simple and direct, and whose love for

God is the whole offering of their complete self, not divided and destroyed but unified and transfigured in "self-naughting" and abandonment to His infinite mercy.

The mystics flourished above all in Yorkshire, the East Midlands, and East Anglia: lands of moors, of rolling wooded hills, or of vast fens laid out under a huge dome of blue sky. Rolle, the Oxford clerk who became a hermit in Yorkshire, is one of the first English vernacular poets. His is a genius of fire and light—and we shall see that for this very reason Knowles tends to question his mysticism. He is a lively and fervent poet for whom the experience of God is essentially "song and sweetness." Another hermit was the anonymous author of the *Cloud*. There is less fire in him than in Rolle, and less sweetness, but no less humor and a great deal more of the hard reality of dark contemplation. Hilton, too, had perhaps lived as a solitary before joining the Austin Canons at Thurgarton. His *Scale of Perfection,* of all the works of the English mystics, comes closest to being a treatise in the tradition of the Fathers, embracing the whole scope of the active and contemplative lives, the first being a "reformation of faith" and the second a "reformation of feeling," that is, of inner experience.

Hilton develops the traditional theology of the restoration, in Christ, of man's "lost likeness" to the divine image. Christ came to rescue man from a state of "forgetfulness and ignorance of God and monstrous love of himself." It is possible that Hilton was following Ailred of Rievaulx in his distinction between the image partially restored "in faith" and that more perfectly restored "in feeling," that is, in contemplative experience. But, in any event, the treatment is common to the medieval writers in the tradition of St. Augustine.

The *Scale of Perfection* is a "ladder" and hence it has steps or degrees, but Hilton, in this more characteristically English than Benet of Canfield, does not insist too much on analyzing and measuring out the precise stages through which the spiritual man is assumed to pass, on his way to mystical union.

Hilton has too much respect for the existential realities of the spiritual life to violate their integrity by formal schematization.

He is at once more theological and less poetic than Rolle, and when he warns against attachment to "sounds or sweet savour or any other sensation" in mystical experience, he was quite probably reacting directly against the popularity of Rolle's poetic fervor, which may perhaps have appealed inordinately to the imagination and to the emotions of untrained beginners.

Detachment from a craving to "see" and "experience" divine things in a crude or human manner is then part of the "reformation of feeling," which is completed when one has attained to a purity of love that no longer reflects on itself or desires anything for itself. But this cannot be attained without a long, difficult struggle with that "obscure and heavy image of your own soul which has neither light to know God nor affection to love Him." [10]

The Cloud of Unknowing

Although he is anonymous, the author of the *Cloud of Unknowing* is no less arresting a personality than any of the other English mystics. His voice has the same ring of sincerity and humor, of frankness, discretion, and sobriety. He is at once more learned, more sophisticated, and more shrewd than Rolle, who is not always moderate. The author of the *Cloud* is a professional in the tradition of "dark contemplation" that reached Europe from the Orient and flourished in the fourteenth century, especially in the Rhineland. The author of the *Cloud* invites comparison with Eckhart, whose influence he must have felt. The brilliant metaphysical improvisations of the Master of Rhenish mysticism and his bold figures of speech are not for the author of the *Cloud*. He speaks in quieter tones, for a strictly limited audience, in a doctrine too unassuming to make enemies. The *Cloud* of course quotes Pseudo-Dionysius—and this is practically the only one of the Fathers it quotes at all. The author even wrote a commentary on the *Mystical Theology* ("Hid Divinity") of the Areopagite. This book is, then, representative of the pure Dionysian tradition and has little in it of Augustinian speculation.

The thing that is most striking, perhaps, about the *Cloud of Unknowing* is the serene and practical assurance with which the author speaks of the "work" that he proposes to his hermit disciple. This is not merely a way of prayer, a manner of devotion: it is a *way of life*. It is a rare grace, a life to which one can only be called by God. It is not so much an exalted way as a rare one: rare by its very simplicity. It implies a peculiar sense of responsibility, a special gift of humility, an unusual common sense. It does not demand peculiar intellectual gifts, or unusual natural aptitudes. But it does require a special fidelity and, one might say, an extraordinary spiritual tact. It is a way of life (we call it, by way of cliché, the "contemplative life"), in which one must learn to act by not acting and to know by not knowing: to have one desire alone which is not really a desire but a kind of desirelessness, an openness, a habitual freedom in the sense of self-abandonment, a realization that all God asks is "that you turn your attention to Him, and then let Him alone. You must only guard the windows and doors for flies and enemies who may intrude. And if you willingly do this, then you will need only to speak quietly and humbly in prayer and soon He will help you." [11] Later, the author adds that this speaking in prayer says little or nothing: and one of the chief preoccupations of the disciple led into the "cloud" is to bear down upon understanding and put aside clear ideas and definite wishes in order to attend, in perfect mindfulness, to the God who is not seen and not known:

> Think of nothing but God Himself, so that nothing will work in your mind or in your will but only God Himself. You must then do whatever will help you to forget all the beings whom God has created, and all their works . . .[12]

This would seem to be the exact opposite of the paragraph we quoted earlier from Traherne. But are Traherne and the *Cloud* really so far apart? In mysticism, opposites tend to meet and coincide, for the realm of spiritual experience is no longer the realm of strict logic in which A and not-A are irreconcilably set apart and opposed. In point of fact, it is by forgetting the immediate data of sense and letting go all preoccupation with material concerns that one enters into the kind of cosmic fellowship and unity with all beings that Traherne spoke of.

Here the author of the *Cloud* simply says: "All of mankind living on earth will be helped by this work in wonderful ways of which you are not even aware . . . And you yourself are cleansed and made virtuous by no other work as much as by this. And yet this is the simplest work of all, the easiest and the speediest to accomplish, if the soul is only helped by grace of feeling a strong desire to do it. Otherwise it is hard, and a marvel if you do it." (p. 62) "For this is a work . . . that man would have continued to do if he had never sinned. And it was for this work that man was made as all things also were made to help him and further him in this work, so that by means of it man shall be made whole again." (p. 65)

There is, in fact, in all the English mystics a characteristic realization of wholeness, of restoration, of return to a primitive state of innocence. The English mystics are Paradise men and the more clear and spontaneous their awareness of Paradise, the more truly English is their contemplation.

The author of the *Cloud* is perhaps, for some readers, the most difficult of them all to understand. He might seem to have nothing definite to say. He might seem to be maddeningly elusive. When you ask him precisely what the "work" is and how it is to be done, he says: "I don't know." For this is a way that cannot be understood by mental activity, it cannot be forced by an effort of the will. It is a pure response to the mysterious appeal of a hidden and incomprehensible God. It is a "wrestling with blind nought," and he is at great pains to contradict Augustine and to warn against thinking of it going on "inside" yourself or even "above" yourself. Where then is this work to be done? He answers, "Nowhere!"

Julian of Norwich

It is not so proper to speak of "Juliana" of Norwich as it is to call her by her true name, the "Lady Julian." Lady not because she was noble but because she was a *Domna,* like the Benedictine nuns of Carrow to whom her anchorhold at St. Julian's Church, Norwich, most probably belonged. Of all the English mystics, Julian of Norwich is perhaps the best known and the most charming. She is the English equivalent of Siena's Catherine and Sweden's Bridget, except that, unlike her great contemporaries, she did not concern herself with the problems of kingdoms and of the Church, but lived as a recluse in her quiet corner. Yet Norwich was not so far from the Continent that rumors of its wars and movements did not come through in plenty by way of the wool ports of the North Sea.

There can be no doubt that Lady Julian is the greatest of the English mystics. Not only that, but she is one of the greatest English theologians, in the ancient sense of the word. As Evagrius Ponticus said in the fourth century, "he who really prays is a theologian and he who is a theologian really prays." By prayer, of course, this Desert Father and Origenist meant the "theologia," which was at once contemplation and experience of the deepest revealed mysteries: the mystical knowledge of the Holy Trinity. Actually, in Julian of Norwich, we find an admirable synthesis of mystical experience and theological reflection, ranging from "bodily visions" of the passion of Christ to "intellectual visions" of the Trinity, and from reflections on the creation and providence to intuitions penetrating the inmost secret of the redemption and the divine mercy.

It would be insufficient and inexact to classify the teaching of Julian of Norwich merely as "private revelation." Certainly she did receive "Revelations of Divine Love" equal to those of St. Theresa of Avila or St. Margaret Mary, and that is the title of her book. These revelations, however, must be seen for what they are: as profound and penetrating supernatural experiences of the truths revealed to and taught by the Church. Furthermore, we must distinguish in Julian the record of the experiences themselves, the "sixteen shewings" which took place when she lay at death's door on May 13, 1383, and her subsequent reflections on these experiences, her elaboration of their meaning and of their import. It must be stressed that her whole book is completely objective. Though it is at the same time entirely personal, it cannot be regarded merely as an interesting account of subjective experiences. It is a document that bears eloquent witness to the teaching and tradition of the Catholic Church, and it is a meditative, indeed a mystical, commentary on the basic doctrines of the Catholic faith.

In a word, Julian of Norwich gives a coherent and indeed systematically constructed corpus of doctrine, which has only recently begun to be studied as it deserves.[13]

The theology of Lady Julian is a theology of the all-embracing totality and fullness of the divine love. This is, for her, the ultimate Reality, in the light of which all created being and all the vicissitudes of life and of history fade into unimportance. Not that the world and time, the cosmos and history are unreal: but their reality is only a revelation of love. The revelation itself is not immediately clear, however. A gift of God is required before the light breaks through and the full meaning of the world and of time is seen in its real relation to God and to His eternal and loving designs.

Julian "saw" the whole world as a "little thing the size of a hazel nut which seemed to lie in the palm of my hand." When she wondered what this was, "it was answered in a general way, thus: 'it is all that is made.' " And she adds: "I wondered how long it could last; for it seemed as though it might suddenly fade away to nothing, it was so small." [14] But the importance of this vision lies, paradoxically, in the fact that it shows not the *insignificance* of the created world so much as its *significance*. Though ontologically the being of the world is as nothing compared with the infinite God, yet it is willed and held in being by His love and is thus infinitely precious in His sight. For thus it becomes, itself, a revelation of His infinite love.

> It lasts and ever shall last for God loveth it. And even so hath everything being—by the love of God. In this little thing I saw three properties. The first that God made it: the second that God loveth it; the third that God keepeth it. And what beheld I in this? Truly the Maker, the Lover and the Keeper.[15]

Not only that, but in this same vision Julian sees herself, along with all beings, wrapped and embraced in the love of God so that: "He is to us everything that is good, as I understand it." And: "He is our clothing that, for love, wrapped us up and windeth us about; embraceth us, all beclotheth us and hangeth about us, for tender love." [16]

The divine love manifested in creation is manifested more clearly and on a much deeper level in the Redemption. And here the originality of Julian lies, in her peculiar insight into the deeply personal and gratuitous character of God's redemptive and merciful love. Here we see a new emphasis, not on Christ's work of atonement, repairing the outraged justice of God the Father, but on the contrary, the redeemed sinner becomes the Father's merciful gift to the Son, "his bliss, his prize, his worship and his crown." (p. 83) The theology of Julian of Norwich is a theology of mercy, of joy, and of praise. Nowhere in all Christian literature are the dimensions of her Christian optimism excelled. Christ asks her if she is "well paid" that He suffered for her. It is a deep and illuminating question. Is she "satisfied" with the work He has done, is she "content" with Him? Is she so content that this alone suffices to content her? Is His love enough for her? She answers that it is. And He replies:

> If thou art paid, I am paid. It is a joy, a bliss and an endless liking to me that I ever suffered passion for thee. And if I could suffer more I would suffer more.[17]

This opens up new perspectives in the Augustinian tradition of *amor amicitiae,* disinterested love. Julian's vision of the divine mercy as a "motherly" love for us stems, perhaps, in part from St. Anselm. At any rate, she is not afraid to speak, with an utterly disarming simplicity, of "Jesus our Mother." "Our Savior is our true Mother, in whom we are endlessly borne; and we shall never come out of Him." (p. 157) "God almighty is our kindly Father; and God all-wisdom is our kindly Mother: with the love and goodness of the Holy Ghost; which is all one God, one Lord. And in the knitting and the oneing He is our very true Spouse, and we are His loved wife and fair maiden." (p. 158) "Our Father willeth, our Mother worketh, and our good Lord the Holy Ghost confirmeth." (p. 162)

It can be seen that Julian's mystical theology culminates in the vision and mystery of the Trinity and here there remain depths to be fathomed which we cannot pause to consider here. One last thought: we must emphasize the originality of Julian's intuition of the problem of evil in the light of the divine mercy. This is the subject of the great thirteenth revelation: "Sin must needs be, but all shall be well. All shall be well; and all manner of thing shall be well." (p. 91) We recall the echoes of this sentence in T. S. Eliot's *Four Quartets.*

Julian's vision of sin and mercy is remarkable above all for its realism. She minimizes nothing. She does not try to bolster up an optimistic explanation of redemption by minimizing sin. Such interpretations betray the mystery of the mercy of God revealed in the Gospel. She sees sin in all its tragedy, she sees the full horror and evil of the crucifixion of Christ. Not only that, she sees that sin persists and evil continues in the world. Indeed, it may grow, and there will come a time when "Holy Church shall be shaken with sorrow and anguish and tribulation in this world as men shake a cloth in the wind." (p. 92) She sees, moreover, the sufferings of the just and the crushing humiliations of those who strive to love Christ: their pain, their anguish, their descent into the abyss of near despair.

Here we come to what is perhaps the most personal and unique intuition in the revelations of Julian of Norwich. It is her distinction between the mystery of sin and redemption as proposed "openly" by the Church and Julian's conviction that this also implies "secretly" something that has never been revealed and which no one will know until the end of time. That though there is great evil in the world, though there are devils and a hell, with the damned in it, and though the Church shall be attacked and shaken in a great storm, yet the Lord assures her: "I *may* make all things well: and I *can* make all things well: and I *shall* make all things well and I *will* make all things well: and *thou shalt see thyself* that all manner of things shall be well." (p. 96) This is not a *solution* to the problem of evil. It is an admission that there exists no satisfactory intellectual solution. It is, even in spite of revelation, a problem that has not yet been fully solved and cannot be solved until the end of time when Christ Himself will make known something that has never been revealed before: the secret which He alone knows, and which it is not given us to know, which not even the blessed in heaven have yet seen, because it is not necessary for our salvation. It is the "secret counsel," the "great deed ordained by our Lord from without— beginning treasured and hid in His blessed breast, known only to Himself, by which He shall make all things well. For just as the blessed Trinity made all things from naught, so the same blessed Trinity shall make all well that is not well." (p. 99)

Recent studies

Both in Professor Knowles's study and in Professor Colledge's anthology we meet Margery Kempe. She is no equal to Julian, not because she was not a recluse (for she was married), but because she seems after all to have been a little hysterical, something of a garrulous busybody perhaps: at least, enough of one for Knowles to compare her, surprisingly, with Chaucer's Wife of Bath.

Margery was not quite as earthy as Chaucer's engaging character. But, still, she did not hesitate to tell her husband she felt she had married beneath her station, and decided to improve her financial condition by running a brewery, which unfortunately failed. Her business losses contributed something to her disillusionment with the world. Her life was certainly not without fantastic incidents. Once when she was hearing Mass a stone fell out of the church ceiling and hit her on the head. It bounced off "miraculously," without doing her any notable harm. She tells us it was on the road from York to Bridlington, while she was carrying a bottle of beer and her husband a cake, that she asked him if he would agree to their living thenceforth in chastity, and had her way. In return, she paid all his debts. She was nearly burned alive by a crowd in Canterbury. Doubtless, they imagined her to be a Lollard, because she preached to them against swearing and quoted abundantly from Scripture.

The mysticism of Margery Kempe is admittedly "original," if not strange. Once at the elevation of the Mass, she saw the Host "flutter like a dove" and took this as a prophetic intimation of a coming earthquake. No earthquake came.

She used to utter loud cries when in ecstasy. She believed herself mystically wedded, in a solemn rite, to the Heavenly Father. She heard the Holy Ghost singing like a robin.

It is not surprising that her orthodoxy was questioned, but

an official examination acquitted her of heresy. Nevertheless, she was frequently imprisoned and even denounced from the pulpit, but she also had staunch friends and defenders among the clergy.

Today, E. I. Watkin has undertaken to write "In Defense of Margery Kempe." [18] While admitting that her behavior was odd, he stresses her subjective sincerity and her real virtue, especially her charity. What others have disapproved as "hysteria," Watkin prefers to call "abnormal suggestibility," and even admits that this suggestibility can be regarded at times as "morbid."

While not agreeing completely with Watkin's spirited defense of Margery, we can certainly recognize that it is a realistic estimate of a remarkably interesting figure seen in the context of her time. After all, the fourteenth century was an age of enthusiasm and of exaggeration.

Eric Colledge questions her mysticism more diffidently than Knowles, but both agree that, as a document of unrivaled historic interest, her autobiography is at once fascinating and invaluable.

Finally, there is Augustine Baker, who provides material for one of the most interesting and controversial articles in David Knowles's book. Born of a Protestant family in 16th-century Wales, Baker went to London to read for the bar and during his residence in the Inns of Court used to frequent the theaters, where he saw Shakespeare's new plays. He was converted, not indeed by Shakespeare but by a narrow escape from death, which he considered miraculous. He crossed over to the Continent, entered the Benedictine Order in Italy, but could not adjust to the systems of meditation and piety that were intensively practiced after the Council of Trent. Indeed, he thought they nearly drove him crazy, and when he later became a director of nuns in France, he dedicated all his efforts to rescuing potential contemplatives from the deadly machinery of systems which had their place in the active life but were less helpful in the cloister. He believed the monastic life ought naturally to lead one to "introversion." Never a community man, he led a marginal life as a semirecluse.

Knowles makes a careful study of this restless and complex character, this monastic oddball, born out of due season, in perpetual hopeless conflict with the "active-livers" in the cloister. He resisted them so doggedly that finally one of them, who came to be his superior, decided to get rid of him by sending him, in sickness and old age, to the English mission in a time of renewed persecution. Baker died in his bed, however, a "baffling figure," a "man of whimsies and corners," and, after all, we cannot help feeling that he was a creature of the fourteenth century who would have blossomed as happily as any Rolle or Lady Julian in an East Midland hermitage, but who had the misfortune to be born two centuries late. Since then, how many other such men have there been in England? We have mentioned William Blake: what would he have been in the fourteenth century? Perhaps the equal of Tauler, or Eckhart—or, more likely, Boehme. But nothing could stop Blake from being Blake. There is no century possible in which Blake would not have seen angels.

What is to be said of Knowles's treatment of the English mystics? It is an excellent, interesting, and well-written book, but its judgments are too rigid and too strict. It suffers from a kind of scholarly compulsion to deny and to reject, as if the most important task of the student of mysticism were to uncover false mystics. Indeed, Knowles is so cautious that, out of six "mystics," he ends up by accepting only three as fully genuine. Margery Kempe, of course, he dismisses as "sincere, devout, but very hysterical," after a consideration of her vision of "many white things flying all about her on every side as thick as motes in a sunbeam." After a patient examination of Baker, Professor Knowles concludes that he never developed into "a genuine mystic." This judgment has been vigorously and I believe rightly disputed by E. I. Watkin. There will certainly be few to accept without question Knowles's minimizing of Richard Rolle as a "beginner."

Knowles clings firmly to a single standard in judging mystics: it is the Dionysian standard of "unknowing." Therefore, he cannot accept as genuine a mystic of light like Rolle. The "fire, song and sweetness" of the hermit of Hampole are, by Knowles's standards, merely the consolations that precede and prepare for the serious business of dark contemplation.

But is it, after all, realistic to cling arbitrarily to a single set standard in such a thing as mysticism, in which the great rule is that there are no rules? The Holy Ghost takes temperaments as He finds them and does what He pleases with them. The history of mysticism, including patristic mysticism, gives us plenty of room for accepting the "fire of love" in Rolle as something more than "sensible consolation." After all, does not Cassian speak of the "prayer of fire" among the Desert Fathers? (Admittedly, this is an illumination that pertains more to *theoria physike* than to perfect mysticism.) But, more serious than this, to reject a mysticism like Rolle's would mean rejecting the mysticism of the Oriental Church.

As a matter of fact, Rolle resembles the Hesychast mystics of Sinai and Mount Athos in more than one point. Not only does he experience the presence of the glorified Saviour in a flood of light, but his ordinary prayer, besides the Psalter, is the meditative and loving repetition of the Name of Jesus. More exactly, it is a constant mindfulness of the Holy Name present as a living and sanctifying power in the depths of the heart. *"Ponder [this Name of Jesus] in thy heart night and day as a special and dear treasure. Love it more than thy life, root it in thy mind . . ."* (R. Rolle, *The Commandment*).

Here we have a close parallel to the famous "Prayer of Jesus" propagated not only in monastic but also in lay circles throughout Greece and Russia by the *Philokalia*.

A study of the controversy between Barlaam the Calabrian and Gregory Palamas will warn us not to be too adamant in clinging to the apophatic standard in mysticism. Indeed, *apophasis* (the mysticism of darkness) and *cataphasis* (the mysticism of light) are simply correlative to one another, and

Pseudo-Denys makes clear that "mystical theology" rises above both of them and completes them both in a darkness that is "superresplendent." The "light of Tabor," which is at the heart of Athonite mysticism, surely seems to bear witness in favor of Rolle, and when we read about Seraphin of Sarov visibly transfigured by the in-dwelling Spirit, we must hesitate to dismiss this prayer of fire without any other reason than that it does not correspond with the standards of the *Cloud of Unknowing.* After all, according to St. John of the Cross, to whom Knowles turns as a court of last appeal, it could be argued that the author of the *Cloud* was simply a "beginner" in dark contemplation.

A more moderate judgment of Rolle is that of Father Conrad Pepler, O.P., who admits there is no doubt of the genuine mystical character of Rolle's experience. It is an "infused" and "mystical" gift, granted to an "exceptionally devoted man" who had lived a heroically ascetic life. But, says Father Pepler, "his life and teaching are characteristic of the illuminative way rather than of the supreme heights." [19] This fits in with the language of St. John of the Cross, who, in the *Spiritual Canticle,* describes relatively advanced mystical states as "the illuminative way," reserving the term "unitive way" for that transforming union which presupposes the rare and intense purification brought about by the dark night of the spirit. And there is no evidence of this dark night in Rolle. One finds in him perhaps too much passion, too much poetry, too much of an active "self" who rises to the occasion and justifies his mystical love in the flames not only of ecstasy but of controversy. Not a few saints have done the same: so who are we to weigh and measure and, with extreme exactitude, to mark out degrees? Too much nicety, and too many preoccupations in judging the mystics make it impossible for us to enter, by empathy, into a valid appreciation of their experience, and thus we can no longer really judge it.

To reject Rolle as an undeveloped mystic is, finally, to reject that which seems distinctly characteristic of the northern

English solitaries, as exemplified by the twelfth-century hermit, poet, and predecessor of Rolle, Godric of Finchale, in whose heart "there was a gentleness greater than anything else, in his mouth a sweetness sweeter than honey or the honeycomb and his ears were filled with the melody of a great jubilation." These words of a medieval hagiographer are borrowed from a sermon of St. Bernard, yet they serve to express a characteristic type of mystical experience. However much we may ourselves prefer the mystics of darkness, we cannot hastily reject the mysticism of light.

Though this is no slight criticism, it does not alter our admiration for Knowles's book or for its author. This is a work of singular excellence. No one who loves the English spiritual tradition can read it without passionate interest and deep concern.

Conclusions

This brief introduction will have given us a good idea of the main characteristics of English mysticism. When we consider the fourteenth-century "school" of English mysticism, we find in it first of all a certain coherence and unity of temper, even though there may be wide differences between the individual mystics. This coherence is due perhaps above all to the fact that it is a small school, in an island nation. Influences from abroad undoubtedly arrive and lead some of them into new directions. This is probably particularly true of the *Cloud of Unknowing*, which we may perhaps owe to a current of Dionysian spirituality from the Rhineland. Yet it is not absolutely necessary to account for the *Cloud* by tracing it to Eckhart and Tauler. There was after all the school of St. Victor in Paris, with Richard of St. Victor, a Scot and one of the medieval theorists of dark contemplation, who was widely read in England. But we are not here preoccupied with influences, since whatever they may have been, these influences were absorbed into peculiarly English minds and doctrines.

Whether they are mystics of darkness or of light, the masters of the English school are all equally positive, optimistic, simple. The author of the *Cloud* talks of "darkness" and "nothing" and yet he does not strike us as much less luminous than Rolle with his "fire, song and sweetness." The mysticism of darkness is not a mysticism of gloom. We must remember how these mystics appropriated the verse of the psalm, *Nox illuminatio mea in deliciis meis* (Night is my light in my delights). It is a darkness illuminated by joy and by the presence of the Lord, all the more joyous precisely because the night brings Him nearer and unites us to Him more intimately than any light.

The masters of the English school, each in his own way, teach a doctrine of simplicity and joy. One finds in them nothing tragic, nothing morbid, no obsession, no violence. Of course, one must make an exception for Margery Kempe. She was odd and she made a lot of noise, but nobody took this seriously or encouraged her to do so. There is in the English school less blood and anguish, less hellfire and horror, than is to be found in any other school of Christian mysticism. Not that the physical sufferings of Christ on the cross were not real to them, witness the first shewing of Lady Julian: but the light of mercy and the joy of life in the Risen Saviour transfigure even the vision of the Crucified. And this is, of course, as it should be.

English mysticism is, then, always positive, always affirmative, even when, like the *Cloud,* it negates. For what is negated is the accidental, the relative, the inconsequential, in order that first things may be put first, and the great, eternal truths affirmed. One finds relatively little of the devil in English mysticism: not that he is ignored, but the English mystics were more impressed with the power of Christ than with the power of Satan.

English mysticism is a mysticism of praise, and consequently it tends to take an affirmative view of God's creation and of human existence in the world. Not that it is what men now call a "world-affirming" spirituality, concerned with establishing the Kingdom of God in a solid political and economic setting. It is rather a "paradise spirituality" which recovers in Christ the innocence and joy of the first beginnings and sees the world—the lovely world of moors and wolds, midland forests, rivers and farms—in the light of Paradise, as it first came from the hand of God. Even the author of the *Cloud*, who is less disposed than the others to "see" these things, does not ignore them.

As people, the English mystics are always very human, and, we may add, very individual. One might perhaps even be tempted to call them "individualists," but that word has overtones that would not be true in the case of men and women who in no way lived for themselves or centered on themselves. The English mystics were certainly aware of themselves as autonomous persons loved and redeemed by God. They attached great importance to this fact, and they recognized it with great simplicity, dignity, and gratitude. They recognized their personal vocation as a gift of wonderful meaning and value. They sought above all to be faithful to the grace of their calling. They took the gift of contemplation seriously, and were not too concerned with the possible approval or disapproval of other men. One senses in them a fine respect for individual differences in these matters. Sometimes this respect was bought and defended with a great price.

Finally, it can be said without exaggeration that the chief characteristic of the English school of the fourteenth century, its homogeneous, simple, optimistic, and personal quality, is perhaps due above all to the fact that it developed out of the English monastic tradition. The mysticism of the English school is basically Benedictine and Cistercian. This does not mean to say, as Dom Cuthbert Butler once held, that it is purely and simply a "genuine Western mysticism" rooted in

Augustine and not in the writings of that dubious Oriental, the Pseudo-Areopagite. It means, on the contrary, that it goes back to the same root as Pseudo-Denys: through Cassian and Gregory the Great to Evagrius Ponticus, the Desert Fathers, and Origen. Of course, Augustine has a great deal to say in and through the English mystics. His Trinitarian psychology is there, the doctrine of image and likeness is there, and the introversion by which we enter into ourselves and then go on above ourselves is also there. True, also, the *Cloud* goes direct to Pseudo-Dionysius and makes a special point of attacking the Augustinian psychology of contemplation. But these varieties were already present within the monastic tradition itself. It may be argued that the English mystics were, for the most part, either solitaries or oriented toward the eremitical life. This does nothing to disprove that their mysticism is rooted in the medieval monastic tradition of England, since the English hermits were, obviously, the full flower of the monastic tradition. Yet, at the same time, the hermit had been from the beginning more a "layman" than a "clerk." That is to say, even if he may have been a priest, his separation from the monastic and liturgical community life put him in a certain sense on a level with the simple layman. The hermit life, properly understood, is a life without exaltation, a life not at the top of the ladder but in a certain sense at the bottom. For more than anyone else the hermit has to be a humble man. This combination of simplicity, individuality, and humility, not without ever present elements of humor, is proper to a spirituality of men and women who have gone apart to live alone with God.

SELF-KNOWLEDGE IN GERTRUDE MORE
AND AUGUSTINE BAKER

It is now well known that the traditional monastic ascesis differs considerably from modern asceticism. Monastic ascesis is a *disciplina* rather than a "method" or a system. That is to say, the monastic life is traditionally regarded as a school in which one is taught by God and by those who bear in themselves by doctrine and example the living tradition which they pass on to their disciples, in the name of God.

In this school one does not learn a method of attaining perfection which one then proceeds to apply, but rather one learns to live as a perfect Christian, as a child of God guided by His Spirit. "For whoever are led by the Spirit of God, they are the sons of God. Now you have not received a spirit of bondage so as to be again in fear, but you have received a spirit of adoption as sons, by virtue of which we cry, 'Abba! Father!' The Spirit himself gives testimony to our spirit that we are sons of God. But if we are sons, we are heirs also: heirs indeed of God and joint heirs with Christ, provided, however,

we suffer with him that we may also be glorified with him"
(Romans 8:14–17).[1] "Behold what manner of love the Father has bestowed upon us, that we should be called children
of God; and such we are. This is why the world does not know
us, because it did not know him. Beloved, now we are the
children of God, and it has not yet appeared what we shall be.
We know that, when he appears, we shall be like to him, for
we shall see him just as he is. And everyone who has this hope
in him makes himself holy, just as he also is holy" (I John
3:1–3). "As for you, let that which you have heard from the
beginning abide in you. If that abides in you which you have
heard from the beginning, you also will abide in the Son and
in the Father" (I John 2:24).

In living this life "in the Spirit," one is purified of inordinate passion, becomes humble, pliable, docile to the divine
teaching, and eventually perfect in charity. "Then, when all
these degrees of humility have been climbed, the monk will
presently come to that perfect love of God which casts out all
fear: whereby he will begin to observe without labour, as
though naturally and by habit, all those precepts which formerly he did not observe without fear: no longer for fear of
hell, but for love of Christ and through good habit and delight in virtue. And this will the Lord deign to show forth by
the power of his Spirit in his workman now cleansed from
vice and from sin." [2]

The monk is sanctified by living the monastic life in all its
fullness, all its wholeness, considered as a *conversatio,* which is
not only a new way of behavior[3] but, one is almost tempted to
say, a whole new mode of being. He who acts according to his
new being, as a *monachos* who has renounced the world and
offered himself to the Father in the mystery of the Passion
and Resurrection of Christ, will at the same time be sanctified
by all his actions and will, in them, find the God Whom he
came to the monastery to seek. One might say that the monk
is not so much one who denies himself and practices virtue in

order to find God, but one who is more or less fervent in his monastic *conversatio* in proportion as he realizes that he has found God in it.

The vow of *conversatio morum* implies an intention and desire to seek and to find God in the monastic life (insofar as one can possibly do so) in its traditional wholeness, simplicity, and purity. Without a genuine monastic spirit, the vow of *conversatio morum* tends to become at once incomprehensible and frustrating, a doom and a confusion, relegating the unfortunate monk to a limbo of varied and almost arbitrary "ascetic practices," which are not seen in any living relation to one another or to God, and which represent the monk's given and isolated will to "become more and more perfect every day." But as soon as the vow of *conversatio morum* is interpreted in the light of authentic tradition, its inner meaning begins to be apparent. It is an awakening to the sound of God's voice calling us to the path of life, to the way of humility and obedience, not merely because they are ascetic exercises, but because they are characteristic of the life of sonship and discipleship which the monk lives in the school of the Lord's service.

Conversatio morum implies, then, not only the will to exert oneself in the service of God (which, of course, it certainly does) but also a certain illumination of faith which enables one to find God while serving Him, and to see that in responding to His will one is at the same time entering into His presence and His light: *apertis oculis ad deificum lumen.* And finally, *conversatio morum* means a consciousness of one's union with Christ crucified, in the ordinary works and duties of the monastic life: perseverance in patience being a mark of fidelity to the teaching of the Master in the monastic school: "As we progress in our monastic life [*processu vero conversationis*] and in faith, our hearts shall be enlarged, and we shall run with unspeakable sweetness of love in the way of God's commandments; so that, never abandoning his rule [*magisterio*] but persevering in his teaching [*doctrina*] in the monastery until death, we shall share by patience in the sufferings of Christ, that we may deserve to be partakers also of his kingdom." [4]

The monastic ascesis is by no means abstract, or "purely interior." It is certainly very concrete in its insistence upon fasting, obedience, humility, silence, labor, penance, vigils, psalmody, and above all solitude and renunciation of the ways of the world. In fact, monastic *disciplina* is generally more concrete than modern ascetic methods, which tend to be compounded of certain exterior mortifications and interior, psychological techniques based on the analytical study of specialized treatises on virtue and vice. These mortifications and techniques demand the expert guidance of a director who is a specialist trained in performing the most delicate surgical operations on "corrupt nature," or a trainer who brings out, in "the soul," the *highest possible capacity to produce results,* whether in the apostolate or in the interior life.

The monastic ascesis does not reject the *exterior* observances (silence, labor, fasting, etc.) which are the "body" of the monastic *conversatio*. It insists that this body be seen as it really is: a living organism vivified by a spirit of charity and by the sense of the divine presence. The difference between this ancient traditional ascesis and modern asceticism is the difference between a sacramental, living, and objective view of the spiritual life, on one hand, and a psychological, technical, abstract, and subjective view of it on the other.

It has been pointed out[5] that as the Benedictine life in the High Middle Ages became a more elaborate and complex structure of devotions and observances that obscured the simplicity of the monastic *conversatio* and destroyed the balance of the life as it had been conceived by early tradition, there was a natural tendency to seek unity and sense in the interior life by withdrawing from the multiplicity of duties and occupations in order to concentrate on the simple interior *spirit*. The monk's day of prayer was so complex, and the necessary business of the monastery introduced so many secular ele-

ments into the cloister, that *one could no longer simply en-
trust oneself to the life as it was actually lived,* forget his cares,
and praise the God who was so palpably near at hand. On the
contrary, one had to struggle to find Him in the busy and
sometimes worldly confusion of the monastery itself.[6] This is
the background of the spirituality of writers like Jean de
Fécamp and St. Anselm, which is usually recognized as more
"affective" and "subjective" in its tone than that of the early
Fathers. The dialectical mind of St. Anselm favored a considerable amount of discursive activity in prayer, and his notion
of the examination of conscience is identical with that which
became common in the late Middle Ages and the Renaissance: "Let nothing draw thy mind away from self-custody.
Let it work out with all care [*sollicite discutiat*] the gains it
has made in day-to-day progress lest, God forbid, it should be
losing by falling back." [7] Here the emphasis is on discovering,
by logical self-examination and reasoning, some evidence of
progress.

An active and "technical" approach to the spiritual life is
more or less necessary and even to a certain extent inevitable
wherever a Christian is left alone to face the confusion of an
active life in the world—or in a monastic society that has become increasingly active and complex. Our ideal view of the
primitive monastic *conversatio* may not, in many cases, be re-
alizable except to a small degree. We must certainly know
how to take care of ourselves and make use of first aid in our
own spiritual life. And when we are unable to be carried
along by the stream of a fervent simple observance that is
completely ordered according to the best and most living tradition, then we must know how to help ourselves. When the
stream is dry, we must know how to leave our boat and walk.
The fact remains that it is simpler, easier, more secure, and
ultimately more perfect if a monk can live purely according
to the spirit of his vocation, interested in his monastic *conversatio* more than in his own interior reactions, and more concerned with the love of God and his brethren than with the

incessant quest for signs of virtue in his own conduct. Practices which are in themselves useful and laudable may, in some circumstances, turn to a harmful obsession with one's own self and ruin one's capacity to enter simply into the stream of the monastic life.

One of the familiar and so to speak "standard" practices of late medieval and modern asceticism is the detailed and systematic examination of conscience, used as a specific and analytical technique, aimed at achieving certain very definite practical results and thus to produce more or less immediate fruits of perfection. This practice is now prescribed for monks in the same terms as for all other religious, with the specification that a definite time is to be set apart for an explicit and perhaps even detailed analysis of one's conscience.[8]

There is no question whatever that self-knowledge is fundamental to all spiritual life. The Benedictine Rule enumerates, among the instruments of good works, that custody of heart by which we become attentive to the character of all our acts: *actus vitae suae omni hora custodire.* The first degree of humility which is treated in great detail, with many Biblical texts, shows that the whole structure of the monastic *conversatio* rests on the monk's capacity and willingness to see himself constantly as God sees him, and to judge himself at every moment, considering not only his actions but also their motives and indeed his inmost desires and thoughts in the light of that fear of the Lord which is the beginning of wisdom. The whole monastic life is ordered to purity of heart: a term which means much more than simply peace of conscience, which, however, it certainly includes. There can be no order, no tranquillity, and above all no true knowledge of God, where unknown or half-known roots of sin still grow and flourish in the spirit of a man. The light of knowledge, awareness, and faith must be brought to play upon the inmost recesses of the self, in order that we may learn to renounce our self. This is the main task of the monastic ascesis.

In this connection, the monk will frequently remember

and lament the faults of his past life and will never forget that he stands before God as a sinner in need of mercy.[9] Because of his sinfulness, he will immediately make known his hidden faults and sins of thought to his spiritual father, and will publicly accuse himself of more external faults in the presence of his brethren.[10] It was also understood that the *Opus Dei* itself was a most excellent way of acknowledging one's faults before God, weeping for one's sins both ancient and recent, and offering Him satisfaction for them. For a monk who seriously attends to the meaning of the office of compline, the examination of conscience which follows may well seem a little superfluous, though it may have more point for one who never adverts to the meaning of what he sings in choir.

We may, therefore, seriously ask whether the monk should necessarily apply himself to *some special psychological or ascetical method of self-examination at fixed times.* The silence, the recollection, the solitude of monastic life should normally enable the monk to live all day long in the presence of God, and consequently he should be able to learn how to know himself, to identify and judge his sinful motives the very moment they reach his consciousness. For the monk, there should be only a minimum of separation between psychological consciousness and moral conscience: the two should function as one, not in a strained fury of vengeful concentration upon one's semideliberate acts, but in the simplicity and compunction of a truly humble heart.

As a matter of fact, though the formal exercise of examination of conscience at fixed times was practiced in pagan antiquity by Stoics, Pythagoreans, and others, and though it had an important place in Rabbinical and Moslem spirituality, this ascetic practice is seldom mentioned in the writings of early Christianity. It first appears after the Peace of Constantine when the Christian had to mix in the life of the world and face its many temptations. St. Ambrose, St. Augustine, and St. Gregory recommend a daily examination of conscience. Yet St. Gregory attributes more importance to *habit-*

ual self-custody, living in the presence of God, and a general spirit of prayer, than to psychological self-analysis at fixed times. Finally, in early monastic tradition, though the examination of conscience is mentioned once or twice, it has no real importance. The whole attention of the monk is aimed at the "discernment of spirits" (*discretio spirituum*) from moment to moment. He does not examine himself for faults after the fact, but by attention and prayer he seeks to control the passionate thoughts from which faults may eventually arise. When sin has been committed, the monk concentrates not on examining the causes or estimating his degree of guilt, but on sorrowful compunction of heart before God. In all cases the attention of the monk is directed to God Himself, and not to a minute examination of dubious psychological motives.[11] However, it is true that in the twelfth century and after, greater and greater emphasis is laid on the daily examination of conscience.

It is interesting in this connection to study a monastic text of the seventeenth century, precisely because it represents a conscious return to the early monastic tradition and registers a protest against the arbitrary imposition of complex methods upon a monastic community that had no need of them.

The text is from Dom Augustine Baker's *Inner Life and Writings of Dame Gertrude More.*[12] To appreciate it fully, we must place it in its historical setting. Augustine Baker (see page 146) studied law in the London of Shakespeare and Queen Elizabeth I. Reconciled to the Catholic Church in 1603 and clothed with the Benedictine habit at Pavia in 1605, he became a spiritual disciple and descendent of the great English mystics of the fourteenth century. Baker wrote a commentary on the *Cloud of Unknowing,* and his *Holy Wisdom* (*Sancta Sophia*) is a compilation of various treatises on the contemplative life and contemplation, written in the spirit of Hilton and the *Cloud* for the English Benedictine nuns of Cambrai.[13]

One of the foundresses of this Benedictine community in

exile was the great-great-granddaughter of St. Thomas More, Dame Gertrude More, who, with Dame Catherine Gascoigne, first abbess of the community, was one of Dom Augustine's most accomplished disciples.

Dom Augustine's life of Dame Gertrude is at the same time an exposition and justification of his own doctrine and of the English and monastic tradition of mysticism. Though he was not a scholar of the caliber of Mabillon and the other Maurists, who were about to begin their great work of "returning to the sources" of monastic, liturgical, and theological tradition, Dom Augustine had been nourished by the monastic fathers. His teaching on prayer is substantially the same as that we find in the Ninth and Tenth Conferences of Cassian, and in the works of St. Gregory the Great. But Baker not only had studied the ancient monastic doctrine on prayer. He had lived it, and from this experience he had recovered the original understanding of the monastic *conversatio* which was perhaps lacking to some of his fellow monks, trained by post-Tridentine spiritual methods for the active, lonely, and perilous life of the English mission.

The English Benedictine nuns in France and Belgium were troubled and divided by the fact that they were taught many "modern" techniques in prayer and asceticism which were entirely alien to their simple contemplative spirit.[14]

This was definitely the case of the newly founded convent of Our Lady of Comfort at Cambrai. The novice-foundresses were being formed by three nuns from a convent in Brussels who had been brought up according to the "new" methods. Dame Gertrude More was reduced by these methods to a state of frustration and confusion bordering on despair. Only the wise guidance of Dom Augustine Baker saved her, and perhaps the convent, from collapse. He preserved the vocations, indeed perhaps the sanity, of the nuns, two of whom at least, by following "Father Baker's way," recovered the ancient monastic spirit and fully experienced the flowering of their monastic vocation in contemplative prayer.

Dom Augustine of course had no special "method" other than the old traditional way of the monastic *conversatio*. He did consent to sketch out a more or less systematic teaching on the ways of prayer, but the whole purpose of this teaching was to make clear that one was free to follow the Holy Spirit in these matters, and indeed should do so, for He is the only true Director and Master in the life of prayer. Baker gave the following description of the spiritual life:

> A spiritual life consists in following the Divine light and impulses, in humbling and subjecting the soul to God and to all creatures according to His will, in loving God above all things, in pursuing prayer and performing it according to Divine guidance—all qualities proceeding from the Divine operation, a state into which none but the Holy Spirit could bring the soul.[15]

Baker insisted on fidelity to the light and inspirations, the "impulsions" of the Holy Spirit, particularly in things that were otherwise indifferent, because, he said, only the Holy Spirit could guide one in such matters. A director should sedulously refrain from imposing his own ideas and preferences upon those he was directing, especially in regard to prayer, reading, devotions, penances, and so on.[16]

But, in general, Baker felt that the Holy Spirit would lead men of prayer into a state of greater and greater simplicity and peace, detaching them from a useless "multiplicity" of discordant and unrelated activities. In giving an account of the way of prayer she had learned from Dom Baker, Dame Catherine Gascoigne said:

> I find myself most drawn and moved to a prayer that tends to unity without adhering to any particular image or creature, but seeking only for that one thing which our Saviour said to be necessary, and which contains all things in itself, according to that saying, *Unum sit mihi,*—"One thing to me be all," that is "all in all"; and on this one depends all. This if I shall have, I shall be content, and unless I enjoy it, I fluctuate always, be-

cause many cannot fill me. What this one thing is I cannot say,
I feel myself to desire it, than which nothing is better, nor
greater, and neither can be thought; for this one thing is not
amongst all, but one above all, my God, to Whom to adhere
and inhere is a good thing.[17]

It was in order to preserve this spirit of simplicity that the
nuns, advised by Baker, abolished the daily examination of
conscience in the convent at Cambrai—an act which certainly
seemed to some observers to be quite rash. This was doubtless
one of the reasons why Dom Augustine was delated for teaching pernicious doctrines and summoned to defend his way.

The root of the trouble was, evidently, the jealousy of the
official chaplain of the convent, who resented the fact that
most of the nuns were going to Dom Augustine for direction
instead of to him. (Dom Augustine had been sent by his supe-
riors to Cambrai to live in the convent and give conferences
and direction to the nuns, without however being appointed
chaplain. In actual fact, however, he sometimes had to take
over all the duties of the chaplain, who was frequently absent
on other business.) Emphasizing his own official status, the
chaplain warned the nuns of dire consequences if they did not
follow *his* teaching, which was considerably more harsh and
rigid than Dom Augustine's "way of love." We catch some
hint of the chaplain's misgivings about Dom Baker in these
words of Dame Gertrude:

[They say] . . . that it is perilous to walk in the way of love
and that (as some would seem to prove) *no soul in any other
course or state is in such peril as is a soul that giveth herself to
this pursuit.*[18]

The good sense, the humor, the independence, the spiritual freedom which we meet everywhere in Dom Augustine
and in his spiritual children were apparently well calculated
to disturb those who knew nothing but a kind of rubrical authoritarianism in the spiritual life. At any rate, the fact that

the nuns, even when threatened with hellfire, did not devote five minutes twice a day to a strictly logical analysis of their conscience, seemed to some people to be a very grave disorder. Some evidently took this as sufficient indication that the sisters had totally abandoned the path of perfection and had thereby violated their vows of conversion of manners.

Such, of course, was by no means the mind of Dom Augustine Baker.

Basing himself firmly on the Benedictine Rule, Dom Augustine argued that where the monastic life is being lived as it should be lived, a formal and explicit examination of conscience at fixed times is superfluous. He is not saying that a monk should not learn to know himself, but that his monastic *conversatio* is designed to furnish him with *much more effective ways of knowing himself* than could be provided by a few minutes of concentrated introspection and self-analysis.

It is, of course, clear that he is speaking of the contemplative life, apart from the world, and not of an active life in the world, for "it may well happen that active Orders pursue a different course here from those who exercise contemplation." For those in the active life, "express, direct examination of conscience at fixed times" is "inculcated" as necessary. But for contemplative nuns, an examination made "indirectly and virtually" is not only more "in keeping with their state" but also "more beneficial to their souls." [19]

Dom Augustine knew that the nuns, especially Dame Gertrude, suffered from a strong "tendency to desolation and obscurity" and were moreover plagued with scruples. Too much self-examination was not only useless but harmful for them, because it induced a fruitless obsession with a psychological activity that could not by any stretch of the imagination do them the slightest good. Why? Because it was not a question of detecting and correcting faults which they could see, but rather of combating hidden tendencies of which they could be obscurely aware but which they would never be able, by dint of self-examination, to identify and deal with adequately.

One of the most original thoughts in this treatment of conscience, by Dom Augustine, is this: he clearly distinguishes between deliberate sins, and obscure, hidden tendencies to imperfection and semideliberate sin which good and fervent nuns may still have without being able to discover precisely where they lie hid. Doubtless, they must know how to identify and to correct all conscious and deliberate faults. The compunction and silence, the regularity, obedience, and prayer essential to monastic *conversatio* make this self-knowledge easy and habitual. But should one go beyond this and try to uncover all the hidden roots of secret and unrecognized sinfulness in the soul? Should one implacably persecute every natural tendency that might conceivably lead to disorder? Even the best religious have faults and weaknesses which are, materially at least, reprehensible: but their roots are too hidden and too deep for conscious control. Hence, there is no formal guilt for these faults. Normally, the only way to be rid of such failings is to hand them over to the purifying action of God's love, as St. John of the Cross teaches.[20] Peace, patience, humility, love, and trust are of more avail in these cases than self-examination.

Dom Augustine declares that no amount of self-examination can reach the hidden roots of imperfection which so often exhaust and discourage the fervent monk. The best thing to do about them is to rise above them and above the level of passion in prayer, submitting them entirely to the merciful and secret love of God.

> Nor does it matter whether we discover the defects or not, for they *may be amended without being known; nor is there any need to know them.* Indeed, there are some faults so secret and so spiritual that they cannot be perceived by sense. . . . Though there may be many secret and spiritual impediments which God does not discover [to the soul], still, in spite of her ignorance, she in time gets rid of them. . . . Such minute and secret sins and imperfections are best removed . . . by acts of

love, or a general act of contrition, or by turning our regard
upon God rather than upon the sins themselves. There is indeed no other way that will remove them so effectually; and
much searching for them and minute examination of them will
only obscure the mind and confound the soul without any corresponding gain.[21]

Here, as a matter of fact, we see Dom Augustine's principal
complaint against an unwise and too insistent effort at self-
examination. While it may be quite true that a thoughtless, negligent, and "extroverted" person needs to acquire a
knowledge of his deliberate faults in order to correct them,[22]
those who are leading silent and recollected lives, who are
well aware of their faults, and are habitually given to prayer,
need to realize that excessive self-examination will produce in
their spirit only darkness and not light. This itch to discover
all the hidden roots and motives of all their acts, to see everything clearly, and to correct all their natural and indeliberate
weaknesses is itself no small imperfection. Speaking of the
scrupulous, who persist in unearthing what they imagine to
be roots of sin in themselves, Dom Augustine says:

What other ground can there be of such disorder but only self-
love deeply rooted in corrupt nature, and ofttimes the suggestion of the devil, to which such souls by reason of their disordered imaginations and passions are miserably exposed? They
had rather confess their virtues for faults . . . than their really
greatest fault which is their self-judgment and disobedience.

He goes on to explain that such a person (and this person
was quite possibly Dame Gertrude More) should realize that:

More harm comes to her and incomparably greater impediments in her exercise of prayer etc., by indiscreet confessions,
or examinations made merely to satisfy scrupulosity, than by
all the defects that she would confess, which, being generally
incurred out of frailty, do far less to estrange her from God

than such confessions do, by which she is habituated in self-will, self-judgment, and servile fear; all which are more perilous inasmuch as they have a pretence of duty to God . . .[23]

Modern psychiatry will doubtless substantiate a great deal that Dom Augustine is saying here. But the point for us to remember is that ascetic practices which may be quite useful and even necessary in the active life can become, to persons who have been formed by silence, solitude, and monastic *conversatio,* a real obstacle to further progress. It may well confirm them in attachment to a willful and otiose exercise of their natural faculties and lead them to a morbid obsession with their own psychological reactions. This, certainly, is a most undesirable kind of subjectivity.

Dom Augustine's teaching on self-examination is based on Walter Hilton among others. At the end of the first section of *Holy Wisdom* (Sect. I, Ch. 6), Baker quotes at length the "Parable of the Pilgrim," which fills three chapters of Hilton's *Scale of Perfection.*[24] A paragraph from this long quotation will give us all the information we need about Dom Augustine's exact thought on this subject:

> This same humility is to be exercised not so much in considering thine own self, thy sinfulness and misery, (though to do this *at first* be very good and profitable) but *rather in a quiet loving sight of the infinite and endless being and goodness of Jesus:* the which beholding of Jesus must be either through grace in a savorous feeling knowledge of Him, or at least in a full and firm faith in Him. And such a beholding when thou shalt attain to it, will work in thy mind a far more pure, spiritual, solid and perfect humility, than the former way of beholding thyself, the which produces a humility more gross, boisterous and unquiet.

In summary: Dom Baker does not teach that examination of conscience is absolutely useless and that it has no place in any kind of spirituality. It may be necessary for beginners and it will probably remain necessary for "extroverts." But for those who have been fully formed in the monastic *conversatio,* who are therefore habitually aware of their own motives, avoid occasions of sin, and have learned that *discretio spirituum,* or discernment of spirits, which is absolutely necessary in the monastic life, a formal psychological exercise in self-analysis at fixed times, practiced with the idea that one can thereby come to penetrate and understand hidden and half-conscious psychological motivations, is normally useless, and perhaps more often than not harmful. As he said of Dame Gertrude:

> The defects of such souls are usually certain inordinate inclinations of nature which are reformed rather by grace and spiritual working than by promises, resolutions, or a violent haste; for the confidence of these souls is not in their own working but in the Divine Operation. Such was Dame Gertrude's method and she found it successful.[25]

It does not necessarily follow that all the ideas which were put into practice by the Benedictine nuns of Cambrai in the seventeenth century should become the norm for monasteries today. A practice which is recommended by the Church and prescribed in our present Constitutions cannot be summarily dismissed as ridiculous. It may have its place in our life. But we will understand that place much better if, with Dom Augustine, we are able to return to primitive sources and see the incongruity that results when this practice is introduced arbitrarily and without understanding into the setting of monastic *conversatio.*

In the long history of monasticism, when the ascetic implications of ancient and more essential observances (psalmody, silence, manual labor, manifestation of conscience to the spiritual father, etc.) are no longer understood, they come to be duplicated by more modern practices which attempt to fulfill the same function in a different and more congenial or more efficient way. Thus, monastic observance becomes a clutter of half-understood or completely misunderstood "exercises," which follow one another mechanically and pell-mell, until they culminate vociferously in some peripheral and non-essential devotional act which everybody "understands." One might compare such observance to a low Mass before the Second Vatican Council, in which nothing was followed and comprehended, until at last the faithful joined lustily in the Hail Mary and the Leonine prayers. One would have thought that this was the climax of the liturgy!

So, too, in the monastic life: in our psalmody, our *lectio,* our silence, our work, our fasting, our separation from the world, we live, or should live, in a habitual atmosphere of self-knowledge, humility, and compunction before the face of God. What is our office of compline but a prayer of compunction and a plea for grace? In such a setting, our examination of conscience should not become an ecstasy of self-castigation, fit only to stir up the embers of a neurosis that would otherwise go out by itself. Examination of conscience in our life should normally be very simple and should not consist principally in an anxious and overactive search for hidden faults, still less in a presumptuous effort to analyze and comprehend all our secret motives. It should rather be a simple gaze of compunction and love which enables us to see our own failings in the light of God's merciful love for us, in such a way that our sins may be consumed by His love.

True *conversatio morum* is not self-preoccupation, but self-forgetfulness, in a total and self-abandoned love for God. Such a love has little concern with the trivialities and minutiae of our day-to-day psychology. It says, with Hilton's pilgrim, quoted by Dom Augustine Baker: "I have nothing, and am nothing, and desire nothing but to be with Jesus in Jerusalem." Let us now turn to the text from Dom Augustine Baker.

TEXT
From the *Inner Life of Dame Gertrude More*[26]

"To turn now to another matter, in which the practice of
Dame Gertrude differed from that taught in many books, and
pursued by many modern Congregations whose state is active
rather than contemplative. I refer to the subject of examination of conscience. It may well happen that active orders
pursue a different course here from those who exercise contemplation. Active orders usually inculcate the necessity of express, direct examination of conscience at certain fixed times
during the day. But this teaching was not accepted or followed by Dame Gertrude and her Sisters. Their examination
was made indirectly, virtually, in a way more in keeping with
their state, and much more beneficial for their souls. This was
brought about by a combination of four or five general practices.

"The first was to have a continual care of themselves, both
interiorly and exteriorly, not scrupulously or anxiously, but
prudently and sweetly, observing the counsel of our Holy Father—'to keep guard at all times over the actions of one's life.'
This can be done with comparative ease in a Contemplative
Order, where the occupations are not very distracting; and
more especially in our convents for women, where every facil-
ity is given for such continual vigilance over themselves, and
where very distracting business, which is the usual cause of
serious lapses, is excluded.

"This, then, is one thing that renders an express examination less necessary, as it tends to take away the cause and matter of examination. For we all see that it is better by watchfulness to avoid falling into a fault than to give occasion for
search by the neglect of such care. Moreover, the faults into
which spiritual souls fall are commonly too spiritual and secret to be discovered by the senses and imagination; for it is

by these that the examination is made. But spiritual defects are best cured by spiritual means—by the elevation of the spirit to God. By such means the soul is cleansed from all spiritual defect incurred, and which, on account of their secrecy and subtlety, she never could have discovered or corrected by her senses. Thus such faults are amended, as far as they can be amended, even before they are known. Further, our holy Rule and Order tend towards solitude, both interior and exterior, discouraging external activity as much as may be, so that we may not only avoid the occasions of sin, but also be able the better *vacare Deo et Divinis*—be at leisure to attend to God and Divine things.

"For these reasons our Holy Father prescribes no express examination of conscience in his Rule, but his teaching tends to cut off the occasions of sin by means of solitude, and the custody of the soul herself over her actions. Hence our Holy Father in the first degree of humility says that the disciple should 'always keep the fear of God before his eyes, avoiding all forgetfulness. . . . And keeping himself at all times from sin and vice, whether of the thoughts, the tongue, the hands, the feet, or his own will. . . . Let him also consider that he is always [*semper et omni hora*] beheld from Heaven by God, and that his actions are everywhere seen by the eye of the Divine Majesty, and are every hour [*omni hora*] reported to Him by the angels.' Also, in the twelfth degree, St. Benedict requires that a religious should in all places and at all times 'think of the guilt of his sins, and imagine himself already present before the terrible judgment-seat of God,' that by this means he may avoid further sin.

"From these and other passages in the Rule it is clear our Holy Father relies for the progress of his disciple on his internal custody of himself; and this watchfulness a good soul will retain in all the external employments which necessarily fall to her. And this is the way Dame Gertrude proceeded, and the way all other souls advance that pursue a similar interior course. To such souls these words of the canticle may be ap--

plied: 'I sleep'—that is, I cease for the time to elevate my will to God—'but my heart is watchful' of Him, and keeps itself in good dispositions, to be ready when the time comes to unite itself to Him.

"The first substitute, then, for examination of conscience consists partly of solitude and a limitation of distracting occupations, by which means the occasions of sin are diminished, and, consequently, the need of examination; and partly of watchfulness over our thoughts, words, and deeds, by which we may avoid sins; and these are best practised in Contemplative Orders.

"The second substitute for examination of conscience is an interior propensity, provided the soul is in a state of life in which she can work on her propensity. Such souls do not easily fall into great sins: and if they appear to fall, there may be no sin, or only a slight one in their case, because their affection is turned rather to God than to the sinful object, and this preserves them from a serious fall or injury. This grace proceeds from their profound recollections, which numb or mortify the affection for all that is not God, and cause their external indulgences and pursuits to be performed with little adhesion, and often with little or no sin. Such was the case with Dame Gertrude. Her recollections were so profound and her love of God so firm and constant that her external occupations were discharged with but little attachment, and consequently with less fault than appeared to be the case.

"The third substitute is the practice of a recollection, or mental prayer, which the Sisters perform twice daily. The morning recollection practically covers the whole of the forenoon, as it is in a measure passed in interior solitude and recollection; and the other time of prayer is in the evening. Although the Sisters do not make an express examination of conscience, still it is virtually made, for either the conscience or the Holy Spirit within it brings to their mind all sins and imperfections of moment incurred since the last recollection, just as surely as if they had made a careful examination. For

we all, however spiritual, daily fall into various sins and imperfections, which we neither do nor can observe, they being
so secret and subtle. Concerning these the prophet says:
'Cleanse me, O Lord, from my secret sins' (Ps xviii 13). And
in another place the Scripture says: 'Seven times (yea, seventy-
seven times) a day falleth the just man' (Prov xxiv 16). Such
sins may be removed from the soul by other means as well, if
not better than, by calling the sins to mind. For they are ordinarily of a kind that cannot be amended save by taking them
up by the root, by breaking the habit from which they spring;
and this can be done only by rising out of the state of nature
and of sensibility, and by getting more into the spirit. And we
get into the spirit in course of time by frequent profound ele-
vations of the spirit during our recollections, and for this purpose a propensity to the interior and Divine grace are of great
help. Souls who are without this propensity can only lop off
the branches which daily spring up again; but the former in
time take the tree up by the roots.

"It is of the nature of these recollections to discover to the
soul the impediments between herself and God. And these are
not so much the actual sins we commit as the deliberate and
habitual affection we have for them. The correction, therefore, of the fault is not sufficient, for the soul may, and usually
does, continue in the same affection and habit of sin as before,
and so she makes no progress. But in her recollections the soul
is able to correct any want of resignation, any inclination to
self-will, and all inordinate affections. For these are presented
to her mind by a certain presence of God, Who is all light,
and Who enlightens the soul to see these imperfections, which
are of themselves but darkness and as nothing. Indeed, the soul
is ordinarily in darkness concerning these things, but in her
recollections she is enlightened concerning them by the Divine presence and light; and thereupon she profoundly re-
signs herself to God, and conforms herself to the Divine will,
and by this means weakens the habit of irresignation and inordinate affection. Without such recollections the soul is in

darkness, and cannot see the impediments which stand between herself and God. It is for this reason that souls who are
in the immediate exercise of the will towards God can discover and correct their faults better than those whose exercise
is in the imagination and discourse. For these are more occupied with the images of the things about which they discourse
than they are with God; so that they are less able to see the
impediments than the former, who in a manner regard God
immediately, and thus see and remove any impediments that
stand between God and themselves. Those that use their imagination and discourse do not perceive the hidden impediments between themselves and God, *for it is the regarding
God and His presence, and not the consideration of creatures
and their images, that enlightens the soul* and enables her to
see her hidden inordinate affections. More palpable sins the
soul can perceive by her internal senses and natural reason,
and these she can amend. But the root or affection remains
unseen, unknown, and will again break out into act when the
soul least expects it. The root of such failings is almost beyond
the scope of the senses and natural reason, or, if the root is
perceived, the soul cannot remove it for want of the proper
means.

"But the contemplative soul does not examine herself or
her want of resignation or other deordinations, but immediately regards God, and God enlightens her so as to perceive
her imperfections, in so far as He sees fit, and to amend them.
Thus the soul acts, according to a certain writer, as one that
looks at a wall in front of him. He not only sees the wall, but
all that lies between him and it. Even so does the soul, regarding God, perceive all the impediments between herself and
Him. And though there may be many secret and spiritual impediments which God does not discover to her, still, in spite
of her ignorance, she in time gets rid of them. And this she
accomplishes by transcending all her natural desires and inclinations in her recollections—a method which is as effectual
as if her faults were visible to her sight. Nor is a reformation

of soul or perfection obtained otherwise than by getting out of the natural man and his ordinary desires; nor does it matter whether we discover the defects or not, for they may be amended without being known; nor is there any need to know them. Indeed, there are some faults so secret and spiritual that they cannot be perceived by sense; hence this is the only way to remove them, unless God bestow on the soul an extraordinary, unusual, supernatural light. Thus God concurs in, or causes, the reformation of the soul by helping her to transcend her inferior nature, and it matters not, as I have said, whether the soul perceives her defects or not.

"A fourth reason why an examination of conscience is unnecessary in the case of a soul that works upon her propensity is that a sin or imperfection which would seem small to another will appear great to her, and will adhere to her and gall her conscience, so that there will be no need to seek for her fault if it be worth remembering; and if it be not, why trouble about it? or why seek for what cannot be found, or when found was not worth the seeking? Such minute and secret sins and imperfections are best removed (as spiritual writers tell us) by acts of love, or a general act of contrition, or *by turning our regard upon God rather than upon the sins themselves. There is, indeed, no other way that will remove them so effectually* and much searching for them and minute examination of them will only obscure the mind and confound the soul without any corresponding gain. If contemplative souls act otherwise, they will find that they labour in vain, that they learn nothing by their scrutiny which they did not know before; and what is worse, they will excite fears and scruples, and imagine sins and defects where there was none. The reason of this is that such examinations are made chiefly by the help of the imagination and the light of nature, and this light is very fallacious. Besides, at such times the soul is not, and cannot be, in a state of recollection. The suitable light for such examinations is obtained only in a state of recollection, when the soul for the time is free from the images of sin and creatures; and this can be only at the beginning of the recollection, and not in the perfection of it, for then no thoughts are admitted but of God Himself. Indeed, women especially are naturally inclined to be timid and scrupulous, and such examinations would only increase their inordinate fears. Experience shows them that the practice of examinations is unsuitable for them, and surely they can judge better of their own case than others in quite different circumstances. In truth, there are few women, even of those who profess to follow the practice of examinations, who really continue long in them, except for more serious sins, to which contemplative souls are not much subject. Besides, such examinations imply a strong resolution of amendment of the sins discovered, and for a contemplative soul to promise herself or God an amendment of such small defects would be impossible. She can only hope to amend them in course of time with the aid of grace and exercises. No industry or violence of her own will be of any avail.

"This was clearly the experience of Dame Gertrude, as may be seen by her words cited on a former occasion. She says that she was to amend her life as she could, and not as she would; that it was God's will that she should await a longer time for a total amendment; that in the meantime she should exercise patience with herself, amending little by little, and as she could, and that if she had proceeded otherwise she would never have corrected anything at all.

"In truth, the defects of such souls are usually certain inordinate inclinations of nature which are reformed rather by grace and spiritual working than by promises, resolutions or a violent haste; for the confidence of these souls is not in their own working, but in the Divine operation. Such was Dame Gertrude's method, and she found it successful."

RUSSIAN MYSTICS

Russian mysticism is predominantly monastic (though one meets an occasional exception like the modern non-monastic mystics, Father John of Kronstadt—recently canonized by the Orthodox Church—and Father Yelchaninov). It therefore thrives in solitude and renunciation of the world. Yet anyone who has even the most superficial acquaintance with Russian Christendom is aware that the monasteries of Russia, even more than those of the West, exercised a crucially important influence on society, whether as centers of spiritual life and transformation to which pilgrims flocked from everywhere, or as bases for missionary expansion, or, finally, as powerful social forces sometimes manipulated—or suppressed—for political advantage. Such struggles as those between St. Nilus of Sora and St. Joseph of Volokolamsk speak eloquently of the age-old conflict, within monasticism itself, between the charismatic drive to solitary contemplation plus charismatic pastoral action, and the institutional need to fit the monastic community into a structure of organized socio-religious power, as a center of liturgy and education and as a nursery of bishops.

Other conflicts, such as that between Eastern Orthodox spirituality and Westernizing influences, play an important part in the lives of the monks and mystics of Russia. Many students of Russian spirituality will be surprised to learn what a great part Western theological attitudes and devotions played in the formation of St. Tikhon in the eighteenth century. The seminary which Tikhon attended was organized on the Jesuit pattern and yet he was not influenced by post-Tridentine Catholic thought. Dr. Bolshakoff identifies him rather with German pietism. In any case, we must not be too quick to assume that St. Tikhon's spirituality is purely and ideally "Russian." Yet, paradoxically, this combination of Western and Eastern holiness is a peculiarly Russian phenomenon. St. Tikhon was perhaps the greatest mystic of the age of rationalist enlightenment.

Russian mysticism is to be traced largely to the greatest monastic center of Orthodox mysticism, Mount Athos. Ever since the eleventh century the Russian monastic movement had been nourished by direct contact with the "Holy Mountain"—interrupted only by the Tatar invasions of the Middle Ages. Liturgy, asceticism, and mysticism in Russia owed their development in great part not to literary documents but to the living experience of pilgrim monks who spent a certain time at Athos, either in the "Rossikon" (the Russian monastery of St. Panteleimon) or in various sketes and cells, before returning to found new monasteries or renew the life of old ones in their country. Periods when, for one reason or another, communication with Athos has diminished have also been periods of monastic decline in Russia.

One of the characteristic fruits of Russian monachism on Athos is the "Prayer of Jesus," the constant repetition of a short formula in conjunction with rhythmic breathing and with deep faith in the supernatural power of the Holy Name. This was a Russian development of the Greek Hesychast way of prayer taught by St. Gregory Palamas. The "Prayer of Jesus" became the normal way of contemplative prayer in Russian monasticism, but, more important still, it was adopted on all sides by devout lay people, especially among the masses of the poor peasantry.

Until recently, Western theologians were highly suspicious of Athonite "Hesychasm" and regarded it as perilous, even heretical. Deeper study and a wider acquaintance with non-Western forms of spirituality have made Hesychasm seem a little less outlandish. It is now no longer necessary to repeat the outraged platitudes of those who thought that the Hesychasts were practicing self-hypnosis, or who believed that, at best, the monks of Athos were engaged in a kind of Western Yoga.

The "Prayer of Jesus," made known to Western readers by the "Tale of the Pilgrim," surely one of the great classics of the literature of prayer, is now practiced not only by characters in Salinger's novels but even at times by some Western monks. Needless to say, a way of prayer for which, in its land of origin, the direction of a "starets" was mandatory, is not safely to be followed by us in the West without professional direction.

The mystical Russian "pilgrim" received from his starets an anthology of patristic quotations on prayer: the famous *Philokalia.* The monastic reformer, Paisius Velichkovsky (1722–94), after living for some time in a skete on Mount Athos during a period of monastic decline, translated the *Philokalia* into Slavonic and introduced it to Russia. It was then done into Russian by another mystic, Bishop Theophane the Recluse.

Paisius and his disciples also translated other works of the Fathers and in addition to this exercised a direct and living influence on Russian monachism through the numerous pilgrims who constantly visited in monasteries reformed by him in Moldavia and Walachia. Here visitors from all parts of Russia encountered not only a pure and austere monastic discipline but also the spiritual direction of specialists in asceticism and Hesychast prayer, who came to be known as *startsy*. The translations of the *Philokalia*, the monastic reform of Paisius, and especially *Starchestvo*, the direction of the startsy, set in motion the great development that was to make the nineteenth century the golden age of Russian mysticism. This was also the time when the Rossikon on Mount Athos reached its peak in numbers, fervor, and prosperity.

One of the best-known (or least-unknown) of the Russian mystics is St. Seraphin of Sarov, who lived the life of a Desert Father in the forests at the beginning of the nineteenth century. He affords a striking contrast to other post-medieval saints and ascetics who have tried to imitate the Desert Fathers. In many of these, together with a sincere ascetic and monastic purpose and devotion to authentic ideals, we seem to encounter a spirit of willfulness that is often violent and artificial even to the point of obsession. As a result, we find a negative, gloomy, and tense spirituality in which one is not sure whether the dominant note is hatred of wickedness or love of good—and hatred of wickedness can so easily include hatred of human beings, who are perhaps less wicked than they seem. The study of ascetic tradition and the passion for austerity do not suffice by themselves to make monastic saints, although it must be admitted that a specious "humanism" which turns its back on all austerity and solitude is hardly more effective in this regard!

Whether or not Seraphin had studied ancient monastic tradition, it is certain that he was a living and spontaneous exemplar of the most authentic monastic ideal. His solitary life in the forest was extremely austere and yet his spirituality was marked by pure joy. Though he gave himself unsparingly to each ascetic exploit (*podvig*), he remained simple, childlike, meek, astonishingly open to life and to other men, gentle, and profoundly compassionate.

He is without doubt the greatest mystic of the Russian Church, and the Hesychast tradition is evident in his mysticism of light. Yet Hesychasm is, so to speak, absorbed in the Evangelical and patristic purity of his experience of the great Christian mystery, the presence of the Spirit given by God through the Risen Christ to His Body, the Church.

Seraphin's simplicity reminds us in many ways of Francis of Assisi, though his life was more like that of Anthony of the Desert. But like every other great contemplative saint, Seraphin had his eyes wide open to the truth of the Gospel, and could not understand how the rest of men could be content with an "enlightenment" that was in reality nothing but ignorance and spiritual blindness. The only contemporary figure in the West who speaks so eloquently and with such ingenuous amazement of the divine light shining in darkness is the English poet William Blake. But there is in Seraphin none of Blake's gnosticism: only the pure and traditional theology of the Church.

Seraphin of Sarov is then the most perfect example of that mysticism of light which is characteristic of the Orthodox Church: completely positive and yet compatible with, indeed based on, the apophatic (negative) theology of Pseudo-Dionysius and St. Maximus the Confessor. It is perhaps this which distinguishes Russian mysticism in its pure state. Not an intellectualist and negative ascent to the Invisible above all that is visible, but more paradoxically an apprehension of the invisible as visible insofar as all creation is suddenly experienced as transfigured in a light for which there is no accounting in terms of any philosophy, a light which is given directly by God, proceeds from God, and in a sense *is* the Divine Light. Yet this experience is not a substantial vision of God, because in Oriental theology the light experienced by the mystic is a divine "energy," distinct from God's nature but which can be apprehended in contact with the *Person* of the Holy Spirit, by mystical love and grace.

Thus, it is easy to see that though there are in Russia some instances of a negative mysticism comparable to the Dark

Night in St. John of the Cross, yet they are not characteristic of Russian mystical theology, which is a theology not of suffering but of transfiguration.

Nevertheless, this theology of resurrection and joy is firmly based on repentance and on tears, and one does not easily find in it the impertinences of a devout sentimentality which simply assumes that "everything is bound to turn out all right." The reality of redemption and transfiguration depends on the most basic experience of the evil of sin.

Not all the Russian mystics were able to experience this evil as totally consumed in the flames of Redemptive Love. Bishop Ignatius Brianchaninov, an aristocrat and an army engineer converted to the monastic life, looked out upon the world with profound pessimism. The world of matter was not, for him, transfigured by the divine light: it was purely and simply the subject of corruption. For him (as for so many others in the nineteenth century), science and religion were in conflict, and to know Christ one had to reject all earthly knowledge as false and totally misleading. And yet science does nevertheless contribute something of positive value to the meditations of Bishop Brianchaninov. However, we observe with regret in Brianchaninov a tendency to impose a kind of unnatural constraint upon the body and the mind, and we are not surprised when he informs us that he considers visions of devils rather a usual thing in the monastic life. His pessimism and suspicion toward women as such blend with the rest of his dark view of things. Yet, even where his negative attitude repels us, we must admit he often displays remarkable psychological insight. All in all, Brianchaninov is too rigid, too suspicious of the light, too closed to ordinary human experience to impress us as St. Seraphin does. And yet it would seem that the negativism of Brianchaninov had a deeper influence on nineteenth-century Russian monasticism than the marvelous Gospel optimism of St. Seraphin. The works of Brianchaninov will help us to understand the conservative reaction of Leontiev and of the monks of Optino against Dostoevsky's idealized and forward-looking portrait of Starets Zosima.

This portrait was supposed to have been based on the living figure of Starets Ambrose of Optino, but the monks in general rejected its optimism, its "humanism," as untrue to the genuine monastic tradition of Russia. Perhaps the generality of monks were more disposed to look at life through the embittered and blazing eyes of the fanatical ascetic Ferrapont, in whom Dostoevsky himself evidently intended to portray the kind of negativism typified by the old school, the critics and opponents of the startsy.

It is curious that the Russian revolution was preceded not by a century of monastic decadence and torpor, but by a monastic Golden Age. But if the term "Golden Age" is to mean anything, it must mean a time of vitality. Vitality means variety, and this, in turn, may imply conflict. In nineteenth-century Russian monasticism we find darkness and light, world-denial and loving affirmation of human values, a general hardening of resistance to forces of atheist humanism and revolution, and yet an anguished concern at the sinful oppression of the poor. We cannot with justice dismiss the whole Russian monastic movement as negative, pessimistic, world-hating. Nor can we identify its deep and traditional contemplative aspirations with mere political or cultural conservatism. There was an unquestionably prophetic spirit at work in the movement, and St. Seraphin is only one among many examples that prove this. There was also a profound concern for "the world" and for humanity, a wonderful, unequaled compassion that reached out to all mankind and indeed to all living creatures, to embrace them in God's love and in merciful concern. It cannot be doubted that the great startsy, in their humane and tender simplicity, were sometimes completely identified with the humble and the poor. It would be ludicrous to class them as obscurantists and reactionaries.

On the other hand, there was a less prophetic, but nonetheless amazing spirit of ascetic fervor, of discipline, of order, which while it was undeniably one of the things that made the age "Golden," still had rather more human and even political implications. And here monasticism was, indeed, more deeply involved in social structures and national aspirations, even where it most forcefully asserted its hatred of "the world." Here, too, contempt for the world and pessimistic rigorism were in fact inseparable from social and political conservatism. The ascetic who renounced the city of man in order to lament his sins in the *poustyna* (desert) may well have been giving his support to a condition of social inertia by implicitly affirming that all concern with improvement was futile and even sinful. We may cite as an example Constantin Leontiev, Dostoevsky's adversary and critic, who entered a monastery, gloried in extreme austerity, and doubtless expressed monastic views that were those of most monks of the time.

Leontiev actually stated that the Orthodoxy on Mount Athos depended on the peace of the harmonious interaction of Turkish political power, Russian wealth, and Greek ecclesiastical authority. Most of his compatriots, monks included, were probably too nationalistic to follow this "realist" view all the way.[1] They were Pan-Slavist and therefore anti-Greek as well as anti-Western. But the point is that their monastic fervor formed part of a complex Russian nationalist mystique and contributed much energy to it. The average good monk, who was not raised by sanctity above this level, tended to identify himself and his religious ideal with this mystique of Holy Russia. It would be very interesting to compare this with the ideas of such lay theologians as Soloviev, who was very open to Rome and the West, but space does not permit here.

The doctrine of the Russian startsy of the last hundred and fifty years is rich in monastic wisdom, as well as in ordinary religious psychology and plain good sense. It is interesting to see that they were concerned with many traditional monastic problems which are being rather warmly discussed in Western monasteries today. The answers to the startsy can be of special value to Western monks who are interested in discovering the deepest meaning of their monastic vocation, and ways to live that vocation more perfectly.

The reason for this is perhaps simpler than one might expect. It is not so much that the startsy were exceptionally austere men, or that they had acquired great learning, but that they had surrendered themselves completely to the demands of the Gospel and to Evangelical charity, totally forgetting themselves in obedience to the Spirit of God so that they lived as perfect Christians, notable above all for their humility, their meekness, their openness to all men, their apparently inexhaustible capacity for patient and compassionate love. The purpose of *Starchestvo* is, then, not so much to make use of daily spiritual direction in order to inculcate a special method of prayer, but rather to keep the heart of the disciple open to love, to prevent it from hardening in self-centered concern (whether moral, spiritual, or ascetical). All the worst sins are denials and rejections of love, refusals to love. The chief aim of the starets is first to teach his disciple not to sin against love, then to encourage and assist his growth in love until he becomes a saint. This total surrender to the power of love was the sole basis of their spiritual authority, and on this basis the startsy demanded complete and unquestioning obedience. They could do so because they themselves never resisted the claims and demands of charity.

One cannot refrain from observing, in this connection, how much Pope John XXIII displayed this same charismatic and Evangelical openness. His life as Pope is filled with incidents in which this great warmhearted man unquestioningly obeyed the spirit of goodness that was in him, and met with consternation when he expected others to obey the same spirit with equal readiness! So many Christians exalt the demands and rigors of law because, in reality, law is less demanding than pure charity. The law, after all, has reasonable safe limits! One always knows what to expect, and one can always hope to evade, by careful planning, the more unpleasant demands!

The mention of Pope John naturally suggests a conclusion to this brief article. Pope John's love for the Church of the Orient, of Greece and Russia, is well known. His idea of calling the Second Vatican Council was prompted in large part by this love of our separated Orthodox brothers. Knowledge of the spirit and teaching of the Russian mystics can be of great help to us in carrying on the work of reunion which Pope John has bequeathed to us.

PROTESTANT MONASTICISM

It is no exaggeration to say that Protestantism was in part a result of the monastic crisis of the late Middle Ages. Luther's most characteristic theological doctrines were shaped by his revolt against the limitations of religious life in a community that was, if not totally corrupt, at least subject to serious deficiencies. Sterile devotionalism, attachment to trivial outward forms, forgetfulness of the essentials of the Christian faith, and obsession with accidentals drove Luther to a desperation which may or may not have bordered on the pathological. (It would seem that scrutiny of Luther's psychic condition has been overdone!) In any case, these ills accounted to some extent for Luther's emphasis on *sola fides*. The "works" by which he denied that man could be justified were first of all the monastic observances which traditional Catholic theology had associated with the state of perfection, the life of the vows.

If Calvin and Luther had confined themselves to a theoretical dispute on justification, there might have been some hope of adjustment and reconciliation. In actual fact, the doctrine of justification by faith declared, as a practical corollary, that religious vows were not only reprehensible but invalid. It emptied the convents and monasteries of Germany. From that time on, one might assume that "Protestantism" and "monasticism" were mutually exclusive and that such a thing as "Protestant monasticism" was inconceivable. (It must, of course, be remembered that Anglican monasticism is not "Protestant.")

Yet, since Taizé has found space in the popular press, everyone is aware of the very significant Protestant monastic revival going on today. As a matter of fact, it is perhaps in Protestantism that the more general monastic movement has gathered the strongest momentum and displayed the greatest vitality in the shortest time. One might even hazard the opinion that these Protestant communities are the most telling and hopeful signs of life in the monastic revival today.

There has evidently been a crucially important shift in Protestant perspective. No longer is it universally taken for granted that the monastic way is a purely manmade invention superimposed upon the Gospel of Christ, and diverting attention from the true message of salvation. No longer are vows regarded by all Protestants as useless constraints, mortgaging the future and binding the religious to sterile trivialities instead of fruitful and spontaneous Christian action. Most important of all, Protestant monasticism implies a rediscovery of the contemplative patterns of life characteristic of the ancient Catholic orders. Active works of charity have an important place in the life of the new communities, but it may be said that they are predominantly contemplative. Contemplation and prayer are by no means considered "idleness."

These communities, however, are not committed to *a priori* formulations, Roger Schutz, founder and prior of Taizé, has said: "Experience of the needs of our times and the meditation in common of the Gospels led the brothers to give definite form to their original vocation"—a form, however, which is not yet so definite as to preclude spontaneous development in the future.

The life of vows, under a rule, must not be allowed to sterilize the liberty and spontaneity which they are meant to consecrate to God. "The Rule [of Taizé] must never be regarded as an end in itself or dispense us from ever more seeking to discover God's design, the love of Christ and the light of the Holy Spirit." The original intuitions of the Reformation have not been abandoned. Taizé believes that a rule that surreptitiously took the place of the Gospel would be nothing but a "useless burden."

One of the special qualities of these Protestant communities is their freedom, their flexibility in meeting crucial needs of our time, not in stereotyped institutional ways (schools, clubs, etc.), but with an apostolic spontaneity nourished by monasticity of life.

Father Biot, a Dominican, has written a concise, sympathetic, and very welcome study of this paradoxical new movement.[1] The recently founded communities of France, Germany, and Switzerland are mentioned, briefly described, and placed in their historical setting. The author is, however, not interested in a journalistic presentation of his subject, or in a monastic travelogue. He is chiefly concerned with a theological explanation of the monastic movement in Protestantism, and he sees it *in a general context of theological awakening,* Protestant, Catholic, and Orthodox. It is another aspect of the Christian renewal which is manifest in the Liturgical, Biblical, and Ecumenical movements.

Father Biot demonstrates, first of all, that the sixteenth-century reformers did not absolutely exclude a dedicated life. The possibility of a special vocation and of vows was generally conceded. The renunciation practiced by the third-century ascetes and the early monks was sometimes admitted as having had value. The decision against vows was made in a definite historical context, in which the Reformers saw the vows violated on every side. They were convinced that modern men and women could not meet the obligation of lifelong chastity. But vows were not always regarded as intrinsically impossible or un-Christian. A life of renunciation remained theoretically possible, even though impractical.

Though Karl Barth has always defended the classic doctrines of the Reformation and is therefore not inclined to overestimate the value of asceticism as a way of Christian perfection, he still recognizes a vocation to celibacy, and esteems monasticism insofar as it seems to him to have been, historically, a protest against the secularization of the Church. Barth approves the call to special renunciation and to liberty in Christ which monasticism issues to Christians in the world, and he asks, "Is there not a need to establish a pattern in which the place of the solitary life will always be assured?" It is precisely the notes of community in solitude, renunciation, and prayer that interest Protestant theologians of monasticism today.

The Protestant monastic movement is, then, much more than a pietistic diversion for a few enthusiasts, a quixotic imitation of Catholic observance. It is just as much a sign of true life and of Christian renewal as the other movements that have come into such prominence in the era of the Johannine Council. This is made evident by the close association of Protestant monasticism with liturgy, the Bible, and ecumenism, as well as by the authenticity of the monastic life that is being led in the new communities.

Protestant monasticism is not interested in merely *imitating* Catholic communities, but in discreetly helping and encouraging monastic reform wherever it is needed and possible. This implies no specific criticism of any set form of monasticism. But Taizé does offer a model of simplicity, spontaneity, openness, and vitality which can be profitably considered by the Catholic orders that have, perhaps in the course of centuries, become a little rigid. Above all, the Protestant communities can help Catholic monasticism to preserve its own authentic sense of values. There is a real danger of confusion in our own monastic communities, where a sense of uneasiness and insecurity often seeks to pacify itself by expedients that threaten to alienate us from our own inner truth. The fidelity of the new Protestant communities to genuine monastic values should reassure us, and encourage us to cling fearlessly to the ideal of solitude, prayer, renunciation, poverty, and work that ought to be ours.

Again, it is Prior Roger Schutz who tells us: "The reformation which ought to have taken place on the inside of the Catholic Church can penetrate it via the medium of charity, and succeed not by demolishing it but by causing those within it to recenter their attention on the essential treasures which it has always possessed."

The monastic life is one of those essential treasures. There is certainly great significance in the lesson which is being taught us by an apparently ironic Providence: that the Reformation which began by demolishing a whole segment of a tottering monastic fabric should now be seeking to help us rebuild it according to its primitive lines. This is a fact of capital importance in present-day ecumenism, and we can be grateful to Father Biot for making it clear. His book offers great encouragement to a monastic and ecumenical dialogue which has been going on for several years and is growing in importance and interest all the time.

PLEASANT HILL

A Shaker Village in Kentucky[1]

The Shakers, or rather "The United Society of Believers in Christ's Second Appearing," were most active in New England and upper New York State in the first half of the nineteenth century. They have almost completely died out today. At the time of their greatest expansion, they reached westward and established communities in Ohio, Indiana, and Kentucky. The simple, spacious buildings of the Kentucky Shaker colonies still stand: some of those at South Union were for a time occupied by the Benedictine Priory of St. Maur's. Those at Pleasant Hill, popularly known as "Shakertown," near Lexington, are being restored as a public monument.

As their official title suggests, the "Believers in Christ's Second Appearing" were people who had entirely forsaken secular society to set up a religious and prophetic commune, believing in the imminent end of the world. With them, as perhaps with some of the early monks, celibacy was held to be symbolic of the futility of generating any more human beings in a world ready for destruction and for renewal on an angelic plane. The term "Shakers" is due not only to the dancing and ecstatic experiences which marked their common worship, but perhaps especially to their belief that when the Holy Spirit was present He made Himself known by "shaking" the whole community in a kind of prophetic earthquake. The eschatological charity of the order produced an inward power which, they believed, would "shake" the world and prepare it for the millennial renewal.

The extraordinary theology of the Shakers, with its emphasis on the "Second Appearing" of Christ in a Woman, is only fully to be understood when we recognize its spiritual affinity with Gnosticism and Montanism. Yet there is a great independence and originality in the Shaker spirit. The "Woman," the embodiment of divine Wisdom in the last days of the world, and Daughter of the Holy Spirit, was Mother Ann Lee, who came to America from England with eight companions and landed in New York on the sixth of August, 1774. After gathering a small community at Watervliet, New York, in 1776, she laid the definitive foundations of her society at New Lebanon in 1779.

For many reasons, "ordinary" Americans of those revolutionary times found the Shakers disturbing, and subjected them to persecution. In the first place, the Shakers were pacifists. They refused to participate in the Revolutionary War on either side, which meant that they were considered "agents of the British" by patriotic Americans. Their fervent love of celibacy was closely connected with pacifism, for they held that lust and cruelty went together, and that unchastity led to avarice and attachment to worldly goods, which were protected or acquired by force. "Marriage," they declared, "is not a Christian institution, because the community of goods cannot be maintained therein . . . Wars are the results of lusts for lands and women. *Those who marry will fight.*"

The Shakers, being fully determined to do neither of these things, lived in peaceful, cenobitic communes, in which the sexes were kept firmly apart. In each "Family House," the men had their common dwelling on one side, the women on the other, and they used separate stairways to reach their isolated dormitories. In the last analysis, the real significance of their celibacy was their belief that they had been completely regenerated and were living the perfect risen life in and with Christ. "We have actually risen with Christ and travel with Him to the resurrection [i.e., of all flesh]," said one of the first Elders. But this rebirth to the angelic life could only be achieved by embracing perfect chastity, without which one could not be a genuine Christian. We can detect echoes of Catharism and Montanism, which, like the religion of the Shakers, placed a great emphasis on virginity and prophetic inspiration and attacked institutional religion. Like the Albigenses, the Shakers believed that the conventional organized "churches" had been reduced, by continual compromises, to complicity with the world in its lusts, its greed for money, and its appetite for power.

They felt that this was amply demonstrated by the social injustices and inequalities which were not only tolerated by most Christians but actively encouraged by them. Therefore, they concluded that the Kingdom of God had not yet been established on earth since the professed followers of Christ were obviously not imitating Him. A Shaker of the Harvard Community wrote in 1853:

> [Jesus] was no speculator in stocks, trades, or estates. He could not be distinguished by the carriage He rode in or the palace He dwelt in, nor the cloth He wore, by the multitude of His servants, golden ornaments, nor refined literature . . .

Jesus was a simple carpenter, the apostles were working men, Mother Ann and the early Shakers were all simple working-class people. The Shaker communities lived an austere and disciplined life of renunciation and labor and it was their hard work that eventually won them the respect of their neighbors. Yet at the same time they were shrewd and practical in their dealings with the wicked world, and they sent their most businesslike representatives to market to buy and sell, so that even Emerson remarked caustically on their ability to drive a hard bargain.

We cannot safely judge the Shakers by what was said about them, especially in the beginning. They were accused by their enemies of everything from nudism and debauchery to being "the principal enemies of America." They are famous for the dancing which characterized their worship, and this dancing was a source of grave scandal to other Protestants, who felt that such "bodily agitation" was distinctly "Catholic." In fact, though the Shakers themselves believed that the Church of Rome was the Great Whore of Babylon, along with all the other established institutional forms of Christianity, they themselves were considered to be "Papish" because public general confession of past sins was a prerequisite to admission, and after one was in the Society he had to obey the Ministers in perfect simplicity—a "Romish" practice.

In actual fact, their written records, their simple songs, and especially their "concentrated labor" show these believers to have been sincere, honest, modest people, minding their own business, devoted to their faith in the Second Coming of Christ, living already in another world in which they felt themselves close to the angels and to the Lord of angels, along with Mother Ann, who would soon usher them into the New Creation, the definitive Kingdom.

The most eloquent witness to the Shaker spirit is the fruit of their labor. Anyone who knows anything about furniture realizes that today a mere stool, a coat hanger, a simple box made by the Shakers, is likely to be worth a good sum: and this not because an artificial market for such things has been created, but because of their consummate perfection, their extraordinary unselfconscious beauty and simplicity. There is, in the work of the Shakers, a beauty that is unrivaled because of its genuine spiritual purity—a quality for which there is no adequate explanation, but which can be accounted for in part by the doctrine of the Shakers themselves and their monastic view of manual work as an essential part of the Christian life.

Like the earliest monastic documents, they spoke of the "work of God" which they were called upon to do: the work of building God's "Millennial Church." (In pre-Benedictine documents, the *opus Dei* is not just the liturgy but the whole life of monastic conversion and transformation in Christ.) "God," said one of the Shaker Elders, "is the great Artist and Master Builder; the Gospel is the means; the Ministration are his Laborers, and instruments under his direction. We must labor in union with them to cast all rubbish out of and from around the building, and to labor to bring everything both outward and inward, more and more into order."

This allegorization of Shaker spirituality in terms of "work" represents, of course, no mere abstract fantasy. The Shakers were meticulous workers, with a passion for order, cleanliness, simplicity, practicality, and economy of means. In their "Millennial Laws" they decreed that "Believers may not, in any case, manufacture for sale any article or articles which are superfluously wrought, and which would tend to feed the pride and vanity of man," and "Buildings, mouldings and cornices which are merely for fancy may not be made by Believers." Not only were mirrors, silver spoons, gold and silver watches, and silver pencils banned from the communes as "superfluous," but also "silver tooth picks, three bladed knives, superfluous whips, gay silk handkerchiefs, checkered handkerchiefs made by the world, superfluous suspenders of any kind, and flowery painted clocks." Speaking of a frivolous and "showy" taste for ornament, an Elder said: "The divine man has no right to waste money upon what you would call beauty in his house or daily life, while there are people living in misery." The words unconsciously echo a famous passage in St. Bernard's *Apologia* for Cistercian austerity against Cluny. Yet the Shakers, like the first Cistercians, while giving no conscious thought to the *beauty* of their work, sought only to build honest buildings and to make honest and sturdy pieces of furniture. In doing so, they produced buildings and furniture of extraordinary, unforgettable beauty. True, this beauty has not always been obvious to everyone. Dickens thought Shaker furniture looked "grim," and the spiritual loveliness of Shaker simplicity is not evident to the eye that has submitted passively to the perversion of form by commerce (for example, the absurdities of American automobile design in the fifties).

The mind of the Shaker was directed not merely to the good of the work, the *bonum operis*, or to the advantage of the worker, the *bonum operantis*, but to something that transcended and included both: a kind of wholeness and order and worship that filled the whole day and the whole life of the working community. "Put your hands to work and your hearts to God," said Mother Ann, and again, "Clean your room well, for good spirits will not live where there is dirt. There is no dirt in heaven." The Shakers worked well because their work was a worship offered to God in the sight of his angels—a Biblical phrase which sets the tone for the life of the monks according to the Benedictine Rule. As a matter of fact, the early Shakers expressed a belief that their furniture designs and other patterns had been given to them by the angels and that they manifested heavenly forms, not belonging to the world of fallen men. In point of fact, as E. D. Andrews shows, the Shaker designs were derived from early American colonial patterns which were purified and perfected by the zeal of the Shakers for "primitive rectitude" and their "religious care."

In this perfect fusion of temporal and eternal values, of spirit and matter, the Shakers were in all truth living according to a kind of inspired eschatology in which ambition, personal gain, and even quick material results were not considered important. Of course, whatever was made was made for *use*, and consequently the quality of the work was paramount. What was to be used, was made for "the Church," and in order to share the fruits of labor with the poor and the hungry. The workman had to apply himself to his task with all skill and also with the necessary virtues of humility, patience, and love, contributing thereby to the peace and order of the common life, and "supporting the structure of fraternity."

In no case was work to be done in a hurry or under pressure, or indeed under any form of spiritual compulsion. The competitive spirit was banned because of its occult relationship with lust and violence. Overworking was frowned upon. The workers were encouraged to engage in a variety of tasks, to escape obsession and attachment. At all times their work had to be carried on at a steady, peaceful rhythm, for, as one of the Elders said: "We are not called to labor to excel, or to be like the world; but to excel them in order, union, peace and in good works—works that are truly virtuous and useful to man in this life." He also said: "All work done or things made in the Church for their own use ought to be faithfully and well done, but plain and without superfluity. All things ought to be made according to their order and use." Therefore, as E. D. Andrews says, "an atmosphere of settledness and repose pervaded the [Shaker] villages, as though they were part of the land itself."

Shoddy and hasty workmanship was condemned as "worldly" and unworthy of those living the divine life. Once, when someone had a vision to the effect that brass doorknobs were useless and "worldly," a brother spent considerable time removing all the brass knobs and replacing them with wooden ones.

Some of the sayings of Mother Ann, and other "Shaker sermonettes," give us more light on this attitude of mind, which consisted fundamentally in a devotion to *truth*. A thing or a person is perfect insofar as it is what it is meant to be. Absolute flawlessness is impossible, and the Shakers had no unrealistic dreams about utter perfection. But they were very realistic in striving to make things as they ought to be made so that they served their purpose well. They strove in all things for truth, and made a point of simply *being themselves.* "Do be natural," one of these maxims tells us, "a poor diamond is better than an imitation." "Do not be troubled because you have no great virtues. God made a million spears of grass where He made one tree." "Do be truthful; do avoid exaggeration; if you mean a mile, say a mile, and if you mean one, say one, and not a dozen." "Whatever is really useful is virtuous though it does not at first seem so." Sometimes the simple Shaker maxims remind one of William Blake. This one, for instance: "Order is the creation of beauty. It is heaven's first law, and the protection of souls." Or especially this other: *"Every force evolves a form."*

When we ponder these statements, we discover that they are full of wisdom. They bear witness to a soundness of judgment and a sanity of vision that help to account for the wonders of Shaker craftsmanship: underlying it all is a quasi-mystical sense of *being* and of *reality* crystallized in this simple maxim, which, for all its technical imprecision, reflects something of the great religious philosophies of all time: *"Sincerity is the property of the universe."*

The Shakers came to Kentucky and established themselves at Pleasant Hill, "the topmost bough upon the tree" and "the cream of Kentucky," in 1806. It was indeed pleasant, rolling farm land, a mile or so from the deep wooded gorge of the Kentucky River. The community consisted of recruits from New York, New Jersey, Pennsylvania, and Virginia. Later members came from Europe, including a large colony of Swedes, who were settled in the West Lot House. In the early days, after surviving the usual persecutions, they built a flourishing little town with workshops rising all around the three main "Families" and the Meeting House. John Dunlavy, one of the first Chief Ministers of Pleasant Hill, is said by E. D. Andrews to have had "a clearer insight into religious communism than any other Shaker writer." He wrote of the "united inheritance" and common life of the Shakers, and explicitly compared it with Catholic monasticism. He viewed the monks with a certain approval for "professing greater sanctity than the Church in general" and for their freedom from marital ties. However, he felt that their dependence on vow instead of "conscience alone" was a weakness, and their reliance on alms led them to be "patronized by public approbation and authority," whereas the Shakers were regarded as outcasts. It is almost certain that Dunlavy must have seen something of the first colony of Trappists established, about this time, only fifty miles from Pleasant Hill, in Nelson County. Unlike the persecuted Shakers, the Trappists were surrounded by the approval and concern of the small Catholic colony, and yet they soon left Kentucky, going to Illinois and then returning to France. They returned to Kentucky to build Gethsemani Abbey in 1848.

The Shakers of Pleasant Hill were harassed and plundered by soldiers of both sides in the Civil War (especially before and after the Battle of Perryville, a few miles away, in the fall of 1862). After the war, vocations began to decline, and in the industrial boom of the late nineteenth century the spiritual and social vigor of the Shakers gradually died out. Since they did not marry, there were no children to carry on the community. A few orphans were adopted, but not all of them took to the Shaker life. Twenty years after the Civil War, registrations ceased at Pleasant Hill and the Family Houses began to close.

As the community dwindled, some members left to consolidate with other communities in the east. The Society at Pleasant Hill was officially dissolved in 1910. A few Shakers remained at Pleasant Hill to conduct a small school. The last Shaker of the Pleasant Hill colony, Sister Mary Settles, a native of Louisville, died there in 1923. For forty years the buildings have been given to other uses or abandoned, but now they are being restored and opened to the public.

After their departure, these innocent people, who had once been so maligned, came to be regretted, loved, and idealized.

Too late, the people of Kentucky recognized the extraordinary importance of the spiritual phenomenon that had blossomed out in their midst. Today there is a general awareness that the Shakers made a unique and original contribution to American culture—but it will take more than nostalgia and sentiment to revive their unique combination of "science, religion and inspiration," which remains to us as a mysterious and fascinating "sign" for our times.

CONTEMPLATION AND DIALOGUE

One of the most important aspects of interfaith dialogue has also so far been one of the least discussed: it is the special contribution that the contemplative life can bring to the dialogue, not only among Christians, but also between Christians and the ancient religions of the East, perhaps even between Christians and Marxists. The present article is nothing more than an attempt to draw attention to the great importance of this neglected aspect of ecumenism, and to take note of some extremely delicate questions that it raises.

The first of these questions is that of contemplation itself. By contemplation here we mean not necessarily mysticism pure and simple, but at least the direct intuition of reality, the *simplex intuitus veritatis*, the pure awareness which is and must be the ground not only of all genuine metaphysical speculation, but also of mature and sapiential religious experience. This direct awareness is a gift, but it also normally presupposes the knowledge and practice of certain traditional disciplines. Thus, we can say that contemplation is both a "gift" (a "grace") and an "art." Unfortunately, we must also admit that it can almost be said to be a "lost art." And for this lost art there is certainly in the world today a definite nostalgia, not unmixed with vague hopes for the recovery of this awareness. But the nostalgia and the desire do not of themselves suffice to make the nostalgic one a contemplative.

Needless to say, the "contemplative," in the context of the present study, is not simply a person who, by vocation, is juridically isolated and cloistered. The mere fact of breaking off communication with the world and of losing interest in it certainly does not make one *ipso facto* a "contemplative." On the contrary, it would seem that today a certain openness to the world and a genuine participation in its anguish would normally help to safeguard the sincerity of a commitment to contemplation.

This having been said, let us turn to ecumenism, which implies dialogue: genuine ecumenism requires the communication and sharing, not only of information about doctrines which are totally and irrevocably divergent, but also of religious intuitions and truths which may turn out to have something in common, beneath surface differences. Ecumenism seeks the inner and ultimate spiritual "ground" which underlies all articulated differences. A genuinely fruitful dialogue cannot be content with a polite diplomatic interest in other religions and their beliefs. It seeks a deeper level, on which religious traditions have always claimed to bear witness to a higher and more personal knowledge of God than that which is contained simply in exterior worship and formulated doctrine. In all religions we encounter not only the claim to (divine) revelation in some form or other, but also the record of special experiences in which the absolute and final validity of that revelation is in some way attested. Furthermore, in all religions it is more or less generally recognized that this profound "sapiential" experience, call it gnosis, contemplation, "mysticism," "prophecy," or what you will, represents the deepest and most authentic fruit of the religion itself. All religions, then, seek a "summit" of holiness, of experience, of inner transformation to which their believers—or an elite of believers—aspire because they hope, so to speak, to incarnate in their own lives the highest values in which they believe. To put it in grossly oversimplified language, all religions aspire to a "union with God" in some way or other, and in each case this union is described in terms which have very definite analogies with the contemplative and mystical experiences in the Christian, and particularly the Catholic, tradition.

We must, however, admit with regret that, in the past, the tendency of Christians has been to regard all non-Christian religious experience as so obviously suspect as to be either too dangerous to study or else not worth the trouble of being studied. Indeed, the characteristic "Protestant" reaction to mysticism has been a basic repugnance. Protestantism has often regarded even professedly Christian mysticism as tainted with pagan eros, as an implicit denial of the Gospel, a "gnosticism" which seeks to improve on the Gospel by adding to it certain Greek philosophical aspirations that are alien to it. Not of course that Protestantism has not emphasized religious experience. But this experience has always been conceived as "prophetic" rather than as "contemplative." The word "contemplation" itself is disliked because of its Platonic resonances. The rejection of the "contemplative life" by many Protestants is consonant with the traditional Protestant rejection of monasticism and all that it stands for (the life of vows, celibacy, cloistered prayer, etc.).

We shall see later in these pages that even modern Catholicism tends, while admitting contemplation as a possible theoretical ideal, to disregard it in practice or to treat it as somewhat irrelevant to the urgent practical problems of our time. Even those Catholics who readily admit the actuality of Catholic mysticism and profess great devotion to the sainted contemplatives of the Western tradition, from the Greek Fathers to the Rhenish, Spanish, and other modern mystics, there has often been a readiness to take the same negative view as Protestants when looking at non-Christian "mysticism." Sufism is then shrugged off as "sensuality" and "self-hypnosis." Hinduism is censured as pagan pantheism, and Yoga is considered simply a technique for inducing contemplative trances. Buddhism is equated with mere quietism and inertia. In short, *all* forms of mysticism other than those encountered within the fold of the Roman Church are sometimes supposed by Catholics to be due to the direct or indirect intervention of Satan. This has even, most regrettably, been applied to the great mystical schools of the Eastern Church, whether Greek or Russian. The Hesychasts of Mount Athos have come in for a special scorn and obloquy as "navel gazers."

Obviously, the dialogue conducted by theologians and bishops on the level of doctrine and of practical adjustment can never have any serious meaning if, in the background, there persists a deep conviction that the non-Christian religions are all corrupted in their inner heart, and that what they claim as their highest perfection and their ultimate fulfillment is in fact nothing but a diabolical illusion. However, I do not think that serious scholars and theologians are really making such sweeping generalizations today.

The Second Vatican Council in its Declaration on Non-Christian religions clearly recognized the validity of the "profound religious sense" which has enabled men of all races and peoples to recognize God, "to contemplate the divine mystery and express it," and to seek liberation from the anguish of the human condition. "The Church rejects nothing which is true and holy in these religions," says the Council, and it adds that the purpose of dialogue should be to combine "the sincere witness of Christian faith with the understanding and indeed preservation and promotion of the spiritual and moral goods found in other cultures." However, the Church in no way abandons her claim to announce the definitive message of salvation to the world in Christ; dialogue, as the Council conceives it, is not merely based on the assumption that all religious truths are equally and indifferently good. Nevertheless, supernatural contemplation is certainly admitted as possible in all religions.

Here we face the first great problem. It is an enormous one, and since it has barely been considered, let alone studied, we can do no more than point to its existence and to its enormity, with the remark that here is where the work must begin. First of all, we must be clear about the soundness of the metaphysical intuitions, or indeed the pre-dialectical and direct intuitions of "being" (described in Hinduism as Brahma or Atman, in Buddhism as "the void" or *sunyata*) which form the ground of Oriental religions. This is relatively simple. But then we pass to the specifically religious level. In what sense do the Asian religious themselves claim to be "mystical" and "supernatural"? Here there will obviously be a great diversity of opinions. For instance, the chief authority on Zen Buddhism, Daisetz T. Suzuki, insists that Zen is "not mysticism," while, paradoxically, the Jesuit author of a standard history of Zen, Father H. Dumoulin, seeks to show that Zen *can* in some sense be called mysticism.

Since in practice we must admit that God is in no way limited in His gifts, and since there is no reason to think that He cannot impart His light to other men without first consulting us, there can be no absolutely solid grounds for denying the possibility of supernatural (private) revelation and of supernatural mystical graces to individuals, no matter where they may be or what may be their religious tradition, provided that they sincerely seek God and His truth. Nor is there any *a priori* basis for denying that the great prophetic and religious figures of Islam, Hinduism, Buddhism, etc., *could have been* mystics, in the true, that is, supernatural, sense of the word.

On the other hand, everyone is aware of the opposite tendency, to loose and irresponsible syncretism which, on the basis of purely superficial resemblances and without serious study of qualitative differences, proceeds to identify all religions and all religious experiences with one another, asserting that they are all equally true and supernatural and differ only in the accidentals of cultural expression. To adopt this view as axiomatic would from the very start guarantee that the interfaith dialogue would end in confusion.

These two extreme *a priori* views, one which denies non-Catholic religious experience all claim to validity, and the other which asserts that all religious traditions are equally true and supernatural in all respects, both proceed from a superficial consideration of the evidence. They are both oversimplifications. Certainly, a deeper and more serious form of research (and such research is beginning to make its results available today in works like those of R. C. Zaehner) will open the way to more qualified solutions.

But the fact remains that as long as the dialogue proceeds merely between research scholars and concerns only the objective study of documents, it will lack its most essential dimension. It is here that we see the need for the Christian contemplative to enter the discussion, in his own modest way, and for the non-Christian contemplative to enter it also.

Here, unfortunately, we are faced with many problems. Contemplatives are by the very nature of their vocation devoted to a somewhat hidden and solitary mode of life. They are not normally found on transoceanic jet planes, though their occasional presence there is by no means excluded. On the other hand, they are far more likely to be living in obscure places, without the benefit of any publicity, and known only to very few. It is also true that they may sometimes lack scholarly and theological preparation, and may indeed have absolutely nothing to say about their inner experience. Or they may, for various reasons, prefer not to speak about their spiritual way and about their tradition, being aware that such information is easily abused and that publicity might tend to falsify and corrupt it. There are, nevertheless, more and more scholars who are not only experienced in their own contemplative traditions, but have had an opportunity to visit monasteries where other living contemplative traditions are still flourishing.

Within the last two or three years, the Abbey of Gethsemani has been visited by men experienced and fully qualified to represent such traditions as Raja Yoga, Zen, Hasidism, Tibetan Buddhism, Sufism, etc. The names of some of these would instantly be recognized as among the most distinguished in their field. Therefore, the question of contacts and actual communication between contemplatives of the various traditions no longer presents very great obstacles. A little experience of such dialogue shows at once that this is precisely the most fruitful and the most rewarding level of ecumenical exchange. While on the level of philosophical and doctrinal formulations there may be tremendous obstacles to meet, it is often possible to come to a very frank, simple, and totally satisfying understanding in comparing notes on the contemplative life, its disciplines, its vagaries, and its rewards. Indeed, it is illuminating to the point of astonishment to talk to a Zen Buddhist from Japan and to find that you have much more in common with him than with those of your own compatriots who are little concerned with religion, or interested only in its external practice.

The reasons for this may be manifold, and one is not entitled to jump to rash conclusions. Nevertheless, however one may explain the fact, one may find in all races and in all traditions both the capacity for contemplative experience and the fact of its realization even on a very pure level. This capacity and this realization are therefore implicit in all the great religious traditions, whether Asian or European, whether Hindu, Buddhist, Moslem, or Christian. That is to say that the spiritual climate of the Christian Middle Ages, and of the patristic period, was basically "sapiential" rather than "scientific," ordered to contemplation above all, and hence it favored a spiritual and intellectual outlook very similar to that of the traditional religious cultures of the East. Since this outlook on life still fortunately exists to some extent in Catholic contemplative monasteries, it follows that our contemplative monks should be predisposed to appreciate and to understand those who come to them with experience in analogous traditions.

On the other hand, since this "sapiential" atmosphere is so far completely absent from modern technological society, and since inevitably the contemplative centers both of the East and of the West are subject to destructive pressures from that society, one can say that there is a certain importance in a dialogue which will enlarge their respective horizons while giving them a deeper consciousness of their gift, their vocation, and their momentous responsibility.

Can one tentatively say what these various traditions have in common? Here we immediately encounter difficulties, for it cannot be said that they all culminate in union with a "personal God." For the Moslem there is no question that God is a Person, but He is so completely and totally transcendent that the idea of union with Him poses doctrinal problems (which, however, the Sufis, in the main, ignore). For the Hindu, union with God on an "I-Thou" level is admitted in *bhakti*, which is, however, considered an inferior form of union. In Buddhism the "impersonality" of God is pushed to the point of *anatta*, in which not even the *Atman* or supreme Self of Hinduism is admitted. But, on the other hand, as soon as one looks a little deeper into the question, one finds that it is extremely complex and that the whole notion of *personality*, whether divine or human, will require considerable clarification before a real dialogue with the East can begin. Note, however, that all this is on the level of doctrine or of metaphysics. What about experience?

Very often, in describing contemplative experience, especially when attempting to do so in a way that will embrace both "Christian" and "Oriental" contemplation, writers tend to do it in a way that raises other serious difficulties. For instance, they will emphasize the element of psychological introversion, of withdrawal from sensible reality, of intense recollection and inner unity, of sublime peace, of spiritual joy above and beyond all sensible satisfaction, and so on. There is certainly a basis for such descriptions, but are they not in the end completely misleading? Do they not present a caricature of contemplation rather than its authentic description? Do they not assert that contemplation is exclusively negative and world-denying, and declare that the contemplative life is one which is totally indifferent to the world, to history, and to time? And in that case, can one avoid the conclusion that contemplation, whether Eastern or Western, is equally useless, selfish, passive, barren, and therefore inadmissible?

This would be the comment of the Marxist as well as of the Christian who, challenged by Marxism, is eager to prove that Christianity is above all active, dynamic, primarily concerned with the realization of God in the world and with His Epiphany in the society of men. In fact, writers of this school simply dismiss all thought of a dialogue between Catholic mysticism and the mysticisms of the East as an anachronistic futility. To take seriously the religions of the East would only serve to perpetuate the errors and illusions which keep the masses of Asia in a state of abjection and starvation. But even without this more intense social concern, this "incarnational" approach to the modern world, the Christian eschatologist would also dismiss such a contemplative dialogue as a dangerous or at best a useless delusion. What is important is that the Word of God has broken through the structures of a collapsing world to establish a new aeon. Contemplation, with its abstraction and its resting within the self in expectation of a pure and gnostic light, is only a refinement of the old and unregenerate aeon, and has nothing to do with the Kingdom of God. We are not called to "purity of heart" or to the gifts of wisdom and understanding. We are not invited to that virginity of spirit which even now apprehends the "light of the Transfiguration." We are simply called to wait in patience for the second coming of the *Kyrios* and for the definitive establishment of the Kingdom. Our "contemplation" should take no other form than the song of praise and the pure and spotless sacrifice which we continue to offer in memory of the Lord "until He comes."

The only answer to all these arguments is that perhaps the division is not quite as simple as all that. Setting aside, for the moment, the other contemplative traditions, we should be quite clear that Christian contemplation is by no means reducible to an experience of withdrawal and recollection, a negation of matter and of sense, a simple folding in upon the mysterious inner presence of God in "prayer of quiet," "prayer of union," "spiritual betrothal," and "spiritual marriage."

Instead of building our ideas of contemplation upon a few superficial modern manuals which, themselves, take only a foreshortened perspective of the Christian mystical tradition, let us remind ourselves of the full, liturgical, biblical, and patristic dimensions of Christian mysticism. Let us realize that Christian *theoria* is, in fact, first of all a response to God's manifestation of Himself in His Word; it is at the same time a contemplative understanding of the whole creation in the light of the Resurrection, the new creation, or, if you like, "the new aeon." It is, in addition to all this, a spiritual awareness of the mystery of God at work in history, and of the Church as the *pleroma* of Christ (Ephesians 1:18–23). Christian contemplation is centered not upon a vague inner appreciation of the mystery of man's own spiritual essence but upon the Cross of Christ, which is the mystery of *kenosis*, the self-emptying of God, the sacrificial submission of the "Suffering Servant" (Isaiah 52) who became obedient "even unto death" (Philippians 2:5–10).

In this mystery we encounter the full Christian expression of the dialectic of fullness and emptiness, *todo y nada*, void and infinity, which appears at the heart of all the great traditional forms of contemplative wisdom. Here too we paradoxically encounter, in the "word of the Cross," the emptying of all human wisdoms (I Cor. 1:18–25) in order that man might directly encounter the light and power of God. Texts such as these, which have so often been invoked as having power triumphantly to destroy all "pagan mysticisms," will then be seen as being, on the contrary, Christian answers to the profound questions raised by all these ancient traditions, which seem to have been grasping at the central truths in their own way. Thus, the full idea of Christian contemplation is a *theoria* that powerfully unites and fuses both "incarnational" and "eschatological" Christianity and then opens out into the realm of divine illumination, the *theologia* in which the highest mystery, the Trinity of Persons in one Nature, is not contemplated as "object" but is celebrated in the hymn of the Spirit, "Abba, Father!" which it is nevertheless not given to the tongue of man to utter in intelligible human speech (Romans 8:14–18; II Cor. 12:4).

The very reasons alleged against the false and insufficient notion of contemplation are the ones which make it imperative for Christian contemplation to take its rightful place in the ecumenical dialogue. But it must be contemplation in its true sense, not consecrated narcissism. It must be able to show the Protestant that the Catholic contemplative is filled with the nourishment offered by the Word of God and that "strengthened by His Spirit with might unto the inward man" he can "know the charity of Christ which surpasses all knowledge and be filled unto all the fulness of God" (Ephesians 3:17–19). It will show, too, that contemplation is not simply an esoteric and quasi-magic technique, but God's gift to the simple through the "foolishness of preaching" in order to confound all presumptuous "wisdoms" which lift themselves up against His Word (I Cor. 1:20 ff). Hence, contemplative wisdom is not a wisdom of the "old aeon," because it is outside the domain of the "princes of the world" (I Cor. 2:6–8) and "the world cannot know the Spirit" (John 14:17) who imparts this wisdom.

Christian contemplation must be able to show the Asian contemplative that the Christian too is aware of the religious dimensions of the Person and of the mystery of Being. At the same time it must show that the Christian does not confuse the person with the individual, and does not consider his relation to the ground of Being as a purely subject-object relationship—that he is not confined to the fussy and materialistic individualism of purely ethical and practical concerns. That he is, above all, dissociated from the crudeness and brutality of a society that seeks to thrive on purely material and scientific exploitation. It must also show modern man that Christianity is deeply aware of the power at work in history while at the same time defending him against the demonic illusion that comes from identifying the Church with the interests of this or that side in the inhuman struggle for political power.

The part that the Christian contemplative can play is then, ideally speaking, quite momentous. Whether or not the contemplative orders are at present able to measure up to such a task is quite another question. The renewal of the contemplative life, called for in the schema on religious proposed to the Council, certainly requires something more than the strict enforcement of the disciplines of enclosure, silence, and regularity in canonical prayer. But at the same time the contemplative orders must take special care to avoid a superficial adjustment which, in the name of a poorly understood *aggiornamento,* would end by depriving them of the authentic riches of their mystical and prophetic tradition.

ZEN BUDDHIST MONASTICISM

A description of the observances of Japanese Zen monasteries might prove entertaining and indeed instructive. But such a description would be worse than useless without some understanding of the nature of Zen. Since Zen is one of the most mysterious of all spiritualities—being so full of impudent paradox that it is at first a real scandal to the rational spirit of the West—it is not at all easy to make it accessible to the modern Western reader.

This article will therefore be divided into two parts. In the first we will consider the meaning of Zen to discover the motivation that brings the postulant to a Zen monastery. The second part will be shorter and will give a description of life in the monastery. Those who would be confused or repelled by the mystery of Zen teaching might read the second part first.

The approach will be one of sympathetic objectivity. Neither the space at our disposal nor the climate of dialogue permit, in such an essay, any destructive criticism of an Asian

religious mentality which is in any case very difficult to understand precisely in our Western terms.

I

Writers with a superficial knowledge of monasticism in
Christianity and in Buddhism sometimes compare the Zen
Buddhist monks with the Cistercians. There are, indeed, obvious analogies. The Zen monks are noted for the simplicity
and austerity of their lives, their uncompromising poverty,
their manual work, the extreme strictness and plainness of the
common life. We frequently encounter in Zen those deliberate and sometimes violent tactics of punishment and humilia-
tion which can remind one of the methods of Abbot de Rancé
and the spirituality of La Trappe. Later in this article we
shall take note of many monastic practices in Zen which recall
to mind some of the most basic monastic traditions of the
West. But it must be said right at the beginning that from a
certain point of view Zen monasticism has a quite different
purpose from ours, and if, in describing the life of the *Zendo,*
we unconsciously project our own monastic ideals, aims, and
problems into the context of Japanese Buddhism, we will certainly fail to understand what Zen is all about, and we will
fail to grasp any possible meaning that Zen might have for
ourselves.[1]

Our own view of monasticism, as Cistercians, is of course
first of all focused on a lifetime consecration to God in a monastery in which, furthermore, we have a vow of stability. The
Zen monk is doubtless no less determined than we are to devote his life to the purpose of attaining salvation. But for him,
the monastery is not what it is for St. Benedict: a permanent
"workshop in which all the instruments of perfection are to
be employed . . . a school in which one perseveres until
death in patience, and in participation in the sufferings of
Christ." [2]

The Zen monastery with its common meditation hall, or

Zendo, is in a sense more like a seminary than a monastic family. It is a place of formation and training. Hence the intensity and pressure of the discipline of the *Zendo* is easier to understand when we realize that it is intended to be lived only for a few years and not for a whole lifetime.

In fact, far from a lifetime commitment to remain in one community, the Zen monk is bound only for a relatively short period, analogous to a scholastic "term." At the end of this he is free to leave for another monastery (as one might change to a different school or university). He is also subject to examinations, and if he fails to meet the standards he is not allowed to return to the monastery and he will even be refused in other monasteries.

The purpose of this formation, as we shall see in a moment, is to give the monk, as quickly and as effectively as possible, a degree of spiritual maturity and liberty which will enable him to stand on his own feet and pursue, on his own, the path to enlightenment by the traditional practice of the Buddhist precepts *(sila),* meditation *(dhyana),* and wisdom *(prajna).* Once he attains this mature formation, he may leave the monastery to dwell as a priest in some city, or perhaps as a hermit in a lonely mountain temple. He may go to another monastery, he may go on pilgrimage, or he may return to business or professional life as a layman. Or he may remain in the monastery to teach and guide others. But, in any case, we see immediately that, in Zen at least, the Buddhist monk is not incorporated for life in one monastic family. In fact, as in primitive Christian eremitism, the Zen monk seeks out a particular monastery more because of a *Roshi,* or "venerable teacher," who is found there, than for the sake of the community or the rule. His aim is to attain to direct spiritual insight that will qualify him to live on his own.

In order to understand something of the spirit of Zen, we might quote a frankly anti-monastic statement attributed to Buddha in one of his last discourses.[3]

Knowing that the Master was about to die, his favorite disciple, Ananda, asked him to leave final instructions, perhaps in the form of a rule, for his disciples. But the Buddha refused to do so. He explicitly refrained from becoming the "founder of an order" which would follow special methods to attain perfection or would deliver an esoteric teaching inaccessible to ordinary people. It will be remembered that in his own life Sakyamuni (Buddha) had been disillusioned with extreme asceticism as well as with the worldly life of hedonism, and followed the "middle path" between them. Now, in reply to Ananda, he said:

> If anyone thinks "It is I who will lead the Order" or "The Order depends on me," he is the one who should lay down instructions concerning the Order. But the Tathagatha [Buddha] has no such thought, so why should he leave instructions?

And the Buddha goes on:

> So, Ananda, you must be your own lamps, be your own refuges. Take refuge in nothing outside yourselves. Hold firm to the truth as a lamp and a refuge, and do not look for a refuge in anything besides yourselves. A monk becomes his own lamp and refuge by continually looking on his body, feelings, perceptions, moods and ideas in such a manner that he conquers the cravings and depressions of ordinary men and is always strenuous, self-possessed and collected in mind. Whoever among my monks does this, either now or when I am dead, if he is anxious to learn, will reach the summit.[4]

The tone of this passage is altogether that of the individualist asceticism of southern (Theravada or Hinayana) Buddhism. We see, of course, how far the Buddhist ascetic ideal is from the Christian dependence on grace, which demands a total self-surrender and a complete dependence on Christ. However, we must be on our guard against interpreting an Asian text in the context of our own Pelagian and semi-Pelagian controversies. The Buddha is warning his disciples against reliance on external means, ritual forms, and ascetic systems. He is by no means telling them to rely on themselves "instead of" on "grace" (a concept which does not enter into consideration at this point). They are to rely on nothing but "the truth" as they experience it directly. Hence, they must not even prefer an authoritative statement by the Buddha to the direct insight into truth in their own lives.

The purpose of the text just quoted seems therefore to be an express prohibition, on the part of Buddha, forbidding his disciples to treat him as a god or as a source of grace, or as a semi-deified monastic patriarch. In Mahayana Buddhism we later find a complete reliance on Buddha as Savior (in Amidism). The spirit of Zen, on the other hand, takes the same view of Buddha that we have seen in this Theravada text.[5] Zen places no reliance upon the authority of scriptures (sutras) as do other Buddhist sects, and it does not place any confidence in special rules or methods, since its main aim is to bring the monk to a state of enlightenment and spiritual liberty in which he has no need of methods because he is in direct and immediate contact with light and reality in their existential source. Zen is, in fact, an Asian form of religious existentialism. It aims at breaking through the conventional structures of thought and ritual in order that the subject may attain to an authentic personal experience of the inner meaning of life.[6]

A famous four-line stanza attributed to the semi-legendary founder of Chinese Zen, Bodhidharma (sixth century A.D.), sums up the Zen program:

A special tradition outside the scriptures
No dependence upon words and letters;
Direct pointing at the soul of man;
Seeing into one's own nature and the attainment of Buddha-
    hood.[7]

Zen discards the elaborate metaphysical speculations that came to China with Indian Buddhism. It can indeed be said to have no doctrine at all.[8] For this reason, the Zen monks have often been accused, as have the Cistercians and for much the same reasons, of being anti-intellectual. Certainly there is some basis to the accusation, if it is understood in the light of the following typical Zen story. A disciple once asked a Zen master: "I wish to read the sutras, and what would you advise me to do about it?" The master replied: "Do you think a merchant who deals in millions would bother about making a few pennies?" [9]

The Zen monks traditionally preferred direct experience to abstract and theoretical knowledge gained by reading and study. But of course they never denied that reading and study could, in their proper place, contribute to the validity of their spiritual training. The harm comes from placing one's whole trust in books and in learning, and neglecting the direct grasp of life which is had only by living it in all its existential reality.

Another Zen master, when asked if a monk should read the sutras, replied in characteristic Zen style: "There are no by-roads and no crossroads here; the mountains are all the year round fresh and green; east or west, in whichever direction, you may have a fine walk." The monk asked for more explicit instructions. The master replied: "It is not the sun's fault if the blind cannot see their way." [10]

Since attachment even to the teaching of Buddha himself could produce spiritual blindness, the Zen masters were very careful to prevent any disciple from becoming attached to their teaching. That is why so many of the sayings of the Zen masters seem to us to be pure nonsense. They were often, in fact, deliberately meaningless from a logical viewpoint. The Zen masters did not want disciples simply to memorize something they had said. Yet, paradoxically, Zen literature consists of almost nothing but quotations of the Zen masters!

One of the Zen masters was asked by a postulant to accept him as a disciple in his monastery and teach him the truth of Buddhism. The master replied:

Why do you seek such a thing here? Why do you wander about neglecting your own precious treasure at home? I have nothing to give you, and what truth of Buddhism do you desire to find in my monastery? There is nothing, absolutely nothing! [11]

We know that the Desert Fathers of Egypt, particularly those in the Evagrian tradition, whose doctrine was transmitted to the West by Cassian, sought a perfect purity of heart, and for this reason they avoided making learning or conceptual knowledge too much of an end in itself. We find in Zen an analogous striving for non-attachment, and an apophatic contemplation which is summed up in the term "no-mind" or *wu nien*. But the "emptiness" and "objectlessness" of the Zen way of "no-mind" must be well understood, for in such a delicate matter the slightest error is disastrous. To become attached to emptiness itself and to an imaginary "purity of heart" that is conceived as an object which one can attain is to miss the target altogether, even though it may seem to be the highest point of the mystical life. Hence, the Zen masters refuse to countenance any deliberate cultivation of a state of negative inner silence, still less of unconsciousness. A Chinese Zen master, Hui Neng, said: "If you cherish the notion of purity and cling to it, you turn purity into falsehood . . . Purity has neither form nor shape, and when you claim an achievement by establishing a form to be known as purity . . . you are purity-bound [i.e., imprisoned by your limited and illusory concept of purity]." [12]

Shen Hui, a disciple of Hui Neng, said: "If disciples cultivate [a state of] unreality and stay put in unreality, then they are chained to unreality. If they cultivate contemplation and stay put in it, the very contemplation enchains them; when they cultivate the silence of the beyond and stay put in it, the very silence of the beyond enchains them." [13]

In other words, Zen, as properly understood, refuses to countenance the deliberate cultivation of a state of inner emptiness from which one might systematically exclude all external images and all concepts in order to experience oneself resting in a well-defined condition of silence, tranquillity, and peace. It is not, as so many Westerners imagine, a mere quietistic cult of inner silence, to be achieved by complete withdrawal from ordinary life. On the contrary, the true Zen enlightenment, according to the Zen masters, is found in action (though not necessarily in activity, still less in *activism*). Zen is a full awareness of the dynamism and spontaneity of life, and hence it cannot be grasped by mere introspection, still less by dreaming. Suzuki says, "Zen must be seized with bare hands, with no gloves on." [14] It requires a real alertness and effort, and one's entire, undivided attention: however, the attention is given not to a theory or to an abstract truth, but to life in its concrete, existential reality, here and now. The Zen masters would doubtless like the maxim *age quod agis*. They seek Zen in the ordinary conduct of everyday life, since "one's ordinary mind is the *Tao*." If one must not vainly seek a special enlightenment in the sutras, one must also avoid the delusion that enlightenment is to be found by sitting for hours in quiet meditation. In truth, one must be free from all bondage to any system whatever. "The whole system of Zen," says Suzuki, "may thus be said to be nothing but a series of attempts to set us free from all forms of bondage . . . [The advocates of inner purity] still have traces of clinging [attachment], setting up a certain state of mind and taking it for ultimate emancipation. So long as the seeing is something to see, it is not the real one; only when the seeing is no-seeing—that is, when the seeing is not a specific act of seeing into a definite circumscribed state of consciousness—is it the 'seeing into one's self-nature.' Paradoxically stated, when seeing is no-seeing, this is real seeing; when hearing is no-hearing, there is real hearing." [15]

A Chinese Zen master, Shu Chou, spoke of two great diseases of the mind which afflict contemplatives. He described these diseases in simple images as "looking for the ass on which you are actually riding" and "having realized that you are riding on the ass, being unwilling to get off." From the Zen point of view, looking for the ass is looking for some special secret of spiritual perfection, some hidden infallible method, some esoteric state of mind which is the property of initiates, making them superior to everyone else. We are already riding on the ass; that is to say, the ordinary experience of everyday life is the "place" where enlightenment is to be sought. "I tell you," says Shu Chou, "do not search for the ass." On the other hand: "Having found the ass, but being unwilling to dismount: this disease is the hardest to heal." Here he means that one becomes attached to the special awareness that one's everyday mind contains the secret one has been looking for. One is now secure that one possesses "the answer," and therefore one clings to it, one puts one's security in the fact of "having an answer." But one must get off the ass, one must forget even that one has the answer. "What I say to you is: do not ride. You yourself are the ass, and everything is the ass. Why do you go on riding? If you do, you cannot dispel your disease." [16] If the whole purpose of Zen training is, then, simply to show the monk that he does not need to look for the ass upon which he is already riding and that he ought to have enough sense to get off the ass when there is no longer any need to ride, one may wonder why the discipline of the Zen monastery is so terribly strict, and why such costly sacrifices are demanded of the monks. Are all these things really necessary, in order merely to bring one to a simple recognition that one can find the answer to life's problems by oneself, since they are right in front of one's nose?

It is at this point that Western understanding of Zen usually breaks down completely and, in some cases, disastrously. The trouble arises from the fact that Western thought is, in one way or another, much more individualistic than Asian thought. Even where Western thought is given a collective and social orientation, and even when its individualism is no longer an enforcement of the "I" but its renunciation, the

"I" nevertheless remains the starting point of everything. It is the subject endowed with freedom and with the capacity to know and to love. For a Christian, of course, the "I" needs to be transformed and elevated by grace. But from the moment one speaks of spontaneity, freedom, etc., the Western mind thinks at once of the empirical ego-subject. Hence, recognizing "the ass" and situating oneself in one's everyday existence is simply recognizing and indeed affirming the empirical self, the "I." This being the case, one would scarcely need the grueling discipline of Zen in order to discover oneself on this level.

But for Zen (backed as it is by a Buddhist ontology), things are just the opposite. The empirical ego is in fact the source and center of every illusion. The "ass" to be recognized in meditation is not the empirical "I," but the ground of Being which the "I" prevents us from recognizing. (Getting off the ass is then a matter of even renouncing one's "experience" and "idea" of the ground of Being conceived as an object.)

Therefore, instead of simply affirming the "I," with its spontaneous desires and joys, the Zen man seeks to accomplish the long and difficult labor of divesting himself completely of this "I" and all its works, in order to discover the deeper spontaneity that comes out of the ground of Being—in Buddhist terms, from the "original self," the "Buddha mind," or *prajna;* in Chinese terms, from *Tao.* This corresponds roughly to the kind of life the New Testament writers and the Fathers describe as "Life in the Spirit," always allowing for the differences involved by a new and supernatural perspective.

Since the work of getting rid of the "I" is in fact so difficult and so subtle as to be completely impossible without the help of others, the disciple must submit unconditionally to the most rigorous obedience and discipline. He must take without question and without murmur every possible difficulty and hardship. He must bear insult, weariness, labor, opprobrium. The attitude he takes toward these things is, however, somewhat different from the Christian attitude, because of his different concept of the self. Where the Christian has Christ and the Cross, the Zen Buddhist has not Buddha as a person but *sunyata,* the Void. This implies very special difficulties and, indeed, unusual dispositions of mind and heart.

Hence, the Zen monk must be persuaded first of all that if he merely relies on his own ability to meditate and to discipline himself, to seek perfection by himself, he is on the way to ruin and perhaps to insanity. Thus, the saying of Buddha—"be lamps for yourselves"—becomes dangerously paradoxical if one takes the "self" to mean simply the empirical "I." In order to become a "lamp for oneself," one must first completely die to one's empirical "I," and to do this, one must submit completely to another who is himself enlightened and who knows exactly how to bring one through the perilous ways of transformation and enlightenment. But in no case must one become attached to the methods, the teaching, the "system" (if any) even of this master.

Western monks who get a taste of Zen by superficial reading and who imagine that it represents a wonderful new world of liberty to do as one pleases without restraint, and indeed to act a little madly at times, if they underestimate the severity and ruthlessness of Zen discipline, are completely misled, and they would do well to recognize that dabbling in Zen will be, for them, a very serious danger.

I I

Having become acquainted with the general principles behind Zen monasticism, we must now consider, in broad outline, the nature of the monastic life and monastic formation in Zen. We shall come across numerous analogies with our own monastic tradition.

The Buddhist monastic life is essentially a life of pilgrimage (*angya*). It is as a pilgrim that the newcomer presents himself at the monastery door, whether he be a monk already experienced and trained in another monastery, or a postulant newly arrived from secular life with a letter from his spiritual father. He comes on foot as a "homeless one," a wanderer, wearing the traditional bamboo hat and straw sandals, carrying all his belongings in a small papier-mâché box slung round his neck. All he has are his clothes, his razor, his begging bowl, and a couple of books perhaps. There is a small sum of money in his box, enough to pay for his burial if he is found dead by the roadside. On his way to his chosen monastery, the pilgrim will spend the nights sleeping in temples or in roadside shrines, if not in the open fields.

The purpose of *angya*, or pilgrimage, is to convince the monk of the fact that his whole life is a search, in exile, for his true home. And he must seek earnestly, not be diverted by the trivial incidents he meets along his way. The "Song of Pilgrimage," composed by a Chinese Zen monk, describes the mentality of the pilgrim monk:

> *His conduct is to be transparent as ice or crystal*
> *He is not to seek fame or wealth*
> *He is to rid himself of defilements of all sorts.*
> *He has no other way open to him but to go about and inquire;*
> *Let him be trained in mind and body by walking over the*
>   *mountains and fording the rivers;*
> *Let him befriend wise men in the Dharma (Law) and pay them*
>   *respect wherever he may accost them;*
> *Let him brave the snow, tread on the frosty roads, not minding*
>   *the severity of the weather;*
> *Let him cross the waves and penetrate the clouds, chasing away*
>   *dragons and evil spirits.*[17]

This pilgrimage, let us repeat it, does not end at the monastery gate. When his period of training has ended, the monk will once again take to the road and continue his search, though now, we hope, it will have a totally new dimension. His whole monastic life is a pilgrimage, and his stay in the monastery is only one of the incidents in his journey. Not even the monastery and the training, the discipline, the teaching and the observance, are permitted to become ends in themselves. However, in practice, it is no longer possible or usual for Zen monks to live the true pilgrimage life that was led by their fathers. Yet, if they return to the world, they must live in it with the mentality of pilgrims.

On arriving at the monastery, the pilgrim, even if he is an experienced monk, receives the same kind of treatment as prescribed by St. Benedict for the reception of postulants. Even though he presents a letter of introduction, the newcomer is politely but firmly told to go elsewhere. There is no room for him here! The aspirant knows well enough that this refusal is not to be taken seriously, so he remains in an attitude of supplication at the gate. When evening comes, he will probably be invited inside the gate for the night. He will pray or sleep on the ground and thus he will undergo a period of probation in the outer court. After about five days he may enter the monastery itself. When he is allowed to come to the *Zendo* or meditation hall, he begins to take part in the life of the community.

The *Zendo* is the place where, for several hours a day, the monk must sit in the lotus posture meditating. Each monk has a small space about three by six feet allotted to him, and when night comes, he unrolls his quilt and sleeps there on the floor. When meditation is in progress, he is not allowed to leave the *Zendo* except to see the spiritual master (*Roshi*). To break the monotony and to relax their limbs, the monks at regular intervals get up together and walk briskly around the hall a few times, then resume their meditation, which, in times of special retreat, can go on for eight or ten hours of the day.

On what does the Zen monk meditate? Here we come face to face with the famous *koan* which is so often bafflingly described in Zen literature. But we must remember that the *koan* meditation is favored only by one school of Zen, that of Rinzai. Hence, we need not devote too much space to it here.

But it must be mentioned, since it is an original creation of Zen. The *koan* is an enigmatic saying which the *Roshi* may assign to the disciple as a topic for meditation. The disciple may spend hours and days trying to analyze the saying, or interpreting it symbolically, but each time he returns to the master he is sent away to continue seeking the "answer." Gradually he begins to realize that the nature of his *koan* is such that it cannot be analyzed or interpreted intellectually. Yet it does in some sense have a "solution," though the solution is not "an answer." It is in fact a solution that can be known only by being lived. The true *koan* meditation is one in which the disciple comes to be so identified with the *koan* that he experiences his whole self as a riddle without an answer. This may be for him an utterly hopeless experience, but if he continues to struggle he may one day suddenly accept himself precisely as he is, as a riddle *without an answer that is communicable to others in an objective manner.*[18] If he is capable of "illumination," he will at that moment taste the delight of recognizing that his own incommunicable experience of the ground of his being, his own total acceptance of his own nothingness, far from constituting a problem, is in fact the source and center of inexpressible joy: in Christian terms, one can hardly help feeling that the illumination of the genuine Zen experience seems to open out into an unconscious demand for grace—a demand that is perhaps answered without being understood. Is it perhaps already grace?

There is also a certain amount of liturgical prayer in the *Zendo,* but it remains very simple. In spite of the fact that the Zen tradition seems to reject the reading of sutras and to despise ritualism, we find that the sutras are nevertheless read. The practice of reading sutras corresponds to our psalmody. There are also other rites, the offering of incense before a statue of Buddha and so on. But the ritual is never very elaborate and there is nothing that would correspond to our conventual Mass.

A daily sermon or conference may be given by the

Roshi. From the literature on the subject, one gets the impression that this has now become a very formal and perhaps artificial exercise lacking the vitality and spontaneity of the exchanges which, in the ancient texts, took place between the *Roshi* and his disciples. Nevertheless, a collection of Zen conferences given in recent years on the Japanese radio can be read in English translation, and they have a very definite spiritual interest.[19]

Undoubtedly, one of the most essential elements of the Zen training is encountered in interviews with the *Roshi*. These are deliberately humiliating and frustrating, for the spiritual master is determined to waste no time tolerating the illusions and spiritual self-gratifications that may be cherished by his disciples. If necessary, he will still resort (as did famous Zen masters in the past) to slapping, kicking, and other forms of physical violence. It may also be mentioned that in the *Zendo* there is always one monk on guard with a stick, with which he does not hesitate to strike the shoulders of anyone who is not manifestly awake. Far from fearing to create tension, the Zen masters deliberately make severe demands upon their disciples, and it is understood that one cannot really attain to enlightenment unless one is pressed to the limit. One might almost say that one of the purposes of the Zen training is to push the monk by force into a kind of dark night, and to bring him as quickly and efficaciously as possible into a quandary where, forced to face and to reject his most cherished illusions, driven almost to despair, he abandons all false hopes and makes a breakthrough into a complete humility, detachment, and spiritual poverty. Unfortunately, however, experience in the monastic life everywhere teaches that this severe training may, in fact, simply make the monk tough, callous, stubborn, perhaps even incurably proud, rather than purifying his heart. This would of course be especially true in a case where the spiritual master, instead of being a genuinely spiritual and holy man, is only a self-opinionated bully with a taste for pushing people around. All methods have their risks!

We must not, however, simply imagine the Zen monk sitting cross-legged and straining his mind almost to the breaking point, with no hope of any relaxation all day long. On the contrary, they have a daily tea-ceremony and occasional recreation in the form of judo wrestling bouts among themselves! Also, on the more serious side, the monks go out to beg, and they also work in the garden or around the monastery. Both begging and manual work are important in Zen monasticism, since they inculcate the spirit of poverty and humility. But, in addition to this, the monk enters into contact with "the world" by his begging and by his work, which is the same as that of the farmers among whom he lives. This reminds him of the realities of life, and he shares in the hardships of the poor, of whom he is one. His meditation and his inner purity are what he offers to the world in return, and he feels that he cannot be entitled to share the bread (or the rice) of the poor if he is not completely serious in his efforts to become enlightened, and open his spiritual "eye of wisdom" (the *prajna* eye). Suzuki quotes a text which brings home to the monk his responsibility to be truly what his fellow Buddhists in the world expect him to be, for in traditional Buddhism the monk has a very important part to play. He indeed is one to whom the rest of the Buddhist world looks for help and for salvation. The Triple refuge of the Buddhist is the *Buddha,* the *Dharma* (law), and the *Samgha,* or the monastic order.

O monks, you are all sons of the Buddha; every thread of the dress you wear comes from the loom of the hard-working weaver, and every grain you consume is indicative of the sweat of the farmer's brow. If your prajna eye is not yet opened, what claim can you ever have on those precious gifts from your fellow beings? Do you wish to know what animals they are that are covered with fur and carry a pair of horns on their heads? They are no other than those monks who accept shamelessly all the pious offerings from their devotees. Monks are not to eat while not hungry, they are not to wear anything more than they actually need. Instead of accepting from their pious-minded devotees fine raiment, a bowl of rice or a hut, let monks wear a dress of red hot steel, make a meal of molten metal, and live in a blazing kiln, if their hearts have not yet burned with the desire to save themselves as well as all beings from the despotism of birth and death, and if they are not straining all their spiritual energy toward the attaining of this end.[20]

Zen monasticism is currently in crisis, as is monasticism everywhere, and doubtless the question of poverty and living on alms as well as work will be a matter of urgent concern with them as well as among us. But the Zen monk has always had a definite sense of being "in the world though not of it," and the mature monk is one who does not shrink from the needs of those who come to him for spiritual help. Another page of a traditional text, moving in its simplicity, tells us this:

Monks ought to behave like a grinding stone: Chang-san comes to sharpen his knife, Li-szu comes to grind his axe, everybody and anybody who wants to have his metal improved in any way comes and makes use of the stone. Each time the stone is rubbed, it wears out, but it makes no complaint, nor does it boast of its usefulness. And those who come, go home fully benefitted; some of them may not be quite appreciative of the stone; but the stone itself remains ever contented . . .[21]

This readiness to be completely "available" to others is more characteristic of the Zen monk's life as priest in the world or as *Roshi* in the monastery. It represents the active side of the Zen life, and does not normally interfere with the *Zendo* training and contemplation.

Zen monasticism, as we have briefly described it here, still exists and flourishes in Japan. It has ceased to exist in China, where it was already in decline before the Communist take-over. In spite of the fact that there has been considerable interest in Zen on the part of Americans and Europeans, the Zen masters themselves feel that the future is not all bright for Zen monasticism. The kind of life we have described is a

life bound up with medieval Japanese culture and it is understandable that modern men who are looking for the answer to
the confusing spiritual problems of our time may no longer
be able, in large numbers, to take on the severe discipline of
the *Zendo,* meditate on the *koan,* or submit to the rough tactics of the *Roshi.* Zen, too, may go through a period of adaptation. It is certain that non-Buddhist students who have been
allowed to participate in the life of Zen monasteries do not
receive all the traditional harsh treatment. Among such
guests of Zen monasteries there has been a Jesuit father,
Enomiye Lassalle, who has written an interesting account of
his experience.[22]

There have been attempts on a small scale to transplant
Zen monasticism to America and Europe. But these remain
study and training centers rather than monasteries where the
Zen life is lived in all its fullness. Yet Zen remains the object
of great popular interest in the West. There are many books
and articles published on the subject, far more, perhaps, than
about Yoga and other Asian spiritualities. These books are
generally of excellent quality and are read in intellectual and
artistic circles. Why? Probably because of the widespread dis-
satisfaction with the spiritual sterility of mass society domi-
nated by technology and propaganda, in which there is no
room left for personal spontaneity. Perhaps also because of
modern man's disgust with all that claims to offer him yet
another final and complete answer to all questions. The
frank, thoroughgoing existentialism and dynamism of Zen
continue to appeal to the kind of men who, suspicious at once
of Marx and of organized religion, live in the existentialist
climate which we owe not so much to Sartre and to the literary existentialists as to Husserl and to Heidegger. Though
perhaps not Christian, this climate does seem to have a certain
spiritual seriousness, as is shown by the fact that Edith Stein,
for instance, began as a disciple of Husserl but became a fol-
lower of St. John of the Cross and eventually gave up her life
at Auschwitz.

Is it enough to say that Zen is a philosophic and existentialist type of spirituality, capable of bringing man into an authentic confrontation with himself, with reality, and with his fellow man, or shall we see in it a deeper religious quality? Without discussing this question in detail, we might at least consider that without this religious dimension it would be hard to see how Zen monasticism could have survived for so many centuries and played such a role in the history of Asian religious culture. But perhaps the most reasonable conclusion would be to reprint here a Zen text of unusual interest, and leave it to speak for itself. The words are those of a Chinese master, Shih Shuang (Japanese: Sekiso), quoted by Suzuki.[23] Another Zen master, Yuan-Wu, comments:

"Stop all your hankerings; let the mildew grow on your lips; make yourself like a perfect piece of immaculate silk; let your one thought be eternity; let yourself be like dead ashes, cold and lifeless; again let yourself be like an old censer in a deserted village shrine.

"Putting your simple faith in this, discipline yourself accordingly; let your body and your mind be turned into an inanimate object of nature like a piece of stone or wood; when a state of perfect motionlessness and unawareness is obtained, all the signs of life will depart and also every trace of limitation will vanish. Not a single idea will disturb your consciousness when lo! all of a sudden you will come to realize a light abounding in full gladness. It is like coming across a light in thick darkness; it is like receiving treasure in poverty. The four elements and the five aggregates are no more felt as burdens; so light, so easy, so free you are. Your very existence has been delivered from all limitations: you have become open, light and transparent. You gain an illuminating insight into the very nature of things, which now appear to you as so many fairy-like flowers having no graspable realities. Here is manifested the unsophisticated self which is the original face of your being; here is shown bare the most beautiful landscape of your birthplace. There is but one straight passage open and unobstructed through and through. This is so when you surrender all—your body, your life, and all that belongs to your inmost self. This is where you gain peace, ease, non-doing and inexpressible delight. All the sutras and sastras are no more than communications of this fact; all the sages, ancient as well as modern, have exhausted their ingenuity and imagination to no other purpose than to point the way to this. It is like unlocking the door to a treasure; when the entrance is once gained, every object coming into your view is yours, every opportunity that presents itself is available for your use; for are they not, however multitudinous, all possessions obtainable within the original being of yourself? Every treasure there is but waiting your pleasure and utilization. This is what is meant by 'once gained, eternally gained, even to the end of time.' Yet really there is nothing gained; what you have gained is no gain, and yet there is truly something gained in this!"

THE ZEN KOAN [1]

The layman Ho asked Basho: "What is it that transcends everything in the universe?" (Another version: "If all things return to the one, to what does the one return?")

Basho answered: "I will tell you after you have drunk up all the waters of the West River in one gulp."

Ho said: "I have already drunk up all the waters of the West River in one gulp."

Basho replied: "Then I have already answered your question." [2]

Such is a typical Zen dialogue (an "example" in the sense of the "esemplo" which the apprentice copies from the master in medieval painting). It contains all that needs to be "known" or "said" about Zen, about Buddhism, and therefore, in the Buddhist context, about everything. The task of the Zen student is to "study" this *koan,* not of course by analysis, or by research, or even by a formal technique of concentration, but by a method that is also a non-method because it cannot be objectively set forth in precise rules. The study of the *koan* has no codified rules and no precise formal answer. Nevertheless, there is a very definite discipline and procedure to be followed in *koan* study. Nothing is arbitrary or left to chance. One either hits the target or misses it entirely. Hitting and missing are not indifferent. The student seeks at all costs to reach the heart of the matter in *koan* study. Therefore, he learns to "work through" the *koan,* to live it as his master has lived it. In fact, the heart of the *koan* is reached, its kernel is attained and tasted, when one breaks through into the heart of life itself as the ground of one's own consciousness. It is then that one sees the "answer," or rather one experiences oneself as the question answered. The answer is the *koan,* the question, seen in a totally new light. It is not something other than the question. The *koan* is not something other than the self. It is a cryptic figure of the self, and it is interpreted insofar as the student can become so identified with the *koan* that it revolutionizes and liberates his whole consciousness, delivering it from itself. How? The fourteenth-century *Roshi,* Bassui, says in a letter:

> When your questioning goes deeper and deeper you will get no answer until finally you will reach a cul-de-sac, your thinking totally checked. You won't find anything within that can be called "I" or "Mind." But who is it that understands all this? Continue to probe more deeply yet and the mind that perceives there is nothing will vanish; you will no longer be aware of questioning but only of emptiness. When awareness of even emptiness disappears, you will realize that there is no Buddha outside Mind and no Mind outside Buddha. Now for the first time you will discover that when you do not hear with your ears you are truly hearing and when you do not see with your eyes you are really seeing Buddhas of the past, present and future. But don't cling to any of this, just experience it for yourself.[3]

Because this is a simple statement, it may be misleading: it contains spatial imagery ("inside," "outside"), which will be a temptation to the Western mind. It uses conventional religious terms, and speaks of "seeing Buddhas" as though they were objects, etc. But the text gives a good idea of the gradual deepening of consciousness that comes with *koan* study. The Zen experience is first of all a liberation from the notion of "I" and of "mind"; yet it is not annihilation and pure unconsciousness (as Westerners sometimes imagine "nirvana" to be). It is, on the contrary, a kind of super-consciousness in which one experiences reality not indirectly or mediately but directly, and in which, clinging to no experience and to no awareness as such, one is simply "aware." This simple "awareness" or "awakeness" is in fact the true identity which the Zen student seeks and for which he, so to speak, immolates his superficial empirical consciousness, his ego-identity with the *koan*. In Miura and Sasaki's *The Zen Koan,* we find in fact that certain types of *koan* are considered appropriate for different steps of this deepening. Hence, it would be superficial to suppose that Zen study ends when one has attained a first *satori,* "enlightenment" (*Kensho*). Enlightenment in this sense of a new identity and awareness is not the end but the serious beginning. The function of the *Roshi* is to guide and test the student, not by elaborate analysis but by brief questions and laconic answers which are always strictly to the "point." In the systematic *sesshin,* this is reduced to businesslike efficiency and the student's aim is to attain *Kensho,* or further enlightenment, and to have this verified by the *Roshi.* Kapleau's *The Three Pillars of Zen* is centered mostly on *Kensho.* In the lectures of the *Roshi* Miura, we are shown further steps in perfecting this original enlightenment.

Such is the traditional Zen practice. What does this mean to the Western mind?

II

The practice of Zen aims at the deepening, purification, and transformation of the consciousness. But it does not rest satisfied with any "deepening" or a superficial "purification." It seeks the most radical transformation: it works on depths that would seem to go beyond even depth psychology. It has, in other words, a metaphysical and spiritual dimension. It seeks the pure ontological subject, at once unique and universal, no longer "individual." Let us set aside the question whether or not it is "mystical," as this is frequently denied by the Buddhists themselves (notably by Suzuki), and in any case creates semantic problems. But from the moment that we are dealing with "consciousness" we face the fact that there is quite probably, as William Haas maintained, a profound difference between consciousness in the East and in the West, at least in the traditions of East and West. The Western consciousness is object-oriented. The Eastern consciousness, says Haas, does not shrink from the possibility of a pure subjectivity *that needs no object.* For the West, consciousness is always "consciousness *of.*" In the East, this is not necessarily so: it can be simply "consciousness." Zen summons one to a realization which will at first confuse and mislead the Western mind. (This becomes very clear in the struggles, the frustrations, and sometimes the neurotic resentments of the Western students in their recorded interviews with the *Roshi*, in Kapleau's book.) Western man sees himself as a subject with various possibilities of fulfillment: a package of desires for things, or states, which can be "attained." What matters is to find and use effective means to get what one wants. Attainment of one's object brings happiness. One rests in the possession of what one has sought.

This is an *individual* project first of all. It is centered in ego-identity, but the autonomy of the individual remains ambiguous. The individual is constituted by his ability to exist in the presence of others, to stand up and differentiate himself from them while at the same time making the necessary accommodation to their demands. Individual happiness is the result of a dialogue which resolves the ever renewed conflicts between one's own desires and the desires of other individ-

uals. Depending on one's philosophy of life, this accommodation can spell itself out variously from a decision in favor of
the highest possible individual self-determination to a total
submersion of the self in the collectivity. In either case, however, the *will* arises out of the individual center and "attains"
its end, which is the consciousness of individual achievement,
the sense that one's individual existence has been justified,
that one's natural desires have been satisfied due to the fact
that one has made "the right choice." One has, in a word,
turned up with a winning ticket in the lottery of life, not only
by good luck but also by an astute and careful selection of a
number that seemed likely to win. Put in these terms, we see
that there is still a great deal of magic in our individualistic
thought, no matter how scientific may be the terminology by
which it is justified.

Such is the project which the Western mind instinctively
sets itself in life. A man sets his mind on something, he uses
his will and energy to get it, and when he has it he keeps it,
enjoys it, rests in it, if necessary protects it. Happiness consists
in the full conscious certitude that he has in fact attained
what he sought, that it is and remains his possession. But the
basic tenet of Buddhism is that an identity built on this kind
of consciousness is false. Such a "self" has no metaphysical
status. If it exists at all, as a valid possibility, it can only be
realized and enjoyed momentarily, and when it passes, it
leaves behind it suffering, death, and the whole train of evils
which are rooted in "craving." Such a consciousness is nothing but the illusory fire which is kindled by craving (*The
Fire Sermon*). The consciousness which lies at the heart of
Zen is quite different from this dialectic of craving, striving,
and rest. It rests not in attainment but in non-attainment,
and, really, the whole question of rest and attainment becomes irrelevant to it. So also do other questions like the conflict between the individual and society, and the casuistical
problems of behavior which result from it. In such a context
the question of ends and means becomes totally different—it

cannot be formulated in our Western terms, which still approach it in terms of cause and effect. Therefore, the *koan* (a paradigm of life itself) cannot be treated as a problem having a solution (end to be attained) which can be arrived at by setting certain *causes* into operation. If the Zen student is pushed to the limit, urged to force himself onward in his struggle with the logically meaningless *koan,* even to the point of near breakdown, it is not in order that he may cause an effect, attain a limited result, but in order that he may learn to get along definitively without any illusory need to attain anything or to rest in anything that accrues to him from "outside" in the guise of an object.

Koan study does not enhance the individual self with a new and special efficiency in attaining its particular ends, in causing its desires to be fulfilled. It seeks rather to liberate the individual consciousness from desires by dissolving its very individuality. Indeed, "individuality" and "desire" are the same thing, in this view of man. It is not as if the "individual" were a hard, substantial, ontological core from which desires proceed, but rather that desires themselves form a kind of knot of psychic energies which seeks to remain firmly tied as an autonomous "self." This knot is certainly real, in the empirical sense of the word—no question about that. But this does not mean that one can draw conclusions such as: "The reality of the knot is an ultimate value to be preserved at all costs" or "It is better for the knot to remain tied than for it to be untied." Buddhism "brackets" all these value judgments by the basic assumption that in the end all the knots will be untied anyway. Hence it denies any special value to the limited and transitory experience of "self" which is constituted by the little knot of desires tied for us by our heredity and our moral history (*karma*). It urges us to dissolve this limited subjectivity—this "consciousness of our self, our desires, our happiness or unhappiness"—into a *pure consciousness* which is limited by no desire, no project, and no finite aim. Such a consciousness will be in a sense "unconscious," but this term must not be negatively understood. On the contrary, the lack of a limited and restricted consciousness, the freedom of the consciousness that has no finite object, is in fact the highest and most positive affirmation. In it, "no" rejoins "yes," and all affirmations and negations are swallowed up in the ineffable —in the famous "Mu" of Joshu's *koan* for beginners:

Question: "Does the dog have Buddha nature or not?"
Answer: "MU!"

Pure subjectivity is then no subjectivity: "Consciousness is void and void is consciousness; void does not differ from consciousness, consciousness does not differ from void. Whatever is consciousness, that is void . . . whatever is void, that is consciousness. Therefore, it is because of his indifference to any personal attainment that a Bodhisattva . . . dwells with his thought completely naked" [i.e., not clothed with forms, objects, or even with a consciousness of self—an ego] (*Prajna-paramita Sutra*).

III

But is all this totally foreign to the West? It is certainly alien to the Cartesian and scientific consciousness of modern man, whose basic axiom is that his "cogitating" consciousness ("clothed with ideas of objects") is the foundation of all truth and certitude. (For the Buddhist, on the contrary, this individually self-aware consciousness is the root of all error and suffering.) Yet in the West there has been a long mystical and apophatic tradition. "Faith," for St. John of the Cross, is a "Dark Night of the Soul," since instead of giving us knowledge of objects, it empties us of all such knowledge in order to lead us to God by unknowing. "If one should say to a man that on a certain island there is an animal which he has never seen, and give him no idea of the appearance of that animal, that he may compare it with others that he has seen, he will have no more knowledge or imagination of it than he had before, however much is being said to him about it." This is a Western text that gives us a rather good insight into the Zen type of consciousness, showing that the same kind of pure consciousness exists in apophatic Christian mysticism. This is in no sense a "consciousness of." He who insists on "imagining" something like the invisible and unimaginable object (of faith) only deludes himself by clothing his mind in "coverings," whereas the consciousness of "pure faith" (and hence of mystical contemplation) is naked and obscure. So, as St. John says, "It is clear then that faith is dark night for the soul, and it is in this way that it gives it light; and the more it is darkened, the greater light comes to it." [4] This is the same kind of awareness as is taught by the Zen doctrine of no-mind. As a Zen master said: "To see where there is no something (object): that is the true seeing, that is the eternal seeing." [5] On the psychological level, there is an exact correspondence between the mystical night of St. John of the Cross and the emptiness of *sunyata*. The difference is theological: the night of St. John opens into a divine and personal freedom and is a gift of "grace." The void of Zen is the natural ground of Being—for which no theological explanation is either offered or desired. In either case, however, whether in attaining to the pure consciousness of Zen or in passing through the dark night of St. John of the Cross, there must be a "death" of that ego-identity or self-consciousness which is constituted by a calculating and desiring ego.

St. John of the Cross says:

The darkness which the soul here describes relates, as we have said, to the desires and faculties, sensual, interior and spiritual, for all these are darkened in this night as to their natural light, so that, being purged in this respect, they may be illumined with respect to the supernatural. For the spiritual and the sensual desires are put to sleep and mortified so that they can experience nothing, either Divine or human; the affections of the soul are oppressed and constrained so that they can neither move nor find support in anything; the imagination is bound and can make no useful reflection; the memory is gone; the understanding is in darkness, unable to understand anything; and hence the soul likewise is arid and constrained and all the faculties are void and useless; and in addition to all this a thick and heavy cloud is upon the soul, keeping it in affliction, and, as it were, far away from God. It is in this kind of "darkness" that the soul says here it travelled "securely."

The reason for this has been clearly expounded; for ordinarily the soul never strays save through its desires or its tastes or its reflections or its understanding or its affections; for as a rule it has too much or too little of these, or they vary or go astray, and hence the soul becomes inclined to that which behoves it not. Wherefore, when all these operations and motions are hindered, it is clear that the soul is secure against straying because of them.

It follows from this that the greater is the darkness wherein the soul journeys and the more completely is it voided of its natural operations, the greater is its security. It follows clearly, then, that by walking in darkness, not only is the soul not lost, but it has even greatly gained, since it is here gaining the virtues.[6]

A modern *Roshi,* Miura, echoes this teaching:

When we enter the Sodo the first instruction we receive is "give up your life!" It is easy to pronounce the words "give up your life!" but to do so is a difficult matter. However, if we do not put an end once and for all to that which is called "self" by cutting it off and throwing it away, we can never accomplish our practice. When we do, a strange world reveals itself to us, a world surpassing our reckoning, where he who has cast away his self gains everything and he who grasps for everything with his illusory concepts in the end loses everything, even himself.[7]

I V

In Rilke's Eighth Duino Elegy we encounter a deep aspiration for pure consciousness:

We've never, no, not for a single day
pure space before us, such as that which flowers
endlessly open into: always world,
and never nowhere without no: that pure
unsuperintended element one breathes
endlessly knows, and never craves.[8]

Since the poet was sympathetic toward Buddhism and curious about it, there is no question that we find here a genuine Buddhist flavor, as in many of his other poems. But this is not foreign to the Western contemplative tradition as expressed, for instance, in Eckhart and the Rhenish mystics. That *"nowhere without no"* (a mysterious expression) is the void of *sunyata* and the emptiness of Eckhart's "Ground" or, perhaps more properly, Boehme's "Un-ground" (*Ungrund*). "God," said Boehme, "is called the seeing and finding of the Nothing. And it is therefore called a Nothing (though it is God Himself) because it is inconceivable and inexpressible."[9] This is more theological than Rilke, who simply reports on the poetic phenomenology of the innocent "out-gazing" proper to the child, against which the child is systematically educated. Culture teaches man to "be opposite," to *stand against* objects, and to be never anything else but a subject confronting objects:

Always facing creation, we perceive there
only a mirroring of the free and open
dimmed by our breath.

The animal simply "gazes out" without any consciousness of a center which gazes.

. . . its own being for it
is infinite, inapprehensible,
unintrospective, pure, like its outgazing.
Where we see future, it sees Everything
itself in Everything, forever healed.

We, on the other hand, have been "turned around," and we are always aware of ourselves as spectators. This spectatorship is a wound in our nature, a kind of original sin (here Rilke is in the Christian tradition of the Church Fathers and the mystics), for which "healing" is urgently required. Yet we refuse healing because we insist on preserving our status as spectators. This is the only identity we understand. Once we cease to "stand against" the world, we think we cease to exist. Furthermore, we manipulate the world as we contemplate it, we rearrange it to suit the whim and yearning of our vision. Always, do what we may, we are condemned to "retain the attitude of someone who's departing." That is to say, we can never really believe ourselves fully at home in the world that is ours, since we are condemned to dwell in it as spectators, to create for ourselves the distance that establishes us as subjects fully conscious of our subjectivity.

> And we, spectators, always, everywhere,
> looking at, never out of, everything!
> It fills us. We arrange it. It collapses.
> We rearrange it, and collapse ourselves.

This throws an admirable light on the "pure consciousness" of Zen, the consciousness that has not fallen into self-consciousness, separateness, and spectatorship. The pure consciousness (as also the apophatic mystical intuition) does not look *at* things, and does not ignore them, annihilate them, negate them. It accepts them fully, in complete oneness with them. It looks "out of them," as though fulfilling the role of consciousness not for itself only but *for them also*. This is certainly a deep spiritual insight on the part of Rilke. The "outgazing" of this Duino Elegy throws important light on the characteristic Rilkean "in-seeing" (*Einsehen*). In-seeing implies identification, in which, according to Rilke's normal poetic consciousness, the subject is aware of itself as having penetrated by poetic empathy into the heart of the object and being united with it. But sometimes, as in the Eighth Elegy,

Rilke carries this further. The poet becomes the conscious expression, not of himself seeing and singing, but of the singing being which is his object and inspiration. He feels *"for,"* sings *"for,"* is aware *"for"* the object. He becomes the subject of the object. In Rilke, then, consciousness *of* is transformed by poetic creativity into consciousness *for,* and this consciousness resides, properly speaking, neither in the subject nor in the object but in the poem which transcends them both, as the expression of that world of inwardness (*Weltinnenraum*) in which both have their true reality.

This unusual ability to yield himself to the object and submit to its ontological and poetic splendor made Rilke very vulnerable. Hence, to protect himself from being absorbed completely by "the other," and especially by the clinging and demanding "love" of other people, he felt he had to defend his own self, his own identity, his own poetic and imaginative consciousness against encroachment by the minds and wills of others. This he explains in his version of the Prodigal's Return (*The Notebooks of Malte Laurids Brigge*). The Prodigal (Rilke!) runs away when he realizes that his imaginative and creative world is not enough protection against the will and the demand of parents, seeking to impose on him *their* intentions and projects for his being. He returns home when he is strong enough to protect himself against their love, and they interpret his gesture of refusal and self-defense as an appeal for forgiveness. This shows, incidentally, how fully the poetic identity in Rilke remains an ego-identity.

These notes on Rilke are appropriate here because the Rilkean poetic consciousness is sometimes confused with the "pure consciousness" of Zen. This is a mistake. It is true that Rilke could aspire, as we have seen, to pure and innocent consciousness, to liberation from a limited ego-identity, to that "not-face which belongs to our darkness" and which we might share with the animals.[10]

But, unfortunately, his consciousness is exclusively poetic, aesthetic, and for the reason that we have seen, he must defend this poetic identity, because, if he did not, it might simply be submerged in Dionysian feeling. This vulnerability to feeling and to ecstasy made it impossible for Rilke to attain definitively to the "out-gazing," which would possibly, in fact, have silenced his poetic voice. Instead, he wrote his greatest poems in honor of the Orphic savior. For Rilke needed a Savior, to lift him above the torrent of feeling. But Zen is a way of insight rather than a way of "salvation." If insight is itself regarded as salvation, it comes from within the ground of being, not from a gift of love, as in Christianity.

V

At this point, since we are discussing insight and enlightenment, or "ways of seeing," it may be well to speak of the testimony of "seeing" which has been left to us by paleolithic cave art. It seems to me wrong to speak of this art as merely representational, photographic, realistic, and so on. Still more absurd to explain it exclusively in terms of the pseudo-causality of magic. Is it not a much more valid hypothesis to suppose that here we have the witness of "pure seeing" and "out-gazing" not yet complicated by subjective awareness and reflection? Certainly this may have been part of a religious and animistic context, but it is not until the formal patterns and the sense of design of the neolithic art that we can speak of the beginning of a specifically *artistic* consciousness. The great paleolithic art was quite possibly what we ought to call pre-artistic. Was it not a conscious pre-artistic celebration of pure visibility? What is expressed in cave art is not the "realistic" shape of the animal (the more realistic, the better, since the ability to "make real" the image supposedly gives the hunter power over the real animal, etc., etc.). The extraordinary vitality of cave art springs from the *realization of seeing*. Cave art does not tell us merely what a bison looks like (there is all the difference in the world between a cave painting and a photograph). This is not the bison of the zoologist, nor is it simply the bison of a supposed (and utterly nonexistent) self-conscious paleolithic man who dwells on the fact that he likes bison meat. Cave art neither represents the object nor expresses the reaction of the subject: it celebrates the *act of seeing* as a holy and transcendent discovery.[11] It embodies that discovery in the work, the image. The creation of the image is not then simply ordered to the exercise of a causal (magic) power over the "reality," but is a reality in itself. It "is" the animal which is not only hunted but also worshipped at the same time, not only killed but also venerated in an act of communion with life (upon which of course primitive man would be the last to "reflect"). It "is" the animal itself *as seen,* as made luminous and transcendent by the act of vision. If we think of cave art in the light of the pure consciousness which is the aim of Zen practice, we will, I think, get rid of the preposterous theory of magic cave-art advertisements for bison meat. We will also see how in fact paleolithic art seems to have transmitted its spirit to Chinese (then Japanese) calligraphy and painting, more than to the more formal and design-conscious arts of the West (which was perhaps more subject to neolithic influences).

There is no lack of *koans* that express this kind of "pure seeing," not in the negation of images but in a simple, concrete image, poetic or otherwise.

A monk once said to Foketsu Osho: "Speech and silence tend toward separation [from It] or concealment [of It]. How shall we proceed so as not to violate It?"

Fuketsu replied with the following verse:

"*I always remember Konan in the spring*
The partridges crying and flowers spilling their fragrance." [12]

Riku No said: "The Dharma Master Jo has said: 'Heaven-and Earth and I have one and the same source; the ten thousand things and I have one and the same body.' Is this not extraordinary?"

Pointing to a flower in the garden Nansen replied: "When men of today look at this flower, it seems to them like a dream." [13]

VI

Zen meditation is not quietist tranquillity, and Zen practice is not tolerant of drifting. It repeatedly demands and even forces an active response. That is the function of the *koan,* of the long periods of *zazen* meditation (upon the *koan*), and the frequent interviews with the *Roshi* in which the student reports on his progress in *koan* study. What does the *Roshi* look for, and often provoke, even with a certain violence? *Personal response.* The purpose of *koan* study is to learn to respond directly to life by practicing on the *koan,* that is to say, by striving to meet the *koan* with an adequate and living response. What the *Roshi* wants is not a correct answer or a clever reaction but the *living and authentic* response of the student to the *koan.* If he finally responds directly and immediately to the *koan,* he shows that he is now able to respond fully, directly, and immediately to life itself.

Jade is tested by fire, gold is tested by a touchstone, a sword is tested by a hair, water is tested by a stick. In our school one word or one phrase, one action or one state, one entrance or one departure, one "Hello!" or one "How are you!" is used to judge the depth of the student's understanding, to observe whether he is facing forward or backward. If he is a fellow with blood in his veins he will immediately go off shaking his sleeves behind him and though you shout after him he will not come back.[14]

The last lines of this quotation must not be understood to mean that mere rudeness is an adequate indication of Zen enlightenment. It refers to the student's ability to "move on" and not stop at the question or the answer or the logical implications of words and acts. If he is alive, he will move. To study a *koan* is to learn not to be stopped by it, not to hesitate in the presence of a difficulty which is only illusory. To know where to go next without interminable figuring and discussions. To have no plans for "causing effects" and "getting results."

In other words, the *Roshi* does not want an analysis of the flower, or a poetic description of the flower, but existential proof that the disciple has really seen the flower and is no longer dreaming. Hence the famous *koan:* "Why did Bodhidharma come from the west?" (i.e., "What is the secret or the ultimate meaning of Zen?"). Answer: "The cypress tree in the courtyard," or even "That post over there." What is required is not the ability to repeat some esoteric formula learned from a book or from a *sesshin* in the monastery but actually to *respond* in a full and living manner to any "thing," a tree, a flower, a bird, or even an inanimate object, perhaps a very lowly one. Zen masters frequently took their examples from the monastery latrine, just to make sure that the student should know how to "accept" every aspect of ordinary life and not be blocked by the mania of dividing things into holy and unholy, noble and ignoble, valuable and valueless. When one attains to pure consciousness, everything has infinite value. (This is important to note, as opposed to the general idea that Buddhism simply negates and abstracts from all concretely existing things. Nothing could be more misleading.)

Here we must remember that *response* is something more than *reaction*. Response involves the whole being of man in his freedom and in his capacity to "see" and "move on." Reaction is nothing more than the mechanical, perhaps astutely and dishonestly improvised, answer of one's superficial self. And this reminds us of the importance of a *Roshi* in Zen practice.[15] The *Roshi* is skilled and experienced enough to tell when the student is merely reacting and when he is really responding. But here a problem arises: there are hints everywhere, especially in Kapleau, that many *Roshis* have failed to measure up to their responsibility in this matter. If a *Roshi* too easily certifies that a student has attained a *satori* enlightenment when in fact he has not, this will have a telling effect on Zen itself. The one who is now supposedly "enlightened" may go forth and teach others in his turn, and their enlightenment will be no better than his. Indeed, Kapleau even suggests that in certain monasteries monks have been known to "sell" to students the answers that will get them by the *Roshi*. This is understandable in the case where the student is not really interested in enlightenment but simply wants to pass his course so that he can be ordained and get his own temple as a Zen priest. It is also understandable where in fact a recognized Zen-attainment gives one a clear identity and status in a certain social or cultural context. Where this is the case, "replies" and "solutions" may easily come to acquire an orthodox classification. Then *koan* study tends to be formalized and institutionalized. One wonders if the "Zen Phrase Anthology" of over forty pages, in Miura and Sasaki's work, though very interesting, does not represent a danger of this kind of formalization. In other words, does not too rigid an emphasis on *koan* study lead to the student's forging himself an official identity as "one who has attained" something, realizing an idealized image of himself as securely "enlightened"? A misuse of the *koan* would lead to a further reinforcement of the "self" it is supposed to liquidate. Instead of opening the way to a spontaneous and immediate grasp of being, it would set up an impassable block between the mind and reality, enclosing the student in a little arbitrary world of formulas, gestures, habits, and routines. The end would be the thinly disguised boredom of a formalized existence justifying itself with verbal gymnastics and half-understood rituals. Ultimate meaning is sought no longer through the insight of a fully liberated consciousness but in the devoted and correct use of means which become ends in themselves. In all forms of institutional religion we find this same tendency to formalism and degeneration. Bassui said this in the fourteenth century:

One who lacks a genuine thirst for Self-realization digs up old Koans and reasoning out "answers," considers himself enlightened. You must not become attached to anything you realize, you must search directly for the subject that realizes. Thus, like something burnt to a crisp or slashed to bits, your preconceived notions will all be annihilated. You will perceive the Master only after you have probed "What is it?" with your last ounce of strength and every thought of good and evil has vanished. Not until then will you feel like one who has actually been resurrected.[16]

The context of this statement is interesting. In a letter of "direction" (as we would say) to a nun, Bassui is warning her that mere resting in a state of peace and tranquillity is not enough. Even this tranquil state of mind must be broken through to find "the Master" who is further "within" than this sensible peace.

VII

To sum it all up: the purpose of the Zen *koan* is to bring the student by ardent and severe interior practice, and the guidance and supervision of his *Roshi,* to a state of pure consciousness which is no longer a "consciousness of." The *koan* is a means of breaking through the following problems and false solutions. First, the intellectual "answer" that merely produces a formal explanation of the content of the *koan.* Then the sentimental, emotional, or simply affective reaction of feeling, whether religious or aesthetic, joyous or despairing, positive or negative.

Intensive meditation on the *koan* in a monastic setting tends to break in upon the historical continuity of a social and conventional self and to initiate a new and more deeply inward personal "history" of more sincere searching and response, in isolation from ordinary social pressures and stimuli. From this viewpoint, the *koan* provides a kind of phenomenological "bracketing" of ordinary, accepted life-views and versions of one's own self-significance. It is a more drastic application of Husserl's epoché. But the *koan* also cuts across the incursion of visions, hallucinations, or seemingly extraordinary supernatural experiences. The *koan* is a rock on which these are dashed to pieces (as St. Benedict would have the young monk dash to pieces all selfish thoughts on the "Rock" which is Christ). The *koan* also prevents one from remaining tranquil in a peaceful, thoughtless void, analogous to what is called in the Western tradition the "prayer of quiet." It seeks to break through even this contemplative peace, good though it may be. Peace is not enough. There is always danger of narcissism and regression. Nor is the first stage of self-realization, the grasp of "one's original face before one was born," in *Kensho,* quite sufficient. On the other hand, the absolutely pure consciousness of the Zen experience is not negation and annihilation of concrete existent beings. It implies the complete acceptance of them as they are, but with a totally transformed consciousness which does not see them as objects, but which, so to speak, "gazes out" from the midst of them. The final awakening of the Zen consciousness is not simply the loss of self, but the finding and gift of self in and through all.

The terms in which all this is expressed are those of what may be called in general a philosophic monism. The first instinct of the Western reader is to tag it as "pantheistic," but I would hazard the suggestion that one of the functions of the *koan* is also to break through this "pantheist" ideological crust which so easily forms around the Oriental type of inwardness. It would seem that in effect the true Zen consciousness, as described, ought to be so ontologically sound a grasp of being that the metaphysical vagueness of pantheistic rationalizations would no longer suffice to describe it. What is it, then? Hakuin says:

> Never ask your teachers to explain. But when your activity of mind is exhausted and your capacity for feeling comes to a dead end, if something should take place not unlike the cat springing upon the mouse or the mother hen hatching her eggs, then a

great flash of livingness surges up. This is the moment when the phoenix escapes from the golden net and when the crane breaks the bars of its cage.[17]

The importance of this Zen intuition of reality is, in my opinion as a Catholic, its metaphysical honesty. It refuses to make a claim to any special revelation or to a mystical light, and yet if it is followed on, in line with its own vast and open perspectives, it is certainly compatible with a revelation of inscrutable freedom, love, and grace. In point of fact, we must always remember that Zen is situated in the religious context of a Buddhism which seeks the "salvation" of all creatures by insight. In this context, insight is extraordinarily well defined and salvation extremely vague. In Christianity the revelation of a salvific will and grace is simple and clear. The insight implicit in faith, while being deepened and expanded by the mysticism of the Fathers and of a St. John of the Cross, remains obscure and difficult of access. It is, in fact, ignored by most Christians. Zen offers us a phenomenology and metaphysic of insight and of consciousness which has extraordinary value for the West. But the cultural accretions and trappings of Zen, the customs and mores of the *Zendo*, while retaining a special interest, no longer have the living power they had in the Middle Ages. Like the Catholic liturgy, Zen practice calls for an *aggiornamento*.

THE OTHER SIDE OF DESPAIR

Notes on Christian Existentialism

Ten years ago, conservative writers were already engaged in a definitive summing up of the "existentialist revolt." What had begun, they said, in the eccentric religiosity of Kierkegaard had ended in the open rebellion of Sartre against all that was decent and sane: and now it had even penetrated Catholic thought with the contagion of situation ethics. But the Church was on the watch, the warning had been sounded. Indeed, the encyclical *Humani Generis* may have been the reason why Gabriel Marcel repudiated the title "existentialist." After a short and competent mopping-up operation in the theological reviews, another victory would be enshrined in the revised editions of the theological manuals, and all would continue in good order. And there can be no question that the existentialism of the forties and fifties was dangerous to Catholicism in many ways. Atheistic existentialism still is!

Outside the Church, even the existentialist philosophers were tending to close up accounts. In 1949, F. H. Heinemann was already asking, "What is alive and what is dead in existentialism?" He was concluding, not without some justification, that existentialism regarded *as a philosophical system* is a contradiction in terms, and was therefore dead even before it tried to live. He added that what was alive in existentialism was the metaphysical problem it raised. However, in asking a somewhat tedious question Heinemann gave us further reason to complain, as Mounier had done, that "a philosophy whose purpose is to drag us away from our idle gossiping" itself tends to degenerate into gossip.

The question Heinemann asked was: "Are the existentialists the spiritual leaders of our time?" This is resolved into another question: "Are they leading us out of our crisis or into a blind alley?" The answers were respectively no and yes. Sartre, the most influential of the existentialists, is for Heinemann at best a pseudo-leader. On the other hand, he does not concern himself with Camus, who, he says, is "not an existentialist." But by 1965 Camus was exercising a very positive influence in America, especially on those concerned with civil rights and avant-garde political positions. And his influence was certainly as "existentialist" as Kierkegaard's, for instance.

However, since these questions belong to the realm of journalism and of academic gossip, I do not intend to get sidetracked into a discussion of them. The fact that existentialism is *less discussed* today than it was in 1950 or 1955 does not mean that it has ceased to be active. However, its activities, I would say, can be soberly estimated today as far less nefarious and perhaps a great deal more useful than they were then thought to be. We can now safely admit the existence of a Christian existentialism active not only in philosophy but also in the renewed Biblical theology which has been so eloquent and so salutary in the years of Vatican II.

If, in talking about existentialism, we distinguish between the "movement," the gossip about the movement, and the cogent reality of existentialist thinking, we can perhaps say that both the movement and the gossip about it are a great deal less actual now than they were ten, fifteen or twenty years ago.

The "existentialist movement" ("revolt") is associated in the popular mind with the French literary existentialists, especially the austere and ironic genius of Camus, lost to us in death, and the bitter Sartre of World War II, also to a great extent lost, or transformed, in his own current brand of Marxism. It is true that, in canonizing Genet, Sartre has shown an undiminished aspiration to meet the popular need for existentialism to be scandalous, and, in refusing the Nobel Prize, he has improvised a hasty defense against being identified, himself, with the French literary establishment.

Is Sartre perhaps caught in his own vicious circle? He is probably right in saying that society *needs* people like Genet to be what they are. But is he right in assuming that the free acceptance of this evil lot, and the total commitment to evil as an act of revenge, is the way to authenticity and liberation? Is it not the logical fulfillment of society's perverse demand that the criminal be totally evil? Is it not then a final capitulation? Sartre should have accepted the reward which our confused and distraught society offered him! He earned it, in his own way.

The existentialism which is most active and of most vital interest to the Church today is neither as well publicized nor as thoroughly discussed as the literature of those earlier days: it is the existentialist theology, both Protestant and Catholic, which owes so much to Heidegger.

We must at once admit that the loaded word "existentialist" must here be used with great circumspection. It is still a term of opprobrium among Catholics, and people are still in the habit of blaming everything they fear or dislike upon it. To suggest that Karl Rahner, for instance, might be tinged with "existentialism" (he is to some extent a disciple of Heidegger) would in some circles be quite enough to damn him, but it would hardly be enough to convict him of being nothing more than a Catholic Sartre. That is the trouble with gossip. Since for various good reasons existentialism is still regarded as "dangerous," and since the function of gossip is, among other things, to permit people to enjoy danger vicariously, at no greater risk than that of being misled, we shall try in this article neither to excite nor to mislead.

Existentialism is still in the air. It influences the climate of theology, and before we dismiss it as completely pestilential, let us at least try to find out what it is.

Of course this is both difficult and deceptive. Existentialism is an experience and an attitude, rather than a system of thought. As soon as it begins to present itself as a system, it denies and destroys itself. Non-objective, elusive, concrete, dynamic, always in movement and always seeking to renew itself in the newness of the present situation, genuine existentialism is, like Zen Buddhism and like apophatic Christian mysticism, hidden in life itself. It cannot be distilled out in verbal formulas. Above all, the journalistic clichés about existentialist nihilism, pessimism, anarchism, and so on, are totally irrelevant, even though they may have some foundation in certain existentialist writings. It is my contention that these writings cannot fairly be taken as representative of genuine existentialism.

Rather than attempt still another abstract and technical definition of something which, in itself, is neither abstract nor technical, let us begin with a concrete example. Existentialism has expressed itself most unambiguously in literature, where it is free from technicalities and quasi-official formulas. Literature offers us an example quite close to home, in the novels and short stories of Flannery O'Connor. I can think of no American writer who has made a more devastating use of existential intuition. She does so, of course, without declamation, without program, without distributing manifestoes, and without leading a parade. Current existentialism is, in fact, neither partisan nor programmatic. It is content with the austere task of minding its own literary, philosophical, or theological business.

A casual consideration of the "good" and the "bad" people in Flannery O'Connor will help us to appreciate the existentialist point of view—that point of view which is so easily obscured when it presents itself in terms of a program. For example, in her story, "A Good Man Is Hard to Find," evil is not so much in the gangsters, so fatally and so easily "found," as in the garrulous, empty-headed, folksy, sentimental old fool of a grandmother. Not that she is deliberately wicked, but the fact is, she does get everybody killed. It is her absurd and arbitrary fantasy that leads them directly to the "good man" and five deaths. She is a kind of blank, a void through which there speaks and acts the peculiar nemesis that inhabits (or haunts) the world of Flannery O'Connor—and doubtless ours too, if we could but see it as she did. This frightening action of Sophoclean nemesis in and through the right-thinking man who is null and void is spelled out in its full and public identity in types like Rayber, the positivist schoolteacher in *The Violent Bear It Away*.

The first thing that anyone notices in reading Flannery O'Connor is that her moral evaluations seem to be strangely scrambled. The good people are bad and the bad people tend to be less bad than they seem. This is not in itself unusual. But her crazy people, while remaining as crazy as they can possibly be, turn out to be governed by a strange kind of sanity. In the end, it is the sane ones who are incurable lunatics. The "good," the "right," the "kind" do all the harm. "Love" is a force for destruction, and "truth" is the best way to tell a lie.

Rayber is, by all standards, the kind of person our society

accepts as normal, not only a sane man but a kind one. A teacher, a man with forward-looking and optimistic perspectives, illuminated and blessed with a scientific world view, he is acquainted with all the best methods for helping people to become happy and well adjusted in the best of all possible societies.

It is he who sees through nonsense, prejudice, and myth. It is he who gets the Bible student to sleep with the frustrated girl from the woods, to relieve her tensions and open her up to a more joyous and fulfilled mode of life. It is he who, when their child is born, wants to protect him against the fanatic uncle, the prophet and believer. It is he who suffers permanent damage (deafness) trying to liberate the boy from the awful trammels of obscurantism and superstition. Rayber is our kind of man, is he not? A sound and practical positivist, well adjusted in a scientific age. True, he is not a Catholic, but we have plenty of Catholics who think more or less as he does, and he could perhaps be persuaded that we too are reasonable.

Yet as we read Flannery O'Connor we find an uncomfortable feeling creeping over us: we are on the side of the fanatic and the mad boy, and we are against this reasonable zombie. We are against everything he stands for. We find ourselves nauseated by the reasonable, objective, "scientific" answers he has for everything. In him, science is so right that it is a disaster.

Such is the dire effect of reading an existentialist.

Rayber wants to help the wild boy to find himself, to forget the madness he learned from the prophet, to become a docile and useful citizen in a world of opportunity where he can at last have everything. Rayber will not count the cost in sacrifice that must be paid. "Now I can make up for all the time we've lost. I can help correct what he's done to you, help you to correct it yourself . . . This is our problem together."

It was perhaps not kind of the boy, Tarwater, to be so suspicious of the world of reason, psychiatry, and togetherness, or to look with such an ugly glint upon the teacher's hearing aid. ("What you wired for?" he drawled. "Does your head light up?")

Alas, we share his cruel satisfaction. We have come to agree that the positivist Mephistopheles from Teachers College is a pure void, a mouthpiece for demons.

> "I forget what color eyes he's got," the old man would say, irked. "What difference does the color make when I know the look? I know what's behind it."
>
> "What's behind it?"
>
> "Nothing. He's full of nothing."
>
> "He knows a heap," the boy said. "I don't reckon it's anything he don't know."
>
> "He don't know it's anything he can't know," the old man said. "That's his trouble. He thinks if it's something he can't know then somebody smarter than him can tell him about it and he can know it just the same. And if you were to go there, the first thing he would do would be to test your head and tell you what you were thinking and how come you were thinking it and what you ought to be thinking instead. And before long you wouldn't belong to yourself no more, you would belong to him."

This, in brief, is the existentialist case against the scientism and sociologism of positivist society. It is a brief for the person and for personal, spiritual liberty against determinism and curtailment.

The old man was doing Rayber no injustice. This is precisely what his *hubris* consists in: the conviction that the infinite rightness and leveling power of "scientific method" has given him a mandate to transform other people into his own image: which is the image of nothing. And though he is "nothing," yet others, he knows it well, must do things his way since he has science on his side.

If, for Flannery O'Connor, the mild, agnostic, and objective teacher is not so much evil as pure void, and if this is what it means to be a villain—this will to reduce everyone else by an infallible process to the same void as oneself—we begin to understand existentialism in its passionate resistance against the positivist outlook. We also begin to see why, after all, existentialism is no immediate danger in a society almost entirely inclined to the consolations of sociometric methods.

Existentialism offers neither attractions nor peril to people who are perfectly convinced that they are headed in the right direction, that they possess the means to attain a reasonably perfect happiness, that they have a divine mandate to remove anyone who seems inclined to interfere with this aim. Existentialism calls into question the validity, indeed the very possibility, of such an aim. But, for positivism, its rightness is never in question. Nor, indeed, is its nature. The positivist does not even need to be quite sure where he is going. The direction must be the right one, since it is determined by his processes and by his scientific method. For him, the only question that really matters is *how* to keep on moving faster and faster in the same direction. Philosophy reduces itself to knowing how: *know-how*. The question *what* is relatively insignificant. As long as one knows *how*, the *what* will take care of itself. You just initiate the process, and keep it going. The *what* follows. In fact, the *how* tends more and more to determine the *what*.

The question *who* also turns out to be irrelevant except insofar as it is reducible to a *how*. That is to say that what matters is not the person so much as the position he occupies, the influence he wields, the money he makes, and his general usefulness in getting things done, or at least his place in the machinery of society. Thus, a man is identified not by his character but by his function or by his income, not by what he is but by what he has. If he has nothing, he does not count, and what is done to him or with him ceases to be a matter of ethical concern.

Pragmatism and positivism are therefore interested in the question *how*. Traditional metaphysics, whether scholastic (realist) or idealist, is interested in the question *what* (the essence). Existentialism wants to know *who*. It is interested in the authentic use of freedom by the concrete personal subject.

The objective truth of science remains only half the truth —or even less than that—if the subjective truth, the true-being (*Wahrsein*), of the subject is left out of account. This true-being is not found by examining the subject as if it were another object. It is found in personal self-realization, that is to say, in freedom, in responsibility, in dialogue (with man and God), and in love. Existentialism is, in other words, concerned with authentic personal identity, and concerned with it in a way that behaviorist methods and psychometry can never be. (The tests are neither interested in nor capable of finding out *who* thinks, only with describing *how* he reacts.) The chief complaint that sets existentialism over against positivism in diametric opposition is this: the claim of science and technology to expand the capacity of the human person for life and happiness is basically fraudulent, because technological society is not the least interested in values, still less in persons: it is concerned purely and simply with the functioning of its own processes. Human beings are used merely as means to this end, and the one significant question it asks in their regard is not *who* they are but *how* they can be most efficiently used.

At this point, we might go back a hundred years to consider a prophetic page of Kierkegaard's, from *The Present Age*. Here he describes the process of "leveling" and of "reflection," related to what has come to be called "alienation" and "estrangement" in more recent existential thought.

The process which Kierkegaard calls "leveling" is that by which the individual person loses himself in the vast emptiness of a public mind. Because he identifies this abstraction with objective reality, or simply with "the truth," he abdicates his own experience and intuition. He renounces conscience and is lost. But the public mind is a pure abstraction, a nonentity. "For," says Kierkegaard, "the public is made up of individuals at the moments when they are nothing," that is to say, when they have abdicated conscience, personal decision, choice, and responsibility, and yielded themselves to the joy of being part of a pure myth. The mythical being which thinks and acts for everybody, and does the most shameful of deeds without a moment of hesitation or of shame, is actually no being at all. Those who take part in its acts can do so insofar as they have abstracted themselves from themselves and have surrendered to the public void, which they believe to be fully and objectively real: this collective self whose will is the will of nobody, whose mind is the mind of nobody, which can contradict itself and remain consistent with itself. "More and more individuals, owing to their bloodless indolence, will aspire to be nothing at all—in order to become the public." Therefore, Kierkegaard concludes, the public is an "abstract whole formed in the most ludicrous way by all the participants becoming a third party (an onlooker)." This process of leveling, of self-abandonment, of abdication of identity, in order to dare what nobody dares and to participate in the unthinkable as though one were an innocent bystander, sweeps through the world as a "hopeless forest fire of abstraction." "The individual no longer belongs to God, to himself, to his beloved, to his art or his science; he is conscious of belonging in all things to an abstraction to which he is subjected by reflection (estrangement) just as a serf belongs to an estate . . . The abstract leveling process, that self-combustion of the human race produced by the friction which arises when the individual ceases to exist as singled out by religion, is bound to continue like a trade wind until it consumes everything."

The existentialist is aware of this danger above all. He tirelessly insists that it is the great danger of our time, since it is completely prevalent both in the capitalist positivism of

America and in the Marxist positivism of the Communist countries. For this reason, the existentialist is condemned everywhere for a wide variety of reasons which usually boil down to this one: he is a rebel, an individualist, who, because he withdraws from the common endeavor of technological society to brood on his own dissatisfactions, condemns himself to futility, sterility, and despair. Since he refuses to participate in the glorious and affluent togetherness of mass society, he must pay the price of fruitless isolation. He is a masochist. He gets no better than he deserves.

Of course, this criticism implies considerable overemphasis on one particular kind of existentialism—that of Sartre, for instance—which lends itself to facile caricature as lawless, negative, profligate, and generally beat. The moral conclusion drawn from this by the mass media, for example, is that nonconformity is, today more than ever, fatal. Not to submit to "leveling" is to become a weirdie. Only the public is fully human. The private sphere can no longer be human except at the price of admitting the abstract and the general into its own intimacy.

To prove your docility, you have to be totally invaded by the public image and the public voice. If you do this, however, you will be repaid by a certain negative privacy: you will not be forced into a disturbing *personal* confrontation with other human beings. You will meet them as strangers and as objects that make no direct demand for love—or, if they do, the demand is easily evaded. So you play it safe by never turning off the TV, and never, under any circumstances, entertaining a thought, a desire, or a decision that is authentically your own. It is in the general void, the universal noise, that you remain alone.

All the existentialists have protested against this state of affairs. To cite two typical works: Karl Jaspers's *Man in the Modern World* and Gabriel Marcel's *Man Against Mass Society*. Authentic "existence" (in defense of which one becomes an "existentialist") is contrasted with the bare inert *Dasein,* the "being there" of the lumplike object which is alienated man in the mass, man in the neuter, *das Mann. Dasein* is the passive, motiveless mode of being of the individual who simply finds himself thrown arbitrarily, by inscrutable fate, into a world of objects. He is a die in a crap game. He neither accepts nor rejects himself, he is incapable of authentically willing to be what he is, he submits to the process. It is the only reality he knows. He is intent on one thing above all: the mental and social gymnastics by which he remains at the same time a participant and a spectator, public and private, passively involved and emotionally distant in the amorphous public mass in which we are spectators and yet all somehow inexorably perform the enormities which the public "does." All see, all participate as though vicariously in the collective excitement (sometimes even the collective ecstasy) without really "being there" except as things, as fragments of the scene. All are aware, all consent, but consent safely because they are neutral. That is to say, they consent passively, they do not choose, they do not decide. They accept what has been decided by the public, that is, by nobody.

From the moment one elects to exist truly and freely, all this comes to an end. Decision begins with the acceptance of one's own finiteness, one's own limitations, in fact, one's own nothingness: but when one's own nothingness is seen as a matter of personal choice, of free acceptance, and not as part of the vast, formless void of the anonymous mass, it acquires a name, a presence, a voice, an option in the actions of the real world—not the abstract world of the public but the concrete world of living men.

Here we come upon a point that requires immediate clarification. Existentialism is not a withdrawal into unworldliness. It is not "monastic." Quite the contrary, it is a frankly worldly philosophy in the sense that it conceives no other realistic option than that of being a live man in the world of men. But the authentic world of men is, precisely, not the fictitious and arbitrary collective illusion of "the public."

The real contest between existentialism and its opponents is precisely about this: existentialism always claims in one way or another that the accepted, conventional forms of thought and life have in fact attempted to substitute a fraudulent world of unauthentic and illusory relationships for the real community of man with man. This, they would say, is obvious. A system which demands the abdication of personality by that very fact destroys all possibility of community. What we have then is a conflict between two concepts of community: on one hand, a false and arbitrary fiction, collectivist togetherness, in which all possibility of authentic personal existence is surrendered and one remains content with one's neutral quasiobjectified presence in the public mass; on the other, a genuine community of persons who have first of all accepted their own fragile lot, who have chosen to exist contingently, and thereby have accepted the solitude of the person who must think and decide for himself without the warm support of collective fictions. Only between such free persons is true communication possible. At the same time, such communication is absolutely necessary if there are to be free and mature persons, authentically existing, with faces, identities, and histories of their own. The authentic person is not born in stoic isolation but in the openness and dialogue of love.

The clue to this concept of community is found in the word *openness*. The world of *Dasein* is a world where all possibilities are closed to the individual who has *a priori* renounced his choice. As individual he is indifferent: he has surrendered his options, his capacity to determine the future by turning to this possibility or that. He has submitted to the abstract leveling force of "the public," "the party," "science," "business," or what you will. In this case, instead of open communication between personal freedoms, we have the submersion of atomized individuals in a general mass. We have a comforting routine of merely mechanical responses.

True openness means the acceptance of one's own existence and one's own possibilities in confrontation with, and in free, vital relation with, the existence and potentialities of the other. It means genuine acceptance, response, participation. It is here that the famous "I-Thou" of the Jewish existentialist Martin Buber has contributed so much to Christian personalism in our day. The world of *Dasein* and of objects is defined only by the "I-it" relationship. The "I" who regards itself as a purely isolated subject surrounded by objects also inevitably regards itself implicitly as an object. In a world where no one else, no "other," is willingly identified, the "I" also loses its own identity. In practice, the collective life of mass society is a mere aggregate of spurious and fictitious identities. On the one hand, we see the leaders or heroes who sum up in themselves the collective nonentity of the mass and become, so to speak, icons of the public void (see Max Picard's book *Hitler in Ourselves*); on the other, the alienated individuals who fabricate for themselves crude identities by contemplating themselves in the typological hero. Note that the word "alienation" is used by non-existentialists to support the fictions of collective life. For them, the "alienated" man is the one who is not at peace in the general myth. He is the nonconformist: the oddball who does not agree with everybody else and who disturbs the pleasant sense of collective rightness. For the existentialist, the alienated man is one who, though "adjusted" to society, is alienated *from himself*. The inner life of the mass man, alienated and leveled in the existential sense, is a dull, collective routine of popular fantasies maintained in existence by the collective dream that goes on, without interruption, in the mass media.

The freedom by which one delivers oneself from the tyranny of the void is the freedom to choose oneself without being determined beforehand by the public, either in its typological fantasies or in its sociological pressures. What then is the basis of this choice? In what sense can it be called unconditional? In the sense that it is made in and proceeds from the inviolate sanctuary of the personal conscience.

It is precisely here that atheistic existentialism proves itself to be so unsatisfactory and so inconsistent. According to Jaspers, Marcel, and all the other basically religious existentialists, conscience is incomprehensible except as the voice of a transcendent Ground of being and freedom—in other words, of God Himself. Hence, the basic choice by which one elects to have one's own personal, autonomous existence is a choice *of oneself as a freedom that has been gratuitously given by God.* It is acceptance of one's existence and one's freedom as pure gift.

In religious existentialism the blank, godless nothingness of freedom and of the person, Sartre's *néant,* becomes the luminous abyss of divine gift. The self is "void" indeed, but void in the sense of the apophatic mystics like St. John of the Cross, in whom the *nada,* or nothingness of the self that is entirely empty of fictitious images, projects, and desires, becomes the *todo,* the All, in which the freedom of personal love discovers itself in its transcendent Ground and Source which we are accustomed to call the Love of God and which no human name can ever account for or explain.

When this becomes clear, we immediately see why even non-religious existentialism is unconsciously oriented toward a religious view of life (if the word "religious" is qualified, as we shall soon see). For this reason also it can be said both that the religious existentialists probably outnumber the atheists and that even those who make no religious claims are, like Heidegger, spontaneously oriented to a religious view of man's destiny.

Taking a broad, random view of the field of existentialism, we see on the one hand Camus and Sartre, both of whom explicitly class themselves as atheists. We have Heidegger, who is non-religious. On the other hand, we have Jaspers, whose thought is basically theistic and even Christian; we have the Jewish existentialism of Buber, the Orthodox and gnostic existentialism of Berdyaev, the Buddhist existentialism of Suzuki and Nishida, the Protestant existentialism of Bultmann, Tillich, and others, the Catholic existentialism of Gabriel

Marcel and Louis Lavelle. It is true of course that both Marcel and Lavelle, and some others we have named here, have renounced the existentialist label. The fact remains that the most significant religious thought of our day, whether in philosophy or in theology, has been marked by "existentialist" insights into man's current situation. We remember also that Maritain and Gilson, while remaining faithful to St. Thomas and criticizing existentialism from a Thomist viewpoint, have themselves contributed in no small measure to a broadly existentialist Christian perspective (see Maritain's *Existence and the Existent*).

Here we must repeat that the popular connotations of the term are altogether misleading, and we must be quite clear that what we must understand by this is not some supposed infiltration into Catholic thought of negativism, disillusionment, and moral license. Christian existentialism is, on the contrary, associated with the return to a Biblical mode of thought which is entirely concrete and personal and, in fact, much more fundamentally Christian than the rather abstract and intellectualist approach that has been accepted as the "only" Catholic approach for almost seven hundred years.

Let us then consider the basic elements of the new existential theology in its implications for human freedom.

Years ago, Karl Adam, whom no one would think of calling an existentialist, protested against the routine Catholic notion of faith as an intellectual assent to dogmatic propositions, nothing more. Faith, he said, could never be reduced to "a purely intellectual and therefore shallow awareness of the teaching of the Church, and to a mere assent of the mind." Then he added this, which strikes the exact tone of the new Catholic theology and, we may add, the renewed perspective of faith as seen in the light of the Second Vatican Council.

Every "Credo," if said in the spirit of the Church, ought to be an act of complete dedication of the entire man to God, an assent springing from the great and ineffable distress of our finite nature and our sin.

Here we already see formulated the awareness which has been made completely explicit by Vatican II. We see the difference between two concepts of faith and of the Church. On one hand, there is the idea that the Church is primarily an official and authoritative public organization and the act of faith is the intellectual acceptance by the individual of what this organization publicly and officially teaches. Thus, the act of faith becomes a profession of orthodoxy and of regularity, a protestation of conformity (backed no doubt by sincere good will) in order to merit, so to speak, a religious security clearance. One's act of faith is then a declaration that one is a reliable member of the organization, willing to abide by everything that is publicly held by it, and to attack everything that opposes it. Such dogmatic professions of faith are of course necessary and right in certain circumstances. They have their proper place. But, as Karl Adam says, they do not exhaust the possibilities of true Christian faith.

To begin with, they do not take sufficient account of man's "existential situation." It is here that insights such as those of Jaspers and Heidegger can serve the theologian.

One can certainly subscribe in all sincerity to correct dogmatic formulas without the intimate spiritual ground of one's own existence being called into question. One can formally acknowledge that one is created and redeemed by God without showing any deep sense of being personally involved in a religious relationship with Him. Indeed, and this is always tragic both for the individual and for the Church, the mere formal acknowledgment of these truths can come to substitute in practice for any kind of intimate and personal surrender to God. Religion thus becomes a matter of formalities and gestures. "This people honors me with its lips and not with its heart."

In this case, we find ourselves confronted with the kind of

Christianity which Kierkegaard attacked precisely because it transferred into the religious sphere all the facticity, the routine, and the falsity of "abstract leveling." Instead of obeying the Word and Spirit of God living and active in His Church, the body of those who love one another precisely insofar as they have been freed from facticity and routine, one surrenders at the same time one's human and one's religious integrity. In effect, this is a spiritual disaster if we consider that the Church should be the one hope of alienated man recovering himself and his freedom. The Bible shows us, without equivocation, that human society itself is "fallen" and alienated. It estranges man from himself and enslaves him to delusion. The word of God calls man back out of this delusion to his true self. The Church has, as her first function of all, to disturb man and unsettle him in the world of facticity by challenging him to return to himself. *Metanoiete,* repent, change your heart, is the inexhaustibly repeated message of God's word to man in fallen society. He who hears this word cannot rest content with the "leveling" routine of mass society. Unfortunately, we see that, in fact, mass society is more and more curtailing the area of good ground on which the seed of the Gospel can germinate. At best, the soul of mass-man is a plot of thorns. Most of the time he is simply a wayside trampled by a restless and unmotivated multitude.

It is here that the Church, in her anxiety to enter into a dialogue with the modern world, must not hastily and unawares overlook the problem of evil and evade the challenge of atheist existentialism. If in trying to reply to the Marxists we take an exclusively optimistic view of man, of the world of science and progress, and of man's chances of solving all his problems here on earth, we find ourselves accused, by the existentialists, of consenting to certain mystifications that ignore the evils which actually confront man and the despair which meets him at every turn. Seeing this danger, one of the best modern Russian theologians, Father P. Evdokimov, of the Russian Orthodox Seminary in Paris, has written:

We must pay close attention to the existentialist question-ings, which have considerable philosophical strength. They overturn the naïvely joyous optimism of a religious philosophy in which evil serves as a good and hence ceases to exist as evil—a fact which makes the death of God on a Cross incomprehensible. It is precisely Sartre's claim that "God" diminishes the radical character of evil, of unhappiness, and of guilt.

The important thing, therefore, is not for Christians to be found ready, once again, with a glib religious answer for another modern question, but for us to reaffirm, in terms at once contemporary and deeply serious, the Christian message to man's liberty. We must reemphasize the call of the Gospel to healing and to hope, not merely reaffirm that everything is going to be all right because man is smart and will meet the challenge of evil with the best possible solutions.

It is at this point that the current concept of "religion" must be seriously examined and qualified.

If in practice the function of organized religion turns out to be nothing more than to justify and to canonize the routines of mass society; if organized religion abdicates its mission to disturb man in the depths of his conscience, and seeks instead simply to "make converts" that will smilingly adjust to the status quo, then it deserves the most serious and uncompromising criticism. Such criticism is not a disloyalty. On the contrary, fidelity to truth and to God demands it. One of the most important aspects of our current biblical-existential-ist theology is precisely the prophetic consciousness of a duty to question the claims of any religious practice that collaborates with the "process of leveling" and alienation.

This means that such theology will manifest a definite social concern and will, in the light of the Bible, identify and reject anything that compromises the standards of justice and mercy demanded by the word of God. It will identify these precisely by the measure of authentic respect and love for the human person. Thus, for instance, any claim that this or that policy or strategy deserves a "Christian" sanction and the blessing of the Church must be examined in the light of the principles we have seen. If in actual fact it amounts to the support of the abstract organization, granting or blessing a destructive power to coerce the individual conscience, it is to be rejected as fraudulent, as incompatible with Christian truth, and as disobedience to the Gospel commandment of love. In one word, the Church must not implicitly betray man into the power of the irresponsible and anonymous "public." If it does so, it will destroy itself in destroying true freedom and authentic human community.

We must certainly recognize the danger of individualism, but we must also be fully aware of where this danger really lies.

The false community of mass society is in fact *more individualistic* than the personalist community envisaged by the Gospels, the *koinonia* of intersubjective love among persons, which is the Church. Mass society is individualistic in the sense that it isolates each individual subject from his immediate neighbor, reducing him to a state of impersonal, purely formal, and abstract relationship with other objectified individuals. In dissolving the more intimate and personal bonds of life in the family and of the small sub-group (the farm, the shop of the artisan, the village, the town, the small business), mass society segregates the individual from the concrete and human "other" and leaves him alone and unaided in the presence of the Faceless, the collective void, the public. Thus, as was said above, mass-man finds himself related not to flesh and blood human beings with the same freedom, responsibility, and conflicts as himself, but with idealized typological images: the Führer, the president, the sports star, the teen singer, the space man.

It is by rigorously confining him within the limits of his own individual nonentity that mass society completely integrates the individual into the mass. The function of the Church is, then, not to intensify this process, giving it an inviolable religious sanction and tranquilizing the anguish of the alienated mind by injunctions to obey the state. It is precisely to strengthen the individual person against the one great temptation to surrender, to abdicate his personality, to fall and disappear in the void. "Man," says Heidegger, "wants to surrender to the world. He tempts himself. He flees from himself and desires to fall into the world. In his everyday talking and curiosity he prepares for himself a permanent temptation to fallenness." There is in this of course an inescapable element of existentialist jargon, but in substance it recalls the eschatological message of the New Testament.

If in fact the Church does nothing to counter this "temptation to fallenness" except call man to subscribe to a few intellectual formulas and then go his way with the rest of the crowd, she will have failed in her gravest responsibility. If, on the other hand, she misunderstands the seriousness of modern theology and lets herself be carried away with a specious enthusiasm for a space-age image of herself, she will equally fail.

While it is popularly supposed that "existentialism" has no other function than to allow man to do as he pleases, leaving him at the mercy of subjective fantasy and passion, removing him from the protective surveillance of social authority, we see that in fact the shoe is on the other foot. If existential theology is properly understood, we see that it unmasks the spurious social responsibility by means of which man flees from his true self and takes cover in the neutral, fallen world of alienation. The true rebellion against God today is not merely that of the defiant and promethean individual, but much rather that of the massive and abstract collectivity in which man in the neuter, *das Mann,* man in the anonymous mass, becomes serenely convinced of his inviolable security as master of his own destiny and of his world. In finding her place in the modern world, the Church must take care not to embrace or even canonize the *hubris* of technological society.

Where some forms of existentialism fail is in their inability to get beyond the individual's discovery and affirmation of himself standing outside of and apart from the neutral mass, and obliged to defend himself with all his power against exploitation or invasion by others. This is particularly true in the early Sartre, for whom *"L'enfer c'est les autres."* Neither his doctrinaire political positions nor his "cool" relationship with Simone de Beauvior can do anything to modify this judgment of Sartrian existentialism as closed to dialogue and genuine communion.

With Camus the problem is much more subtle and profound. One feels that few men in our time, Christian or not, were at once more soberly aware of the limitation of man in mass society and more open, in compassion and understanding, to his plight. *The Plague* is a novel of crisis and alienation in which a few men manage to prove themselves authentic persons by openness and availability in a mass of thoughtless, stupefied human beings. Here, incidentally, the Church is examined and found somewhat wanting in the person of a Jesuit priest who, in spite of a certain degree of heroism and self-sacrifice, remains insulated from human realities and from other men by the "official answers" with which he has already solved all problems in advance.

An existential theology is not one that claims to know all the answers in advance. It is concerned not with answers or with statements ("what," "how"), but with man's authentic existence (*who*). This depends on his capacity for dialogue with his fellow man, his ability to respond to the need of another, to waive his own anterior rights and claims in order to meet the other on a common ground. In a word, it depends on freedom and on love. Hence, it is by no means concerned (as Sartre appears to be) merely with the cool assertion of one's privacy. However, in existential *theology,* more is at stake than openness to others. Man cannot be genuinely open to others unless he first admits his capacity to hear and obey the word of God, to bear and to understand the inevitable anxiety of an estrangement from God and from his own inner truth. Since this call to authenticity is heard in the depths of the conscience, existential theology emphasizes the formation of conscience. It seeks at all costs to defend the personal conscience against distortion by the all-pervading influence of collective illusion. It is all too easy for conscience to be twisted out of shape by merely attending to the claims of worldly care. The care of one's own privacy and one's own liberty can be included as "worldly."

Existential theology focuses on grace and on love, rather than on nature and on law. It tends to view grace less as a supernatural quality modifying our human nature than as an event, an eschatological encounter with God, who, by His word, restores to us the capacity for authentic personal freedom, and the power to love in a "new creation." Far from being a further development in liberal and rationalistic dilution of the Gospel message, existential theology, because of its Biblical content, strongly emphasizes the obedience of faith, the surrender of the free person to Christ. Far from being a justification of disobedience, existential theology insists that it is only in the obedience of faith that we truly discover our authentic existence, our true selves. Though Heidegger is never explicitly Christian, this element of openness to grace, this capacity for obedience, is implicit in his philosophy, of which John Macquarrie has said: "Although Heidegger does not acknowledge it, his understanding of man brings us to the place where either the divine grace must intervene or all thought of an authentic existence must be given up entirely."

Existential theology is concerned with man in his world and in his time. The word of God, the dialogue of man and God, is not confined to a meditation on the Bible written two thousand years ago. In the light of Biblical revelation, the Christian feels himself challenged, summoned, addressed by God here and now in the events of our own confused and sometimes alarming history. But the Christian existentialist knows precisely that he cannot evade the present and fly from it into a safe and static past, preserved for him in a realm of ideal essences, to which he can withdraw in silent recollection. His recollection will be of no use to him if it merely serves him as a pretext for not being open to his brother here and now. The existential insistence on grace as event, as an ever renewed encounter with God and one's fellow man *now*, in present reality, in dynamic acceptance and availability, disturbs the idealistic and static outlook which treats grace as a "thing," a "commodity," to which one gains access by virtue of a spiritual secret, a ritual formula, or a technique of meditation.

Whatever one may say about it, Christian existentialism is not gnostic. It does not regard grace as a "supply" of light and fuel for the spiritual mansion in which one dwells in complacent isolation. It sees grace as an eschatological encounter and response, an opening of the heart to God, a reply of the Spirit within us to God our Father (Romans 8:15–16), in obedience of faith, in humility and openness to all men. Grace is sonship and dialogue, from which obstacles and limitations, whether of law, of nature, of sin, of selfishness, of fear, and even of death, have all been taken away by the death and resurrection of Christ. Grace is perfect and total reconciliation, in Christ, with one's true self, one's neighbor, and with God.

Writing in *New Blackfriars* (July, 1965), John Dalrymple (not a professed "existentialist") sums this up by saying: "The question is whether we today offer Christ to the world as a liberating person or an agent of restriction. If we are to show forth Christ as a liberating agent then we must first have entered into that liberation ourselves; we must have conquered our primal fears; we must first have prayed. This is the level at which modern theology has its greatest significance spiritually. Its insights draw us powerfully to prayer." This is important to remember because a superficial understanding of modern theology seems to end in restless activism, itself an illusion and an evasion.

Rudolf Bultmann has done much to bring out the Christian implications which he found to be latent in the existentialist philosophy of Heidegger, and Macquarrie says of him: "The whole aim of Bultmann's theology, including his views on demythologizing, is to spotlight the essential kerygma of the New Testament for men and women of our time and to bring it before them as the one relevant possibility that is still open for a bewildered world."

Hence, though the existentialism of Heidegger may seem to end up with stoic heroism in the presence of unavoidable death, Bultmann and other Christian theologians influenced by Heidegger have gone much further. They have convincingly restructured the classic theology of Christian and Gospel hope in the categories of existentialist freedom. This does not mean, however, that the revelation of God in Christ the Incarnate Word means the same to Bultmann as it does to the Catholic Church. Here we would indeed find serious divergences on the level of dogma. But, from the point of view of freedom and grace of *lived* experience, Bultmann's insights have their value for Catholics.

Far from being a negative cult of life-denying despair, existential theology challenges the sterility and the inner hopelessness, the spurious optimism and the real despair which masks itself in the secular and positivist illusion. For the fallen world there can be no genuine future: only death. But for Christian freedom there is an authentic future indeed. In fact, for the existentialists freedom would be worth nothing if it were not constituted by openness to a genuine future—a future liberated from the facticity of life in a depersonalized mass, free from the care and concern with mere "objects," free at last even from death.

At the same time, however, existential theology is recognizing that it must move further and further from the characteristic subjectivity of the early existentialism in order to achieve a genuine relatedness to and full participation in the world of nature and above all the world of man. Where the earlier existentialists regard "the other" with suspicion as a hostile force, and even tended to consider *all* communal life as a threat to individual integrity, the existential theologians look rather for a transformation of communal life by the leaven of Christian freedom and agape. This implies willingness to renounce suspiciousness, to be open to man and to his world, to freely participate in all the most cogent concerns of the world, but with a freedom of spirit which is immune to the forces of "leveling." This, it must be admitted, demands a certain maturity! But maturity cannot be acquired in withdrawal and subjective isolation, in fear and in suspicion. Maturity is the capacity for free and authentic *response*. Once again, this demands something more than psychological adjustment. It calls for divine grace. And our openness to grace is proportionate to our sense of our *need* for it. This in turn depends on our awareness of the reality of the crisis we are in.

The most serious claim to consideration which the existential theologian can offer is the cogent diagnosis of our trouble, and the complete sincerity, the total frankness with which he faces the basic Christian problems of death, sin, the wrath of God, grace, faith, freedom, and love. Where he is still admittedly weak is perhaps in his sense of Christian communion and of the Church. But let us not forget that in his sensitivity to the danger of an alienated and unfaithful church organization, the existentialist has done us a service, and warned us against the ever present peril of institutional complacency. There is no greater danger than this for the Church in the modern world, and we are daily reminded of the fact when we see how easily the faithful, even some of the hierarchy, yield to the temptation to identify the Church with the status quo, the public establishment, and to submerge the Christian conscience in the complex and dubious cares of an existence that is inauthentic because it is sociological rather than Christian.

BUDDHISM AND THE MODERN WORLD

Can Buddhism retain a place for itself in the modern world? Obviously this question cannot be answered intelligently if the ordinary Western clichés about Eastern religion are accepted. It must be admitted that some of the most sensational —and most earnest—efforts of Buddhist monks and nuns who have immolated themselves by fire are often simply baffling to Western man and seem to confirm his suspicion that Buddhism is a religion of nihilism and pure negation. Without commenting one way or the other on this extreme form of protest, we can simply remark that it is extreme and therefore not to be taken as typical. St. Simeon Stylites, too, had something very definite to say about the Gospel, and he said it by sitting on top of a pillar. Yet Christianity can be more calmly understood if we turn to the pages of St. Augustine, St. Thomas, Pascal, or Luther. At the present moment, the Buddhists who seem to have the most to offer the West are Zen-existentialists and phenomenologists. We shall examine here some recent writings, including articles published in Japan and a book published in South Vietnam.

Professor Shin'ichi Hisamatsu writes on "Zen: Its Meaning for Modern Civilization." This article appears in the first issue of *The Eastern Buddhist* (new series), a revival of the magazine published by associates of the late D. T. Suzuki.[1] This article directly and succinctly confronts the problem of a Zen humanism today, and raises typical questions, which it answers quite simply and directly, without recourse to apologetics. In an age in which traditional religious documents are being passed through the sieve of a most refined scientific criticism, the Buddhist sutras are no more fortunate than any other religious canon and may turn out to be in some respects more vulnerable than others. But Zen has always assumed, as one of its basic principles, that the enlightenment of the proficient Zen monk demands a certain freedom with respect to the authority of any literal canonical text. What the Zen man seeks to realize in himself is a "self-sustaining independence," and here the entire question of religious authority is raised. The aim of Zen is, according to Zenists, simply the aim of Buddhism itself, "the ultimate emancipation from duality." Hence, to maintain a concept of authority in which the (limited individual) self of the monk attains to perfection and illumination by remaining face to face with a Buddha who perfects and illuminates him from the outside would be to negate the whole meaning of Budhism. This is why to some Christians Buddhism seems to be "atheistic"— or "pantheistic." Suzuki and his associates claim that it is neither. God is neither affirmed nor denied by Buddhism, insofar as Buddhists consider such affirmations and denials to be dualistic, therefore irrelevant to the main purpose of Buddhism, which is precisely emancipation from all forms of dualistic thought. "The attainment of Buddhahood" is, then, not a matter of becoming "like Buddha" or even "transformed into Buddha." It is an ontological awakening to the ultimate ground of being, or the "Buddha which one is." "For Zen there is no true Buddha outside the man who is awakened to his True Self." This "True Self" (always capitalized in the *Eastern Buddhist*) is the Formless, Original Mind, the void, *Sunyata*. Suzuki has explicitly compared this concept to that of the Godhead in Meister Eckhart and the Rhenish mystics. Hence we have here no "God is dead" mythology.

Professor Hisamatsu is talking of the root problem of social and psychological alienation, a modern and Western term for a condition that Zen has been at grips with since it began: the condition of servile dependence on something which is really one's own but which is experienced as outside, above, more perfect than one's own self. Recent interest in the early manuscripts in which Marx developed this idea, which is taken by Revisionists to be really fundamental to Marxian humanism, shows that the approach of the Zen existentialist is not without a certain timely importance.

The ultimate resolution of the problem of authority, for Zen, is this: "In Zen, true authority is that Self which is itself authority and does not rely on anything. . . . True authority is where there is no distinction between that which relies and that which is relied upon." Comparing this with Marx, we see that the contemporary rigid forms of pseudoreligious Marxian orthodoxy seem to have no comprehension of the real implications of Marx's teaching on alienation and on the ultimate freedom which Communism is supposed to bring about. The great question, not only for Marxism, but for liberal democracy, for Christianity, and for Zen, is how, in practice, such freedom can be the possession of any but the rare few who have undergone the trouble, discipline, and sacrifice necessary to attain it. The pseudofreedoms of those who have bypassed illumination and arrived at pure autonomy in unregenerate dark must always remind us of the reality of this problem. Western literary existentialists have not contributed much to help us see the difference.

Living by the "basic authority which is the True Self," or metaphysically, in direct contact with the ground reality by "freedom from forms," the Zen man does not resolve all being into a pure Void but rather sees the Void itself as an inexhaustible source of creative dynamism at work in the phenomena that are seen before us and constitute the world around us. This world is illusory only insofar as it is misinterpreted to fit our prejudices about our limited ego-selves. This simple, direct approach to reality, this unabashed apprehension of the One in the Many, of the Void in everyday life and in the ordinary world around us, is the foundation for Zen humanism in the world of today.

Hence—and this will probably come as a surprise to Western readers, the very concept of Nirvana itself becomes dynamic and existential, a basically humanistic one. Reviewing Paul Tillich's book, *Christianity and the Encounter of World Religions,* Masao Abe writes: "Nirvana is nothing but man's realization of his existential True Self as the ultimate ground both of his ordinary self and the world opposed to it. . . . Nirvana is not simply transpersonal but also, at once, personal." [2]

According to Professor Hisamatsu, this approach to reality avoids two pitfalls: that of a degenerate, irrational, purely willful and anthropocentric humanism, and that of a return to ancient traditional and mythical concepts which leave no room for human autonomy at all. This traditional approach has become useless because it can do nothing but prescribe evasions and world-denying flights into antiquated and indeed illusory world views, estranged from the problems and needs of our time. The pseudoradical approach is deficient in that it does not attain to the reality which "is there" in the world around us. The Zen view, says Professor Hisamatsu,

will enable us to make a more proper attempt at a radical cure of the human predicament through the Self-awakening of that oneness which, contrary to being in estrangement from civilization, accords with, and is the source and base of civilization. Such an image of man entertained by Zen will also sweep away every internal and external criticism or misunderstanding of

Buddhism which takes it to be world-weary, world renouncing and removed from reality, longing for some ideal world in a sphere other than the historical world of time and space.

Thus, once again, we see that Nirvana is not an escape from phenomena and from the everyday world with its problems and risks, but a realization of that Void and True Self which is the common ontological ground of both personal freedom and the objective, problematical world.

Meanwhile, what about Zen and science? Professor Keiji Nishitani[3] turns demythologizing against science itself. In apparently destroying the teleological character of the universe, science has effectively disposed of anthropocentric myths—but at the same time it has rendered its own brand of humanism empty and ambiguous. How can a basis for a new humanism be discovered in a mechanistic universe that invites only to the creation of new delusions or to surrender and despair? Zen, says Nishitani, does not fear the Void but rather discovers in the Void itself the ground of religious existence which science had apparently dissolved. How? Not by nihilism but by a dialetic of the "Great Death" leading to new life, a life stripped of myth and naked of illusion. This discovery of the "dimension of bottomlessness" behind and in phenomena is, once again, characteristic of Zen enlightenment. But this dimension is never found "in front of us" as object. It is, on the contrary, "behind" us as the very subject or Self which is aware of Itself at once in us and in the world around us. All phenomena are thus accepted and so to speak "held in a bottomless basket." This is beyond the world of mere scientific process and the world of religious myth. In this, both science and religion accomplish a breakthrough to an "ecstatic" consciousness of ultimate reality. This consciousness is the basis and justification for all claims to a Buddhist humanism.

Anyone who heard the Vietnamese monk, poet, and intellectual Thich Nhat Hanh when he visited the United States in May and June of 1966 will be aware that Zen is not a flight from the most urgent problems of the age. Indeed, Thich Nhat Hanh, head of the Institute of Higher Buddhist Studies at Saigon, and a militant in the movement for peace and for the reconstruction of his country, seems to be one of the few men who have anything concrete and positive to say about the plight of Vietnam. His basic principles are exposed in a little book translated from Vietnamese into French,[4] which is a militant criticism of traditional and conservative Buddhism. Traditional Buddhism, formal, rigid, doctrinaire, is sterile, fit for the museum, irrelevant in the modern world, not because it is out of touch with current realities, but because it *is out of touch with human experience itself*. Once again we find ourselves on existentialist terrain, involved in a passionate critique of that alienation which substitutes ideas and forms for authentically experienced realities. This sclerosis is of course common to all arbitrary and purely authoritarian orthodoxies, whether in religion, politics, culture, education, or science.

The basic aim of Buddhism, says Nhat Hanh, arises out of human experience itself—the experience of suffering—and it seeks to provide a realistic answer to man's most urgent question: how to cope with suffering. The problem of human suffering is insoluble as long as men are prevented by their collective and individual illusions from getting directly to grips with suffering in its very root within themselves. To set up party, race, nation, or even official religion as absolutes is to erect barriers of illusion that stand between man and himself and prevent him from facing his own reality in its naked existential factuality. In this case, says Nhat Hanh, the various world views, whether religious or political, may concur in the error of providing man with a refuge, and with stereotyped formal answers which substitute for genuine thought, insight, experience, and love. One must break through these illusory forms and come directly to grips with suffering in ourselves and in others. The aim of Buddhism is then the creation of an entirely new consciousness which is free to deal with life barehanded and without pretenses. Piercing the illusions in ourselves which divide us from others, if must enable man to attain unity and solidarity with his brother through openness and compassion, endowed with secret resources of creativity. This love can transform the world. Only love can do this. It comes as no surprise to know that Nhat Hanh is an intelligent and ardent reader of Camus, as well as of Bonhoeffer.

For Nhat Hanh, therefore, Nirvana is not an escape from life, but is to be found right in the midst of "life, suffering and death." This is, of course, a modern expression of the pure Mahayana ideal, that of the Bodhisattva.

Perhaps the best chapters of this book are those devoted to the phenomenological grasp of reality in Buddhist terms. At the origin of all suffering is the ignorance which, not knowing how to grasp reality, atomizes and distorts it to fit the demands of a perverse, obstinate set of prejudices. In order to see rightly, one must recognize the essential interdependence, impermanence, and inconsistency of phenomena. On the basis of a correct *perception* (not a correct *interpretation,* please note), one may proceed then to correct—that is to say, *realistic* —action.

In his last chapter, Thich Nhat Hanh frankly faces the problem: can there be a Buddhist humanism in a society where a half-dead, half-ossified traditionalism identifies "Buddhism" with a decaying social structure? There is only one answer: a radical renewal of the Buddhist experiential grasp of reality within the framework and context of a bitter, agonizing social struggle, and in terms that are comprehensible to those who are most deeply involved in that struggle. This formula applies not only to Buddhism but to every religion that seeks to find its real place in the world of today.

It must not, however, simply be assumed that Buddhism is now preaching a naïve and activistic doctrine of revolution by force. Masao Abe[5] questions rather astutely the Western acceptance of a "will to transform others" in terms of one's own prophetic insight accepted as a norm of pure justice. Is there not an "optical illusion" in an eschatological spirit which, however much it may appeal to *agape,* seeks only to tranform persons and social structures *from the outside?* Here we arive at a basic principle, one might almost say an ontology of nonviolence, which requires further investigation.

NOTES

Mystics and Zen Masters

1. *Matter and Spirit: Their Convergence in Eastern Religions, Marx and Teilhard de Chardin.* Religious Perspectives, Vol. 8 (New York, Harper & Row; 1963), 218 pp.

2. *Hindu and Muslim Mysticism* (London, 1960).

3. Heinrich Dumoulin, S.J.: *A History of Zen Buddhism,* translated by Paul Peachey (New York, Pantheon Books, 1963), 365 pp.

4. Dumoulin: *The Development of Chinese Zen,* translated by Ruth Fuller Sasaki (New York, First Zen Institute of America, 1953), 146 pp., with additional notes and appendices.

5. *A History of Zen Buddhism,* pp. 200–1.

6. *A History of Zen Buddhism,* pp. 214–15.

7. D. T. Suzuki: *Essays in Zen Buddhism,* Series III (London, 1958), p. 23.

8. The exact meaning of the Chinese is apparently: "The clear mirror is without stand." In other words, the duality, body-soul, is treated as irrelevant to Zen enlightenment.

9. *Essays in Zen,* Series III, p. 25.

10. *Development of Chinese Zen,* p. 51.

11. *Essays in Zen,* Series III, p. 42.

12. Ibid., p. 30.

13. Ibid., pp. 34, 35.

14. Compare the doctrine of Nicholas of Cusa: since the infinite is all, it has

no opposite and no contrary. It is at once the maximum and the minimum, and is the perfect coincidence of all contraries. Hence it explodes the Aristotelian principle of contradiction. Nicholas of Cusa, like the Zen masters, affirms and denies the same thing at the same time, when speaking of the infinite. For him, admission of the coincidence of opposites is the "starting point of the ascension to mystical theology." A remark of Gilson's shows how perfectly Nicholas of Cusa agrees with Hui Neng: "Nicholas exhorted his readers to enter the thickness of a reality *whose very essence, since it is permeated with the presence of the infinite* [i.e., "the Unconscious"], *is the coincidence of opposites.*" (*History of Christian Philosophy in the Middle Ages*, p. 536.)

15. *Esays in Zen*, p. 39.

16. *History of Zen Buddhism*, pp. 91–2. Emphasis added.

17. D. T. Suzuki: *The Zen Doctrine of No-Mind* (London, 1958), p. 26. He adds that for this reason Hui Neng is the true father of Chinese Zen.

18. Ibid.

19. Ibid., p. 28.

20. *History of Zen Buddhism*, p. 156.

21. Ibid.

22. Ibid., p. 159.

23. Ibid., p. 164.

24. Ibid.

25. Ibid.

26. Ibid.

27. St. John of the Cross: *Ascent to Mount Carmel, Dark Night of the Soul*, passim.

28. Suzuki: *The Zen Doctrine of No-Mind*, p. 45.

29. While the proofs of this book were in my hands I received the last piece of writing published by Dr. Suzuki. It was an introduction to a book of a friend, Zenkei Shibayama, *A Flower does not Talk* (Kyoto, 1966). The introduction was written by Dr. Suzuki the day before his death. It closes with these remarkable words, which throw light on the passage just quoted. Suzuki said: "Let us not forget that Zen always aspires to make us directly see into Reality itself, that is, be Reality itself so that we can say along with Meister Eckhart that: 'Christ is born every minute in my soul' or that 'God's Isness is my Isness.' Let us keep this in our minds as we endeavour to understand Zen. . . ." As the final statement of a great Zen master, this gives food for thought.

Classic Chinese Thought

1. *Sources of Chinese Tradition,* compiled by Wm. Theodore de Bary, Wing-Tsit Chan, Burton Watson (New York, Columbia University Press, 1960), 976 pp. Arthur Waley: *Three Ways of Thought in Ancient China* (Doubleday Anchor Book, 1956), 216 pp. Liu Wu-Chi: *Short History of Confucian Philosophy* (Pelican Books, 1955), 229 pp. *Confucius, the Great Digest and the*

Unwobbling Pivot, translation and commentary by Ezra Pound (New York, New Directions, 1951), 187 pp.

2. Quotations from the *Tao Te Ching* are taken from *Sources of Chinese Tradition,* pp. 57 and 59.

3. *Short History of Confucianism,* p. 96.

4. Ibid.

5. *Three Ways of Thought in Ancient China,* pp. 161 and 167.

6. *Summa Theologica,* I, Q. xiv, a. 8.

7. *Religion and Culture* (New York, Meridian Books, 1959), p. 171.

The Jesuits in China

1. George H. Dunne, S.J.: *Generation of Giants* (University of Notre Dame Press, 1962).

From Pilgrimage to Crusade

1. Mircea Eliade: *Myths, Dreams and Mysteries* (London, 1960), pp. 59–72. See also, by the same author, *The Myth of the Eternal Return.*

2. *Le Pèlerinage d'Ethérie,* Latin text and French trans. by Hélène Petré (Paris, Sources Chrétiennes, 1948).

3. *La Vie de Moïse,* Greek text and French trans. by Jean Daniélou, 2nd edition (Paris, Sources Chrétiennes, 1955).

4. Valerius of Vierzo: *Epistola de B. Echeria,* P.L. 87:424. See also the important article by Dom Jean Leclercq: "Monachisme et pérégrination du 9e au 12e siècles," *Studia Monastica,* Vol. 3, fas. 1 (1961), pp. 33–52. This study traces the development from *stabilitas in peregrinatione* to *peregrinatio in stabilitate.*

5. For example, St. Silvinus, St. Ulric, etc., wished to venerate Christ in the very place where He had accomplished the mysteries of salvation. Leclercq, op. cit., pp. 37–9, 43.

6. H. Von Campenhausen: *Die Asketische Heimatlösigkeit* (Tübingen, 1930). Dom L. Gougaud: *Christianity in Celtic Lands* (London, 1932), pp. 129 ff. N. K. Chadwick: *The Age of Saints in the Early Celtic Church* (London, 1961). Professor Chadwick calls this "one of the most important features of Irish asceticism and its chief legacy to after ages," p. 82.

7. *Adomnan's Life of Columba,* ed., with translation and notes, by the late Alan Orr Anderson and by Marjorie Ogilvie Anderson (Edinburgh, 1961), "de Scotia (Ireland) ad Britanniam *pro Christo peregrinari volens* enavigavit," p. 186.

8. *Navigatio Sancti Brendani abbatis,* ed. by Carl Selmer (Notre Dame, Univ. Publication in Medieval Studies, 1959).

9. See quotations from the Icelandic *Landnámbók* (eleventh or twelfth century) in *Christianity in Celtic Lands,* p. 132. Also a quote from *De Mensura*

Orbis by Dicuil (ninth century) in L. Bieler: *Ireland the Harbinger of the Middle Ages* (London, 1963), p. 119.

10. Leclerq, op. cit., pp. 34, 36.

11. Quoted in Chadwick, op. cit., p. 83. Cf. Leclerq, op. cit., p. 36. See also Leclerq: "La Séparation du monde dans le monachisme du moyen âge" in *La Séparation du Monde: Problèmes de la religieuse de d'aujourd'hui* (Paris 1961), p. 77.

12. Leclercq: "Monachisme et pérégrination," passim., esp. pp. 37, 39, 41.

13. Mircea Eliade: *Myths, Dreams and Mysteries.* Cf. Anselm Stolz, O.S.B.: *Théologie de la Mystique* (Chevetogne); Dom G-M Colombas, O.S.B.: *Paraiso y vida angélica* (Monserrate, 1958).

14. Chadwick: op. cit., pp. 82–3. Kathleen Hughes: "The Irish Monks and Learning," *Los monjes y los estudios* (Poblet, 1963), pp. 66 ff. Eleanor Shipley Duckett: *The Wandering Saints of the Early Middle Ages* (New York 1959), pp. 24–5.

15. Adomnan: op. cit., I.6., "(Cormac) tribus vicibus herimum in ociano laboriose quaesivit . . ." pp. 222–4.

16. Bieler: op. cit., p. 119.

17. *Navigatio Brendani,* c. 11. pp. 22 ff.

18. Dom H. Leclercq, O.S.B.: "Celle," D.A.C.L., ii, 2870, and "Reclus," D.A.C.L., xiv, 2149 ff. Rotha Mary Clay: *The Hermits and Anchorites of England* (London, 1914). P. McNulty and B. Hamilton: "Orientale Lumen et Magistra Latinitas—Greek Influences on Western Monasticism (900–1100)," *Le Millénaire du Mont Athos* (Chevetogne, 1963), esp. pp. 197–9, 216. Gougaud: *Ermites et Reclus* (Ligugé, 1928).

19. O. Doerr: *Das Institut der Inclusen in Suddeutschland* (Münster, 1934).

20. Chadwick: op. cit., pp. 36, 37, 50–3.

21. See H. Leclercq: "Pèlerinages à Rome," D.A.C.L., xiv, 53–4. This applies more to Franks than to Celts, who were less enthusiastic about pilgrimages to Rome. Witness this ancient verse: "To go to Rome is great labor. The King you seek you will not find unless you bring Him with you." However, St. Moluca, disciple of St. Maedoc, pleaded with his master for permission to go to Rome: *Nisi videro Romam cito moriar.*

22. J. Leclercq: "Monachisme et pérégrination," pp. 42–3.

23. See M-L Soejstedt: *Dieux et héros des celtes,* quoted in R-Y Creston: *Journal de Bord de Saint Brendan* (Paris, 1957), p. 221.

24. See Kenneth Jackson: *A Celtic Miscellany* (Cambridge, Mass., 1951), pp. 301 ff. G. Murphy: *Early Irish Lyrics* (Oxford, 1956). Bieler: op. cit., p. 57.

25. Aussi la pérégrination continue-t-elle a être présentée comme un forme d'érémitisme, et, comme telle, dans la logique de la vie monastique. "Monachisme et pérégrination," p. 41.

26. L. Vogel: "Le Pèlerinage pénitentiel," *Revue des Sc. Rel.,* XXXVIII, 2, 1964, pp. 113 ff. Poschmann: *Penance and the Anointing of the Sick* (New York, 1964). Chadwick: op. cit., p. 103.

27. Chadwick notes that the Scilly Isles had been a penal settlement in Roman times and that some Priscillianist heretics had been sent there. She also cites the questionable tradition of St. Columba's exile for a sin of violence

(op. cit., p. 102). Vogel (op. cit., p. 127) does not think the medieval penitential practice of exile is traceable to Roman law.

28. Council of Seligenstadt, 1022/23. Vogel: op. cit., pp. 143–4.

29. Vogel: op. cit., p. 118.

30. Numerous references given in Vogel, pp. 130–1.

31. *Canones sub Edgaro Rege*, England, tenth century, quoted by Vogel, p. 127.

32. St. Gregory of Tours: *Hist. Franc.*, VI, 6. H. Leclercq: "Pèlerinages à Rome," D.A.C.L., xiv, p. 52.

33. D.A.C.L. One penitent even carried an identification in Latin verse by Venantius Fortunatus, id. 52, on *litterae tractoriae*. See Vogel, p. 133.

34. D.A.C.L., xiv., p. 60.

35. See penitential of Vinnian, n.23, quoted in Bieler, p. 52. Chadwick, p. 102.

36. Le Pèlerinage pénitential aboutit en fait à sélectionner les pires criminels et à les lancer sur les chemins. Vogel, p. 130.

37. Ep. 289.

38. See the famous letter of St. Boniface to Cuthbert of Canterbury (MGH. Epp. III, 78, p. 354), of which Vogel says that it "constitutes a sociological document of the highest order" (op. cit., p. 140).

39. Rule of St. Benedict, C. 38, cf the quotation of I Cor. 5:5 in the Rule, C. 25.

40. Vogel, p. 126.

41. St. Peter Damian: Opusc. XII., 9–14, 20–25. PL 145:260 ff. G. Peno: "Il Capitulo de Generibus Monachorum nella Traditione Medievale," *Studia Monastica*, 1961, 41 f. J. Leclercq: "Le Poème de Payen Belotin contre les faux ermites," *Rev. Ben.*, 1958, pp. 52 ff.

42. Vogel, p. 145.

43. Ibid., p. 146. Cf. PL 140, 952.

44. Vogel, p. 135.

45. For a complete list of places of pilgrimage, see Vogel, p. 135.

46. *Hagiologium Cistercianse*, Aug. 1.

47. Texts quoted by J. Leclercq: "Monachisme et pérégrination," pp. 40–9.

48. On ne peut s'empêcher de penser que de tels récits étaient, en quelque sorte, les romans d'aventures des moines du moyen âge. J. Leclercq: "Monachisme et pérégrination," p. 40.

49. J. Leclercq, in Leclercq, Vandenbroucke, Bouyer: *Histoire de la Spiritualité Chrétienne*, Vol. II, p. 165.

50. Pilgrims, being foreigners, were naturally suspect, but Moslems usually understood the idea of pilgrimage, which plays a central part in the religion of Islam. St. Willibald was arrested in Edessa in 723 but released when an aged Moslem assured the police that he had many times seen Christians like this one "fulfilling their law." H. Leclercq: D.A.C.L., xiv, p. 163.

51. Vogel, pp. 128–9.

52. Ibid., p. 129, see references.

53. Mourret-Thompson: *History of the Catholic Church* (St. Louis, 1941), Vol. IV, p. 282.

54. J. Leclercq: *Histoire de la Spiritualité Chrétienne,* Vol. II, p. 166. See references to Dupront, Rousset, etc.

55. Ibid., p. 167.

56. St. Bernard: Letter 458 and *De Laude Novae Militiae.*

57. Mourret-Thompson: op. cit., p. 283.

58. Ch. E. Delaruelle: "L'Idée de croisade chez S. Bernard," *Mélanges S. Bernard* (Dijon, 1953), p. 57.

59. St. Bernard: Letter 363. Cf. Bruno James: *Letters of St. Bernard* (Chicago, 1953).

60. Delaruelle: op. cit., p. 58.

61. Oderic Vital: *Historia Ecclesiastica,* ix, PL 188:652.

62. Delaruelle, p. 54.

63. Delaruelle, p. 66.

64. C. Selmer: "The Vernacular Translations of the *Navigatio Brendani,*" *Medieval Studies,* xvii, 1956, p. 150.

65. H. B. Workman: *Evolution of the Monastic Ideal,* reprint (Boston, 1962), p. 196*n.*

66. *De Imagine Mundi,* I., 36, PL 172:132.

67. W. H. Babcock: "St. Brendan's Explorations and Islands," *Geographical Review,* July, 1919, pp. 37–46.

68. *The Book of the Foundations,* in the *Complete Works of St. Theresa,* translated by E. Allison Peers (New York, 1946), Vol. III.

69. Jean-Paul Sartre: *No Exit.* This expression sums up the existentialist's meditation on hell.

70. G. Basetti-Sani, O.F.M.: *Mohammed et Saint François* (Ottawa, 1959).

Virginity and Humanism
in the Western Fathers

1. E. R. Curtius: *European Literature and the Latin Middle Ages* (New York, 1961), Bollingen Series, XXV, p. 315.

2. Epistola XXII, *Ad Eustochium,* n. 30, PL 22, col. 416 (vide infra.).

3. Illustrior portio gregis Christi. St. Cyprian: *De Habitu Virginum,* c. 1. PL 4, col. 440.

4. Op. cit., c. 1, PL 4, col. 440.

5. Clarificemus et portemus Deum in puro et mundo corpore. Idem., 442.

6. St. Jerome: Epistola XXII, *Ad Eustochium,* n. 38, PL 22, col. 422. Also: Vidi viros corrumpentes virgines in doctrinis haereticis et vanam facientes virginitatem earum. A. Wilmart: "Les Versions Latines des Sentences d'Evagre," *Revue Bénédictine,* XXVIII, 1911, pp. 148–51.

7. St. Jerome points out that Christ is not a proud and arrogant Spouse, in implied contrast to men of this world. Epistola XXII, n. 1, PL 22, col. 395. Cf. same letter, n. 2, and n. 18 (col. 405) for allusions to the sufferings of married life, but he goes on to point out that virginal life is also a constant struggle.

8. Estote tales quales vos Deus artifex fecit, estote tales quales vos manus Patris instituit: maneat in vobis facies incorrupta, cervix pura, forma sincera. Op. cit., XXI, col. 459.

9. Servate, Virgines, servate quod esse coepistis, servate quod eritis. . . . Quod futuri sumus jam vos esse coepistis. Vos resurrectionis gloriam in isto saeculo jam tenetis. Op. cit., XXII, col. 462.

10. St. Ambrose: *De Institutione Virginis*, c. 17. Migne, PL 16, col. 331.

11. St. Jerome: Epistola XXII, *Ad Eustochium*, n. 20, PL 22, col. 406.

12. Libertate opus est et audacia. Quae sic in pace metuis, quid faceres in martyrio perpetiendo. St. Jerome: Epist. 130, *Ad Demetriadem*, n. 5, PL 22, col. 1109. Aula regalis est virgo quae non est viro subdita sed Deo soli. St. Ambrose: *De Institutione Virginis*, c. 12, PL 16, col. 324.

13. Stridor Punicae linguae procacia tibi Fescennina cantabit? Op. cit., 1109. This phrase is reminiscent of Catullus, 61:126: Procax fescennina locutio. "Fescenninan songs" were ribald extemporaneous verses sung by the guests at wedding feasts, made doubly offensive, Jerome suggests, by the harsh Punic accent of Roman Africa.

14. Solent miseri parentes et non plenae fidei Christiano, deformes et aliquo membro debiles filias, quia dignos generos non inveniunt, virginitati tradere. Op. cit., n. 6, col. 1111.

15. Migne, PL 16, col. 305 ff.

16. Ubi ergo tres isti integri, ibi Christus est in medio eorum: qui hos tres intus gubernat et regit ac fideli pace componit. Haec igitur tria integra prae caeteris in se virgo custodiat. Op. cit., cap. 2, col. 309. This is the classical tripartite division of man into *anima* (psyche), *animus* (nous), and *spiritus* (pneuma). Cf. William of St. Thierry: Epistola ad Fratres de Monte Dei, Lib. I, cap. V, PL 184, col. 315 ff.

17. Advertimus itaque per mulierem caeleste illud impletum esse mysterium Ecclesiae, in ea gratia figuratam, propter quam Christus descendit, et aeternum illud opus humanae redemptionis absolvit. Unde et Adam vocavit nomen mulieris suae Vitam; nam et in populis per mulierem successionis humanae series et propago diffunditur, et per Ecclesiam vita confertur aeterna. Op. cit., cap. 3, col. 311.

18. Mulier excusationem habet in peccato, vir non habet . . . Culpa tua illam absolvit. Ibid., cap. 4, col. 311.

19. Pro te mulier doloribus suis militat et remunerationem ex pena invenit ut per filios per quos affligitur, liberetur. Facta est itaque gratia ex injuria, salus ex infirmitate. Cum salute itaque parit quos in tristitia parturivit. Ibid., col. 312.

20. Non est vitium mulieris esse quod nascitur, sed vitium viri est quaerere in uxore quo saepe tentatur. Ibid.

21. Non possumus reprehendere divini artificis opus sed quem delectat corporis pulchritudo, multo magis illa delectet venustas quae ad imaginem Dei est intus non foris comptior. Ibid., col. 312.

22. Quotidie mulieres jejunant . . . peccatum agnoscunt, accersunt remedium . . . Semel de interdicto mulier manducavit et quotidie jejunio solvit. Qui secutus es errantem, sequere corrigentem. Ibid., col. 313.

23. Ibid., c. 9, col. 320, 321. For *Ordo caritatis*, see St. Augustine: *De Doctrina Christiana*, Bk. i, cap. 27, PL 34, col. 29.

24. See St. Augustine: *De Doctrina Christiana*, especially Bk. ii., PL 16, col. 36 ff. Cassian: *Conlatio* XIV, "De Spirituali Scientia," PL 49:953 ff.

25. Porta clausa es virgo, nemo aperiat januam tuam quam semel clausit Sanctus et Verus qui habet clavem David qui aperit et nemo claudit, claudit et nemo aperit: APERUIT TIBI SCRIPTURAS, NEMO EAS CLAUDAT: CLAUSIT PUDOREM TUUM NEMO APERIAT EUM. St. Ambrose, op. cit., c. 9, col. 321.

26. Cf. John Cassian: *Conlatio* I, cc. 4–8, PL 49:485 ff.

27. Habeto ergo tecum hunc ignem in pectore tuo qui te resuscitet, ne frigus tibi perpetuae mortis irrepat. St. Ambrose: op. cit., c. 11, col. 323.

28. Semel mundo mortua ne quaeso tetigeris ne attiminaveris quae sunt istius saeculi: sed semper in psalmis et hymnis et canticis spiritualibus abducas te ab hujus saeculi conversatione non homini sed Deo cantans. Et sicut sancta faciebat Maria, conferas in corde tuo. Quasi bona quoque agnicula rumines in ore tuo praecepta divina. Ibid., cap. 16, col. 330.

29. Cibis praeferto doctrinam. St. Jerome: Epist. 22, n. 24, PL 22, col. 409.

30. Ibid.

31. Ibid., n. 17, col. 404.

32. *Speculum Charitatis.*

33. Tenenti codicem somnus obrepat, et cadentem faciem pagina sancta suscipiat. St. Jerome: op. cit., n. 17, col. 404.

34. Op. cit., n. 29, col. 416.

35. Ibid., n. 30, col. 416.

36. Epistola XXVII, *Ad Marcellam*, PL 22, col. 431, 432. Someone counted the number of classical quotations in Jerome's letters before and after this vision. They are most numerous in his later letters. See E. K. Rand: *Founders of the Middle Ages* (Cambridge, 1928).

37. Unde est tibi providendum ne ineptiis blanditiis feminarum, dimidiata dicere verba filia consuescat, et in auro atque purpura ludere: quorum alterum linguam, alterum moribus officit: ne discat in tenero quod ei postea dediscendum est. Epistola CVII, *Ad Laetam*, n. 4, PL 22, col. 872.

38. Ibid., col. 871.

39. Ibid.

40. Ibid.

41. Ibid., n. 9, col. 874.

42. Ibid.

43. Ibid., n. 11, col. 875.

44. Oratio lectioni, lectio orationi succedat. Ibid., col. 875.

45. Ibid.

46. Pro gemmis et serico divinos codices amet. Ibid., n. 12, col. 875.

47. Discat primo Psalterium et in Proverbiis Salomonis erudiatur ad vitam . . . In Ecclesiaste consuescat quae sunt mundi calcare . . . in Job virtutis et patientiae exempla sectetur . . . Ad Evangelia transeat numquam ea positura de manibus . . . Apostolorum Acta et Epistola tota cordis imbibat volunte. Cumque pectoris sui cellaria his opibus locupletaverit, mandet memoriae Prophetas, etc. . . . Ibid., n. 12, col. 876.

48. Ad ultimum sine periculo discat Cantica Canticorum. *Ibid.* Jerome adds that she must "beware of all the Apocrypha." Patristic studies are not to be neglected either: she must concentrate especially on St. Cyprian (Cypriani opuscula semper in manu teneat), Athanasius, and Hilary. St. Jerome is once again most concerned for the purity of virginal faith, which must conform perfectly to the mind of the virginal Church, thus reproducing in the world the faith of the Mother of God.

49. Virum bonum dicendi peritum a prima aetate suscipiens, per cunctas artes ac disciplinas nobilium litterarum erudiendum esse monastravit, quem merito ad defendendum totius civitatis vota requirerent. Cassiodorus: *Instituta*, II, ii, n. 10; Mynors, p. 104.

50. Ut in omnibus sensibus et operibus ejus Christus eluceat, Christum intendat, Christus loquatur. *De Institutione Virginis,* c. 17, col. 333.

51. Cum avum viderit in pectus ejus transiliat, collo dependeat, nolenti Alleluia decantet. Epistola 107, n. 4, col. 872.

The English Mystics

1. David Knowles: *The English Mystical Tradition* (New York, 1961).

2. Hugh Farmer: *The Monk of Farne* (Baltimore, 1961).

3. *The Medieval Mystics of England,* ed. with an introduction by Eric Colledge (New York, 1961).

4. *Un Educateur monastique: Aelred de Rievaulx* (Paris, 1959).

5. Thomas Traherne: *Centuries of Meditations* (New York, 1961).

6. Ibid., Introduction, p. xvi.

7. Ibid., p. 94.

8. Ibid., p. 91.

9. I am indebted to Etta Gullick for permission to quote from her unpublished manuscript of the seventeenth-century English text of Benet's *Rule of Perfection.*

10. *The Scale of Perfection,* in modern English by Dom Gerard Sitwell, O.S.B. (London, 1953), p. 83. See also Dom G. Sitwell: "Walter Hilton," *English Spiritual Writers,* ed. by C. Davis (New York, 1961).

11. *The Cloud of Unknowing,* translated and with introductory commentary by Ira Progoff (New York, 1957).

12. Ibid., p. 61.

13. See P. Molinari: *Julian of Norwich, the Teaching of a 14th Century English Mystic* (New York, 1958).

14. *Revelations of Divine Love,* in a new translation by James Walsh, S.J. (London, 1961).

15. Ibid., p. 53.

16. Ibid.

17. Ibid., p. 83.

18. In *Poets and Mystics* (London, 1953).

19. C. Pepler: "Richard Rolle," *English Spiritual Writers,* ed. by C. Davis

(New York, 1961). Cf. Pepler: *The English Religious Heritage* (London, 1958).

Self-Knowledge in Gertrude More
and Augustine Baker

1. All Biblical quotations are taken from the *Confraternity Version.*

2. *Rule of St. Benedict,* Ch. 7, ed. by Dom J. McCann (Westminster, Md., 1952), p. 49.

3. Dom Cuthbert Butler habitually translated *conversatio* by the expression "monastic life." There is a useful note on *conversatio* in Dom J. McCann's edition of the *Rule of St. Benedict,* pp. 168 & 202. Dom J. Chapman defined *conversatio morum* as "monasticity of behavior."

4. *Rule of St. Benedict,* Prologue (end), McCann's ed., p. 12.

5. Dom Salmon: "L'Ascèse monastique et les origines de Cîteaux," *Mélanges S. Bernard* (Dijon, 1953), pp. 268 ff.

6. Dom Salmon, op. cit., pp. 271–2, quotes Jean de Fécamp: "I beg Thee, liberate the soul of Thy servant from these arguments and contentions, these tumults of litigation and the manifold noise of those who converge upon me; free me from this great worldliness [*ab hoc multo saeculo*] which I suffer in the monastery amid this crowd of brethren . . ." etc. See J. Leclercq and J. P. Bonnes: *Un Maître de la Vie Spirituelle an XIe siècle, Jean de Fécamp* (Paris, 1946). The text of J. de Fécamp's "Lament for Lost Solitude" is given on pp. 195 ff.

7. Nihil sit quod mentum tuam a sui revocet custodiam. Sollicite discutiat quid quotidie acquirat proficiendo; ne, quod absit, perdat deficiendo. St. Anselm, *Epistolarum Lib.* I, n. 2, PL 158, col. 1065. We find much the same spirit in St. Bernard's *De Consideratione,* and St. Bernard develops the idea of examination in *Serm. 58 in Cantica,* n. 12; see J. Leclercq's edition, Vol. 2, p. 135, and *Serm. 93 de Diversis.* However, St. Bernard is speaking of habitual self-custody rather than a formal exercise at a fixed time. Note the various anonymous Cistercian tracts which recommend examination of conscience, in PL 184.

8. *Constitutions O.C.S.O.,* #84. Cf. C.J.C., c. 592 and c. 125–n. 2. No difference is indicated between the obligations of a *monk,* an *active religious,* and a *secular cleric.* Examination of conscience first appears in Cistercian Law in 1601.

9. "Daily in one's prayer with tears and sighs to confess one's past sins to God." *Rule of St. Benedict,* Ch. 4. This refers to *past* sins, but is often improperly alleged as our argument for daily examination of conscience in the *Rule.*

10. Cf. *Rule of St. Benedict,* Ch. 4–n. 50, and Ch. 46.

11. See H. Jaeger, J. Guillet, and J. C. Grey in the article "Examen de Conscience," *Dictionnaire de Spiritualité,* Vol. V., col. 1789 ff. It is true that Father M. Olphe Gaillard, a Jesuit, has said: "All that later tradition will

teach of the particular examen is found in substance in Cassian" ("Cassien," *D.S.*, Vol. II, col. 249 ff.). He is here referring, not to any description of any such exercise, but rather to Cassian's teaching on discernment of spirits and on the twelve principal vices. This must be seen in its *monastic* context of habitual uninterrupted silence and prayer, not in a modern context of activity broken up by moments of introspection.

12. Dom Augustine Baker: *The Inner Life and the Writings of Dame Gertrude More*, revised and edited by Dom Benedict Weld-Blundell, O.S.B., 2 vols. (London, 1910).

13. *Holy Wisdom*, last reprinted in London in 1933, is made up of selections drawn by Dom Serenus Cressy from Baker's collected papers. A list of Dom Baker's works is in the article "Baker, Dom Augustine," by Dom J. McCann, in *D.S.*, Vol. I. Most of Dom Baker's works are still in manuscript. The *Secretum* or Commentary on the *Cloud of Unknowing* was published with Dom J. McCann's edition of the *Cloud* (London, 1924).

14. For a description of the more and more complex methods of examination that came into use in the fifteenth and sixteenth centuries, see Irenée Noye, in *D.S.*, vol. V ("Examen de Conscience"), col. 1820 ff. St. Francis de Sales and St. Alphonsus Liguori will recommend a very *simple* form of examen. Noye, col. 1829.

15. *Inner Life,* p. 143.

16. "Dame Gertrude had no relish for books, sermons or instructions that tie souls down to certain practices that are of themselves indifferent and might lawfully (in themselves) be omitted. She would have contemplatives left to their own call concerning such things." *Inner Life,* p. 187.

"Nothing disgusts a contemplative soul more than to hear exhortations and sayings that would limit or tie the soul down, or urge her overmuch to things not of obligation, and without regard to what the spirit relishes or has a call or inspiration for, be it concerning the matter or manner of prayer, or any other kind of exercise." Ibid., p. 188.

17. *In a Great Tradition,* the Life of Dame Laurentia McLachlan, Abbess of Stanbrook, by a Benedictine of Stanbrook (New York, 1956), p. 16.

18. *Inner Life,* p. 152.

19. Ibid., p. 102.

20. *Dark Night of the Soul,* Collected Works, Book I, Ch. i–vii.

21. *Inner Life,* p. 109.

22. See the important chapter on the "Danger of a Tepid Life" in *Holy Wisdom*, Sect. I., Ch. 5, pp. 54 ff., especially *n.* 5, p. 55.

23. See *Holy Wisdom,* Sect. II, Ch. 11, un. 11, 12, pp. 297, 298.

24. Ibid., Sect. I, Ch. 6, n. 5, p. 60.

25. *Inner Life,* p. 110. Dom Baker describes how spiritual love, implying a perfect aversion from sin, purifies the heart. Ibid., pp. 182 ff.

26. Ibid., pp. 102–10.

Russian Mystics

1. See Igor Smolitsch: "Le Mont Athos et la Russie," in *Le Millénaire du Mont Athos* (Chevetogne, Belgium, 1963), p. 299. Smolitsch calls this opinion of Leontiev's a "somewhat unusual estimate."

Protestant Monasticism

1. François Biot: *The Rise of Protestant Monasticism* (Helicon, 1964), 161 pp.

Pleasant Hill

1. These pages rely heavily on material collected and published by Edward Deming Andrews, especially in his books *Shaker Furniture* and *The People Called Shakers*. The latter (New York, Oxford University Press, 1953) is the best introduction to Shaker history and thought. It is now being reissued in a new edition by the Indiana University Press.

Zen Buddhist Monasticism

1. Dom Aelred Graham, O.S.B., in his *Zen Catholicism* (New York, 1963) has given us a useful demonstration of the value, even for Christians and Christian monks, of a certain Zen way of looking at life. Not that we should necessarily imitate the rather drastic methods of Zen, but there is a directness and a simplicity in the Zen attitude toward life that is spiritually and psychologically healthy, provided of course that it is properly understood. Dom Graham advances the merits of this simplicity as against rigidly artificial and self-conscious programs in the spiritual life.

2. See *Rule of St. Benedict*, C. 4 end, Prol. end, etc.

3. From the *Digha Nikaya*, which is a Pali text belonging to the Theravada (Hinayana) tradition. Zen is of course in the Mahayana tradition. But the text nevertheless throws light on the Zen spirit. The translation used here is taken from *Sources of Indian Tradition*, by De Bary, Hay, Weiler, and Yarrow (New York, 1958), p. 113.

4. Ibid. This translation is also a condensation of the original text and it avoids the technical Buddhist emphasis of the original, conveying instead a genuine idea of ascetic impassibility. This gives it a more "Pelagian" tone.

5. In fact Chao Chou (Japanese, Joshu, ninth century) once slapped a disciple whom he found bowing down before an image of Buddha. The disciple complained: "Is it not a laudable thing to pay respect to Buddha?" Joshu replied: "Yes, but it is better even to renounce a laudable thing!" Suzuki comments (*Introduction to Zen Buddhism*, London, 1960, p. 53): "Does this attitude savour of anything nihilistic and iconoclastic? Superficially, yes, but

let us dive deep into the spirit of Joshu out of the depths of which this utterance comes, and we will find ourselves confronting an absolute affirmation quite beyond the ken of our discursive understanding."

6. Martin Heidegger, the German existentialist, in a conversation with the Japanese writer on Zen, Daisetz Suzuki, remarked on the basic similarity of their purposes. A succinct statement of Heidegger's philosophical aim may be quoted here, as it throws light on Zen. "Heidegger uses Being as the 'inner light,' that illumination through which we become conscious of our meaning or of our existence and of existence itself. The light allows us to know that we are beings. It illumines the ground which makes this knowledge possible . . . The Heideggerian approach forces us to return, and this path of return leads us to a correspondence with the source and primordial structure of all being, the Being of being. Man must seek himself in the ground of life, the *Urgrund,* the Being of beings . . . Man is neither explained economically, rationally nor politically, his meaning lies in the ontological structure of his reality." From the Introduction to Heidegger's *What is Philosophy?* by W. Klubach and Jean Wild (1958), p. 9.

7. See Heinrich Dumoulin, S.J.: *A History of Zen Buddhism* (New York, 1963), p. 67.

8. "There are in Zen no sacred books or dogmatic tenets, nor are there any symbolic formulae through which an access might be gained into the signification of Zen. If I am asked, then, what Zen teaches, I would answer Zen teaches nothing. Whatever teachings there are in Zen, they come out of one's own mind. We teach ourselves; Zen merely points the way. Unless this pointing is teaching, there is certainly nothing in Zen purposely set up as its cardinal doctrines or as its fundamental philosophy." D. T. Suzuki: *Introduction to Zen Buddhism.* This statement must of course be balanced with others made by the same author. We shall see that, in fact, the Buddhist scriptures are normally read and recited as part of the daily life of the Zen monastery.

9. See Suzuki: *The Training of the Zen Buddhist Monk* (New York, 1959), p. 113. The insistence on direct insight rather than speculative knowledge can be compared to the aims and methods of Socrates, except that Zen is never dialectical. "Knowledge of values, in fact, is a matter of direct insight like seeing that the sky is blue, the grass green. It does not consist of pieces of information that can be handed from one mind to another. In the last resort every individual must see and judge for himself what is good for him to do. The individual, if he is to be a complete man, must become morally autonomous, and take his own life into his own control. This is a responsibility that no individual can escape. He can indeed, once for all, accept some external authority and thenceforward treat this authority as responsible for what it tells him to do. But he remains responsible for his original choice of an authority to be obeyed. Socrates held that the judge within each of us cannot depute his functions to another." F. M. Cornford: *Before and After Socrates* (Cambridge, 1960), pp. 46–7.

10. Suzuki: *Training,* p. 113. Once again we can profitably compare this intention with that of Socrates, though the means used are very different. "As with the bodily eye, the soul's vision may be clouded and dim, and it may be

deceived with false appearances. Pleasure, for instance, is constantly mistaken for good, when it is not really good. But when the eye of the soul does see straight and clearly, then there is no appeal from its decision. In the field of conduct, education (after the necessary tutelage of childhood) is not teaching; it is opening the eye of the soul and clearing its vision from the distorting mists of prejudice and from the conceit of knowledge which is really no more than secondhand opinion." Cornford: op. cit., p. 47.

11. Quoted in Suzuki: *Introduction to Zen Buddhism,* p. 49.

12. Suzuki: *The Zen Doctrine of No-Mind* (London, 1958), p. 27. The quotation is from the Platform Scripture (*T'an Ching*) of Hui Neng.

13. Quoted in Fung Yu Lan: *The Spirit of Chinese Philosophy* (Boston, 1962), p. 164.

14. Suzuki: *Introduction,* p. 51.

15. *Zen Doctrine of No-Mind,* pp. 27–8.

16. Fung Yu Lan: op. cit., p. 169. Another Zen master (Yengo) said: "People of the world seek the truth outside themselves. What a pity that the thing they are so earnestly looking for is being trodden under their own feet . . . We see the thing and yet it is not seen; we hear it and yet it is not heard; we talk about it and yet it is not talked about; we know it and it is not known. Let me ask, how does it so happen?" Quoted in Suzuki: *Introduction,* p. 55.

17. Suzuki: *Training,* p. 5.

18. This experience is not, however, regarded as pure solipsism, for it is in enlightenment that the Zen monk also experiences himself as one with other men and with all beings; not in metaphysical immersion or confusion, but also in love above all.

19. See Abbot Amakuki's lectures on Hakuin's "Song of Meditation," published in *A First Zen Reader,* compiled by Trevor Leggett (Tokyo, 1960).

20. A traditional text, quoted in Suzuki: *Training,* pp. 97, 98.

21. Ibid., p. 98.

22. H. M. Enomiye Lassalle, S.J.: *Zen, Weg zur Erleuchtung* (Wien, 1960). See *Collectanea,* Jan.–Mar. 1965.

23. *Introduction,* pp. 46–7.

The Zen Koan

1. These reflections have been suggested by two new books, of which they may serve as a review: P. Kapleau: *The Three Pillars of Zen* (Tokyo, John Weatherhill, Inc., 1965), 363 pp., illus.; and Isshu Miura and Ruth Fuller Sasaki: *The Zen Koan* (New York, Harcourt, Brace and World, A Helen and Kurt Wolff Book, 1965), 156 pp., illus. Besides giving historical and factual information about Zen, both books transcribe instructions given by living *Roshis* both in lectures and in individual interviews. *The Three Pillars of Zen* also presents previously untranslated Zen texts (notably, the letters of Bassui), as well as reports of contemporary Zen experiences, including some by Westerners. Both books are recommended. I would remark, however, that though the light thrown on contemporary and Western Zen is interesting, the

real value of the books is still to be found in the traditional Zen texts and in the admirable drawings of Hakuin reproduced in *The Zen Koan*.

2. See Kapleau, p. 171. This is one version of a well-known *koan*. There are often slight variations in the *koan* texts. Slight twists can be given them to bring out something the student needs to see at the moment.

3. Translated in Kapleau: op. cit. See pp. 171–2.

4. St. John of the Cross: *Ascent of Mount Carmel*, Bk. ii, ch. 4.

5. Suzuki: *The Zen Doctrine of No-Mind*, p. 39.

6. *Complete Works*, Vol. I, "Dark Night of the Soul," Ch. XVI, pp. 448–9.

7. Miura and Sasaki: op. cit., p. 45.

8. Rilke: *Selected Works*, Vol. II, translated by J. B. Leishman (Norfolk, 1960).

9. *Theosophical Fragments*, II, p. 13.

10. Flechen wir zu den Bescheidenden
    nächstens nicht um das Nicht-Gesicht
    das zu unserem Dunkel gehört.
                         Poems, 1906–1926

11. In support of this, see William Faulkner's novella *The Bear*.

12. Miura and Sasaki: op. cit., p. 54.

13. Ibid., p. 59.

14. Hekigan Roku, quoted in Miura and Sasaki: op. cit., p. 49.

15. Both Kapleau and Miura-Sasaki claim to help the student to practice a "do-it-yourself" form of Zen, with abundant material from the actual instructions and interviews of *Roshis* with their disciples. Perhaps this claim is a little more valid than that of those who suggest that a man can psychoanalyze himself. In point of fact, however, the *Roshi* is as important in Zen as the analyst is in analysis.

16. Kapleau: op. cit., p. 186.

17. Miura and Sasaki: op. cit., p. 42.

Buddhism and the Modern World

1. Shin'ichi Hisamatsu: "Zen: Its Meaning for Modern Civilization," *The Eastern Buddhist*, new series, Vol. 1, No. 1 (September 1965).

2. *The Eastern Buddhist*, new series, Vol. 1, No. 1 (September 1965), p. 114.

3. Keiji Nishitani: "Science and Zen," *The Eastern Buddhist*, new series, Vol. 1, No. 1 (September 1965), pp. 79 ff.

4. Nhat Hanh: *Aujourd'hui le Bouddhisme*, trans. from the Vietnamese by Le Van Boi (Cholon, South Vietnam, Editions La Boi, 1965).

5. Op. cit., p. 120.